Stories We Live and Grow By

(Re)Telling Our Experiences as Muslim Mothers and Daughters

Muna Saleh

DEMETER

Stories We Live and Grow By
(Re)telling Our Experiences as Muslim mothers and daughters
Muna Saleh

Copyright © 2019 Demeter Press

Individual copyright to their work is retained by the authors. All rights reserved. No part of this book may be reproduced or transmitted in any form by any means without permission in writing from the publisher.

Demeter Press
140 Holland Street West
P. O. Box 13022
Bradford, ON L3Z 2Y5
Tel: (905) 775-9089
Email: info@demeterpress.org
Website: www.demeterpress.org

Demeter Press logo based on the sculpture "Demeter" by Maria-Luise Bodirsky www.keramik-atelier.bodirsky.de

Printed and Bound in Canada

Front cover image: Hidesy (Getty Images).
Front cover artwork: Michelle Pirovich
Typesetting: Michelle Pirovich

Library and Archives Canada Cataloguing in Publication
Title: Stories we live and grow by: (re)telling our experiences as Muslim mothers and daughters /
Muna Hussien Saleh.
Names: Saleh, Muna (Muna H.), author.
Description: Includes bibliographical references.
Identifiers: Canadiana 20190048042 | ISBN 9781772581751 (softcover)
Subjects: LCSH: Mothers and daughters—Canada—Religious aspects—Anecdotes. | LCSH: Muslim women—Canada—Social life and customs. | LCSH: Muslim girls—Canada—Social life and customs.
Classification: LCC HQ755.85 .S25 2019 | DDC 306.874/3088297—dc23

Bism'Allah Al-Rahman Al-Raheem

For Malak, Ahmad, and Maya.

May the stories we plant together
root and sustain you
the way they sustain me,
and may Allah (SWT) grant you innumerable blessings
in this life and in the next.
I love you.

*And in loving memory of Sittee Charifa (Um Hussein) Bekai,
Jiddee Mahmoud (Abu Hussein) Saleh, Sittee Khadijah (Um Ahmad)
Tarshahani, and my dear cousins and brothers Billal and Yehia Al-Bekai.*

Allah yirhammun wa yija3l mathwahun al Jannah ya Rubb. Ameen.

Acknowledgments

Safaa, Rayyan, Ayesha, Zahra, Layla, and Maya
Being alongside you as a friend and co-inquirer has been one of the greatest honours of my life. Thank you for your love, time, friendship, and for trusting me with your stories—I love you all.

My incredibly loving and supportive husband Wissam El-Haj
Words cannot express how much your love and encouragement have meant to me over the last several years. Thank you for the early morning and late-night Tim's coffee runs, letting me sleep in after countless sleepless nights, and your unparalleled patience. I love you so much.

My beloved parents, Nadia and Hussein Saleh
May Allah (SWT) bless and guide you and keep you in His mercy now and forever. Thank you for your love and everything you continue to do for me. I am who I am because of you.

My beautiful grandmother, Sittee (Allah yirhama), the strongest woman I know
I have been so blessed to have grown up in your light. May Allah (SWT) reunite us in Jannah.

My best friends and sisters Suha, Fatima, and Eman Saleh
Thank you for being mothers to my children and for everything else you do. There is no way I could have engaged in this work without you. I am so blessed by your presence and love.

My brothers Mohamed and Walid Saleh
Thank you for always being just a phone call away (I know you both will understand the reference to the inside joke). Love you both.

Jean, Janice, Vera, and Florence, four incomparable scholars and friends

Thank you for all your time, love, and support during my doctoral program and beyond. I have been so blessed to grow as a scholar alongside you and am forever grateful.

Jinny and Hiroko, the most amazing friends, sisters, and response community

Thank you for your love, the laughs, and for the breakfasts, lunches, dinners, desserts (especially the ones in Toronto!) and – of course – coffees. I have been so blessed to be alongside you both. I know we will continue to be friends/sisters wherever our futures take us.

My wonderful friends and extended family

All my wonderful friends, Aunts, Uncles, and cousins, Alhamdulillah for you all. And especially to A3mty Fatima and A3my Hassan—I am honoured to still think of myself as Muna Abu-Ka3kee. *Allah khaleekun wa yizjeekun kul khair ya Rubb. Ameen.*

My dear sisters of the heart (in alphabetical order)

Amanah, Amany, Angie, Charifa, Cristina, Deebe, Elham, Esra, Fatima, Hiba, Janine, Kali, Linda, Marina, Mariam, Nahla, Nanna, Nariman, Nawal, Nouhad, Rana, Rodaina, Saja, Samar, Siraj, and Zahra. I love you all so much and look forward to many more years of love, laughter, and friendship insha'Allah.

I would also like to acknowledge the generous funding of this research by Killam Trusts

Receiving the Izaak Walton Killam Memorial Scholarship allowed me to focus upon researching alongside co-inquirers for over two years, and I am eternally grateful.

Finally, I would like to gratefully acknowledge the University of Alberta's Faculty of Education for its support in my doctoral studies (this book is a revised version of my dissertation), and Concordia University of Edmonton's Faculty of Education for its support as I continue my love of teaching and research.

Contents

Preface

Spring 2014

It was a busy after-school day. Noor, Yehia, and I had just finished supper, and I was trying to persuade baby Hannah to eat so that we could go cheer Noor on at her soccer game. My cousin Billal (Allah yirhamu[1]) was co-coaching her team this year, and he usually drove Noor and his daughter (Noor's friend and teammate) to the field in time for pre-game warm-up. Yehia, Hannah, and I (and Wissam if he was able to leave work early) would join them later.

I was calling out to Yehia to get the bug spray ready while trying to feed an uninterested Hannah when Noor rushed into the kitchen to fill her water bottle for the hour-long game. She was in full soccer gear, including her team jersey, shorts, shin pads, and knee-length soccer socks. Looking at her I thought, for the umpteenth time since she was a baby, about how fast she is growing (she will be in grade six next year!). A few days earlier, the children and I had visited my childhood home and I told them about the time their Jiddo, Khalto Suha, and I planted my grade one Arbor Day tree seedling some thirty years ago. I thought about how some plant roots can grow deeper/wider than the stem and branches grow tall/wide … and I wondered what stories are alive in Noor. What stories are being planted in her, what stories is she planting, and what stories sustain her as she continues to compose her life?

Unaware of my musings, Noor rushed back out of the kitchen. Before she left the house, however, she yelled out, "Bye Mama, make duaa for us!"

Always my love, I thought as my entire being smiled, always.

---

1   An Arabic phrase for "may God have mercy on him." A glossary of all Arabic and/or Islamic terms is included on pages 299 to 302.

(Experientially) Rooting a Research Puzzle

Neither myself nor my narrative can have, therefore, a single strand. I stand at the crossing point of too many social and cultural forces; and, in any case, I am forever on the way. My identity has to be perceived as multiple, even as I strive towards some coherent notion of what is humane and decent and just.

(Greene 1)

As I reflect on my experiences as a Muslim woman, mother, (grand) daughter, educator, researcher, and scholar, Maxine Greene's words help me to appreciate the intimate ways that experience and identity are narratively connected (Connelly and Clandinin, *Shaping*; Crites; Sarbin). She reminds me that the stories of my being and becoming are shaped by an intricate multiplicity that cannot be understood independently from each other. The stories in the forthcoming autobiographical sections illustrate that I live—and live *in*—multiple interconnected, familial, intergenerational, cultural, temporal, spatial, social, linguistic, institutional, faith-based/religious, and personal stories (Clandinin, "Engaging"). My body knows these stories (Johnson); they have shaped, and continue to shape, me in indescribable ways as I composed my life alongside co-inquirers, family, friends, and others. However, these stories are neither fixed nor frozen. Rather, they are fluid, shifting with time, new knowledge, changed perspectives, diverse places, and relationships. They have been told and retold, lived and relived (Clandinin and Connelly, *Narrative*) innumerable times as I continue to compose my life with improvisation and imagination (Bateson, *Composing*).

Maria Lugones refers to the fluidity and multiplicity of identity as "a plurality of selves" (14). She highlights the movement among and within the selves we embody in particular times, situations, places, and relationships—in various "worlds"—in her discussion of world-travelling. A "world," Lugones elucidates, "need not be a construction of a whole society. It may be a construction of a tiny portion of a particular society. It may be inhabited by just a few people. Some 'worlds' are bigger than others" (10). Reflecting upon my ongoing autobiographical narrative inquiry (Clandinin, "Engaging"; Saleh et al., "Autobiographical"), I think about who I am, who I have been, and who I am always in the process of becoming in the worlds I inhabit. I think about how I have mainly felt a strong sense of belonging, of being at home, in my familial, school, and community worlds. Lugones, however, reminds me that world-travelling can occur with varying levels of ease. While I acquired the ability to travel to, within, and among the worlds I inhabit, there have been worlds where I was constructed in ways that did not fit my construction of myself. As I approached this research, I thought about my travel to, within, and among multiple worlds amidst shifting levels of ease, and I wondered ...

I wondered about Noor, Yehia, and Hannah and how they have experienced—and how they will continue to experience—their childhood worlds. I wondered about the experiences they will have as they compose their lives as second-generation[2] Canadian Muslim children. I wondered especially about my eldest daughter Noor, who at close to eleven years old was poised "at the edge of adolescence" (Brown and Gilligan 1) at the commencement of this research, would experience her time in the spaces between girl and woman. Over twenty-five years ago, Lyn Mikel Brown and Carol Gilligan discussed how adolescence marks a "crossroads in women's development: a meeting between girl and woman, an intersection between psychological health and cultural regeneration, a watershed in women's psychology which affects both women and men" (1). I wondered how Noor experiences the worlds she inhabits and how she will experience the worlds she will inhabit along the way in her transitions to adolescence and womanhood. I also wondered about other second-generation Canadian Muslim girls who, similar to Noor, are transitioning into adolescence. How do they experience this time of great significance in their lives? How are they composing their lives as they experience this transition? What are the stories that root and sustain them?

---

2   While Statistics Canada defines second-generation Canadians as "individuals who were born in Canada and had at least one parent born outside Canada" (my emphasis, 3), my conceptualization of this term is broader. For this research, I attend to the experiences of Muslim girls who are composing their lives in Canada, whether they were born in Canada or elsewhere, and have at least one parent who was born outside Canada.

D. Jean Clandinin highlights that we live *by*, *with*, and *in* stories ("Engaging"). The term stories to live *by* refers to a narrative conception of identity at the nexus of narrative understandings of knowledge and contexts (Connelly and Clandinin, *Shaping*). We also live *in* stories—in the midst of continually unfolding personal, familial, intergenerational, institutional, social, cultural, faith-based/religious, temporal, linguistic, school, and other narratives. Living *with* stories is a relational way of living with the multiplicity of narratives we are always in the midst of. As I prepared for this research, I wondered about the stories Canadian Muslim girls live *by*, *with*, and *in*. How are they storying their experiences as they transition into adolescence? How do personal, school, familial, intergenerational, cultural, temporal, social, faith-based/religious, and other narratives shape them as they compose their lives and identities?

Ben Okri highlights, "One way or another we are living the stories planted in us early or along the way, or we are also living the stories we planted—knowingly or unknowingly—in ourselves" (46). Thinking alongside Okri's words, I play with ecological metaphors of planting, rooting, and growing throughout this work because, like John Dewey, I conceptualize growth as profoundly experiential. As I engaged in experientially rooting my research puzzle, I thought about how the women I love—my mom, Sittee[3] (Allah yirhama), my sisters, aunts, cousins, and friends, have planted so many of the stories that live in me. I thought about other women who, like me, are looking for ways to make sense of mothering Canadian Muslim girls during a time of significant life transition. Who are we in relation to our daughters? What stories of motherhood are we living? What stories are we planting in our familial curriculum making (Huber et al., *Places*)? What stories are being—and have been—planted in us?

These wonderings shaped my research puzzle as I prepared to engage in narrative inquiry alongside other Muslim mothers and daughters. As D. Jean Clandinin and F. Michael Connelly note, "Narrative inquiries are always strongly autobiographical. Our research interests come out of our own narratives of experience and shape our narrative inquiry plotlines" (*Narrative* 121). To root and

---

3   My paternal grandmother, Sittee Charifa (Um Hussein) Bekai, passed away in the summer of 2018. *Allah yirhama ya Rubb. Ameen.*

deepen my personal, practical, and social/theoretical justifications[4] for engaging in this inquiry, different times, relationships, and places in my life are brought in and out of focus with stories, poetry, literature, reflections, and autobiographical narrative inquiry. The following chapters highlight a multiplicity of stories that mother and daughter co-inquirers and I live *by*, *with*, and *in* and the ways personal, familial, intergenerational, cultural, school, linguistic, temporal, faith-based/ religious, and social narratives, among others, shape our experiences and stories of becoming.

4   Clandinin explained that narrative inquiries must be justified personally, in terms of why this narrative inquiry matters to us as individuals; practically, in terms of what difference this research might make to practice; and socially or theoretically, in terms of what difference this research might make to theoretical understandings or to making situations more socially just. ("Engaging" 35).

Chapter 1

Rooting (Autobiographical) Stories to Live By, With, and In:
(place-ing myself with)
A Beginning Story

ully aware that anyone noticing would think I'm a creeper, I slowly drive up the neighbourhood street before coming to a stop in front of the aged yellow- and white-trimmed house. It looks so much smaller than even the last time I visited, about thirteen years ago. Back then, I had driven this way to show my then-fiancé, now-husband, Wissam, my childhood home.

Now, Noor, Yehia, and Hannah sit, tucked in by their seat-belts, as I try to explain why tears are welling in my eyes. I tell them about playing in the areas we have just passed with my siblings and cousins. I tell them about how my beloved cousin, Yehia (Allah yirhamu), lived with us in this house for the first five years of my life. I tell them how he helped teach me how to play soccer and hockey among so many other important lessons. I tell them about the two pine trees that their Jiddo, Khalto Suha, and I once planted, now gone for reasons unknown.

It was the spring of 1986, and I excitedly, but cautiously, stepped off the school bus and quickened my pace. I couldn't wait to get home and plant my new tree seedling! Grade one students in Alberta receive seedlings as part of a long-standing Arbor Day tradition, and I happily received a small pine seedling in school that day. Later that evening, I helped my dad dig a second hole in the front lawn of our home, identical and adjacent to the one that was dug the year before for my sister

Suha's seedling. Reminded to say Bism'Allah, we planted the fragile looking seedling together, and I then showered it with water. Walking back to the house, I silently prayed that it would survive and grow, if even a little bit.

Looking at the places on the front lawn where two pine trees should be proudly standing, I am aware that Noor, Yehia, and Hannah will not view the house and lawn with a remembered landscape layered atop the current one. I smile as I remember how the tree did indeed grow—it grew to be quite large quite quickly! And I loved watching the two pine trees grow, although I do not imagine this was ever a conscious thought as, day after day, I walked by the two trees that grew to be much taller than me. I think the only time I ever really thought of the trees' significance was when I looked wistfully back at my childhood home during our drive away from it and towards our newly constructed home in the spring of grade eight.

Driving away from the house with a heavy heart, I wonder what happened to the trees. Did they grow to be too large? Were the roots disturbing the house or nearby sidewalks? Were they shedding needles, obstructing views, or otherwise deemed to be nuisances? I thought of these possibilities as I quietly mourned them, not realizing until I was driving away how much I had been looking forward to seeing them.

Noor, intuitively perceptive, asks me if I'm disappointed that the trees are not there. I answer truthfully that even though the trees are gone, they have forever changed the landscape. Their long-ago presence is still felt in the soil, in the places once shaded, and in the habitats they once provided to living beings.

Besides, I tell her smilingly, reassuring myself as much as I try to reassure her, how could they ever be truly gone if their roots still live inside of us?

(revisiting) What I Knew First

The narratives we shape out of the materials of our lived lives must somehow take account of our original landscapes if we are to be truly present to ourselves and to partake in an authentic relationship with the young. As I view it, it is on that primordial ground that we recognize each other, that ground on which we are in direct touch with things and not separated from them by the conceptual lenses of constructs and theories.

(Greene 75)

I marvel at how much has changed since I lived in that first home within my childhood familial landscape. I think about some of these changes and wonder at the shifts that have simultaneously occurred within me in unseen yet embodied places. Wondering about and inquiring into the often taken-for-granted shifts and changes of my life propelled me to (re)visit my childhood home alongside my children. I wanted to live and relive, tell and retell some of my stories alongside them. As the opening quote by Maxine Greene illuminates, I needed to revisit what I knew first.[5]

Inquiring into this story, I was originally puzzled about why I felt that the disappeared trees were deeply significant to my stories to live by. Was it because of my belief that, as Keith Basso and Leslie M. Silko so eloquently posit, identity is intricately connected with the land? However, similar to Basso, I also believe that our imagined landscapes—those of the heart and mind—are imbued with moral wisdom: "This ever-changing landscape of the active heart and mind rewards repeated visits. For wherever one journeys in the country of the past, instructive places abound" (4). Along with his assurance that physical landscapes live within us just as surely as we live within them, Basso further helped guide me to the probable root of my dis-ease: "In this convulsive age of uprooted populations and extensive diasporas, holding onto places —and sensing fully the goodness contained therein—has become increasingly difficult, and in years to come, I expect, it may everywhere be regarded as a privilege and a gift" (xvi). Basso's words resonated profoundly for me because only a few months before revisiting my childhood home, I had been sitting with my beloved Sittee (Allah yirhama) discussing some of her life experiences. In what follows, I represent, in poetic and narrative form, my understandings of multiple conversations I shared with my beloved grandmother Sittee (Allah yirhama), over the course of several weeks in the spring of 2014. These understandings stem from several conversations in which Sittee (Allah yirhama) and I shared and inquired into stories alongside each other.

---

5   This is a reference to Patricia MacLachlan's beautiful picture book "What You Know First."

Sittee's Stories of Being Uprooted[6]

My body is a story
a remembrance in the making
sit here next to me love
and I will tell you its tale.

جسدي قصة
اجلسي بجانبي حبيبتي
الذكريات التي أعيشها، سأرويها لك

I am happy that my knees are limber once again
allowing me to travel across this earth
but, in truth, I sometimes long for the ones I was born with
the ones that played in, and sought refuge from, the land flowing
in my veins.

إنني سعيدة لأن ركبتاي
تستعيد حركتهما وتساعداني على السفر حول أنحاء العالم
ولكنني أتمنى بعض الأحيان
لو أن ركبتاي اللتين كنت العب بهما في الارض التي ولدت فيها، وهربت منها

These eyes, ya bintee, are clouded not with the burden of rain
for healing saltwater has oft showered these pores
but with the memory of loved ones from times past
forever alive in the lucid landscapes of my dreams.

عيناي يا إبنتي ليست مملؤة بالدموع
ولكن بذكريات الاحباء
الذين يعيشون في احلامي كالغمامة

The faint borders written across my belly
were stroked by giving life to eleven beloveds
don't be sad, my love, that only nine walk this land
for there are two beautiful birds waiting for me in Jannah insha'Allah.

الخطوط المرسومة في بطني
علامات حملي احدى عشرة مرة
لا تحزني، تسعةٌ منهم يمشون على الارض
وطائرين منهم ينتظراني في الجنة إن شاء الله

6   While our conversations were always in Arabic, I wrote this poem for Sittee
(Allah yirhama) in English to represent the stories she shared with me. My
mom helped me to translate the poem into Arabic. However, as always, some
meaning and nuance are lost in the always incomplete travel between languages.

These lines engraved on my hands and around my eyes
were ploughed with hard work
turned by working the earth, in cleansing waters and generous sun
as I nurtured love with the fruits of my labour.

خطوط العمر المرسومة على يديّ،
وعيناي حفرهما العمل الشاق في الحقول في الصيف الحار
لتربية الثمار التي انجبتها

Every strand of silver is a wistful celebration
of life danced in sweet defiance
to hard-hearted dictators and expectations
playfully reminding me to stay soft and fluid.

الخصل الفضية في رأسي
هي احتفالٌ لي لأنني تحديثُ الصعوبات في الحياة
من الناس والحكام
ولكن تذكّرني بأن أبقى طيبة ومملوءة بالفرح

Let not the bullet lodged in my back grieve you my child
I am at peace with it
for alongside pain came the knowledge of your father
and without his life you would not be here to grieve.

لا تحزني عليّ من الرصاصة المغروسة في كتفي يا ابنتي
انها دائما تذكّرني،أنه من ألمها علمتُ بحملي بوالدك
الذي من دونه لم تكوني لتولدي وتشاركيني حزني.

Ya habibty, smiles and laughter etched the grooves around my mouth
joyful witnesses to a blessed life
for I sit, here, now, embraced by the memory of different times,
places, and people telling one beloved, of many, my body's—for
now—story.

يا حبيبتي،الإبتسامات التي رُسمت حول فمي
شاهدةٌ على الحياة المباركة التي اعيشها، وعشتها.
فأنا هنا، اجلسُ ، أروي لمن أُحب الذكريات التي عشتها،
والتي تعانقني عن قصة جسدي.

(revisiting) What Sittee Knew First

"Muna, I think it will be good to videotape this."

"Yes, I think so too Sittee."

Sittee and I retreated from the cozy chaos of my parents' family room to the relatively quieter living room. I had asked Sittee to sit with me so that I could ask her some questions about her experiences growing up in Palestine. I wanted to create a mini movie or slideshow presentation for her for Mother's Day, and I thought it would be nice to include some of Sittee's early stories of experiences alongside more recent ones. Sittee loved the idea of creating a digital imprint that would bear witness to her experiences. What I thought would be a straightforward Mother's Day project, however, evolved into a series of conversations over the course of several weeks that shifted so many of my stories of Sittee and of our relationship. I wrote the poem on the previous page as one way to honour Sittee and the stories she shared with me.

Sittee had come to live with us in the fall of 1990. I will never forget my excitement as my family and I waited at the Edmonton International Airport for her plane to touch down. Both my grandmothers lived in Lebanon, and I was not yet five years old the only time we had visited, so I was ecstatic that I was finally going to have one of my Sittees living with us. As I think about my excitement that day now, after hearing so many of her stories, I wonder about how Sittee (Allah yirhama) might have experienced that moment, farther away than ever from Palestine, the land she still dreamed about.

Sittee had a far-away look in her eyes as she wistfully recounted some of her stories. She said that her earliest memories were of working alongside her mother and sister on the family farm. With a glowing smile, as if she could still smell the groves, Sittee told me how she loved harvesting the fruits from her family's olive, fig, and date trees. Born in the early thirties in a small village next to the larger community of Safad in northern Palestine, Sittee explained that girls did not really go to school at the time because it just was not part of their traditions. She stressed, however, that many boys were also not sent to school because the nearest school was quite far away and because a lot of villagers felt that it was a waste of time—time that could be better spent helping the family earn a living.

Scattered about Like Leaves

Like many girls of that time and place, Sittee was married at a very young age. She explained that she was not exactly sure how old she was because time was not really tallied according to calendars but by the cycles of the moon and the rhythms of farm life. However, Sittee *thought* that she was about sixteen years old on her wedding day sometime in January of 1948.[7] Sittee recalled how, as a newlywed bride a few months later, she heard the distant sounds of gunfire steadily approaching, and the sounds of men, women, and children screaming, running, and crying. She remembered hearing someone yelling at her to gather a few necessities so they could flee the violence, but she did not remember who yelled it. All she remembers, she somberly said, was the terror and confusion.

With measured tones and resolute grace, Sittee narrated how a bullet struck her in the back as she tried to run alongside friends and family. She depicted some of the horrific scenes she witnessed as she, a few months pregnant with my father at the time, slipped in and out of consciousness as a result of her injuries. Sittee described holding on to consciousness long enough to learn that she was in a makeshift hospital in neighbouring Lebanon, finally able to ask about her loved ones. Hearing that her husband, unborn child, and immediate family were safe brought immense relief. However, she continued, coming to understand that she may never know the fate of so many extended

7   1948 is a significant year for Palestinians. Sa'di and Abu-Lughod describe how the *Nakba* (an Arabic word for "catastrophe") of the 1948 War, where 88% of the indigenous Palestinian population became refugees after their land was confiscated, has become "the demarcation line between two qualitatively opposing periods" for Palestinians (3). That is, Palestinians often use the *Nakba* to differentiate their experiences before Israel was created in 1948 from the harsh ones after. Sa'di and Abu-Lughod outline a series of events that led to the *Nakba* of 1948, including the following: the establishment of the World Zionist Congress in 1897; the Balfour Declaration of 1917 (where Britain announced support for the creation of Israel on Palestinian lands); the British occupation of Palestine during WWI; the Palestinian resistance to British occupation and its subsequent defeat from 1936 to 1939; WWII and the Holocaust; the 29 Nov 1947 United Nation Resolution on the Partition of Palestine; and the 1948 Israeli offensive. Henceforth, what was once known to the indigenous population as Palestine was referred to as Israel post-1948.

family and friends, who had scattered about like leaves in all directions that fateful day, was especially sorrowful. The realization that she may never be able to go back home carried a different kind of pain that would always live at the edge of her consciousness.[8]

Sittee's Stories Live in Me

As part of our familial curriculum making, Sittee (Allah yirhama) had generously shared her stories with me at different times of my life—usually to illuminate the wisdom her experiences have taught her. I had never, however, sat alongside Sittee to narratively inquire into her stories. For this reason, perhaps, her stories lived within me for a very long time, strumming painful chords of recognition from deep within me. The resonant pain I experienced hearing Sittee's stories was a feeling infinitely more complex than empathy. Drawing from her study of three families living in Israel,[9] Rachel Lev-Wiesel explores what she refers to as the "intergenerational transmission of trauma"—that is, trauma that is passed from a first-generation family member who had directly experienced a traumatic event to members of the second and third generation. Participants in her study included a Palestinian family who were forcibly dislocated from their homeland.[10] That event lived on in second- and third-generation family members in the form of sadness, anger, and intent to return to their original homes if the opportunity should ever present itself. They still felt a strong sense of belonging to their original homeplace several years after their family's traumatic displacement in 1948. This resonated profoundly with me as an intergenerational survivor[11] of the *Nakba* of 1948, as a

8   Sa'di and Abu-Lughod note that place is central to the stories and memories of Palestinian people.

9   While Lev-Wiesel refers to this land as Israel, my family members refer to it as Palestine.

10 The family had taken refuge in another part of Palestine/Israel (they were internally displaced).

11 Young similarly discusses intergenerational trauma in her narrative inquiry into the relationships between *Anishinabe* language and identity; she highlights "intergenerational narrative reverberations" in relation to first and subsequent generation survivors of Canadian residential schools.

woman who does not live in Palestine but in whom Palestine lives.

What makes Sittee's story all the more compelling and powerful for me is its sense of unfinishedness. Nearly seventy years later, the *Nakba* is a narrative that is still unfolding (Sa'di and Abu-Lughod). Indeed, another horrific round of violence had erupted in the Gaza Strip as I began writing about Sittee's experiences.[12] The uprooting and continued assault of indigenous Palestinians by occupying forces is an oft-told tale in my family. As important as this familial story is, however, it is only one of the many planted within me, one of many that I must honour as I compose forward-looking stories (Nelson) alongside loved ones.

Reconsidering Sittee's stories as I prepared to inquire alongside three second-generation Canadian Muslim girls and their mothers as girl co-inquirers transition into adolescence, I thought about the many cultural, temporal, and intergenerational stories—embodied and expressed in diverse ways—that are alive within me. I wondered about the stories living within co-inquirers. What are the cultural, temporal, and intergenerational stories shaping their experiences? Thinking about the reciprocal relationship between roots and surrounding soil, I wondered about the ways co-inquirers are (re)shaping the stories planted in them.

As I continued to deepen my understandings of my inquiry puzzle before coming alongside co-inquirers, I turned to another amazing woman I love, my mother, and to the stories that our relationship planted in me. I attempt, through the following sections, to represent my continually evolving understandings of several of the stories my mom has shared with me over time.

12 The Gaza Strip is an area of land in southwest Palestine/Israel that borders Egypt. This region possesses a long history of strife and bombardment, most recently the 2014 Israeli offensive that killed 2,139 Palestinians and injured approximately 11,000 (the majority of whom were civilians), 64 Israeli soldiers, and 6 Israeli civilians (Dearden).

Dear Mama

Your heaven lies at the feet of your mother.
(Prophet Mohammed, Peace be Upon Him)

> my
> mother
> was
> my first country.
> the first place i ever lived.

— *lands,* by Nayyirah Waheed

Mama Teaching Me to See the Forest for the Trees

We had a house full of guests (again!) on a night I will never forget. Suha and I were expected to serve the refreshments, wash the dishes, entertain the younger children, and otherwise help out. While I always wanted to help Mama, I felt annoyed by these almost nightly visits and grumbled about it to Suha as we were washing the latest round of dishes. I did not see that Mama had come into the kitchen and overheard me. I turned around at the sound of her voice, edged with tears and disappointment, as she said, "Muna, don't ever complain about having guests over. You should say Alhamdulillah and be grateful to Allah (SWT) that your father is alive and that people visit this house."

I was in grade six at the time, and yet I do not think I have ever felt as bad as I did in that moment.

(revisiting) What Mama Knew First

"Mom, can I please just ask you a few questions about your experiences growing up to make sure I don't get anything wrong?"

"Of course, Muna, ask me anything."

My mother was born in Bar-Elias, a town in Lebanon's Bekaa Valley. A child of the 60s and 70s, she recalls the big hair and short skirts fad that gripped the then-small town, which had become more than a temporary home to the hundreds of Palestinian refugees who still lived there decades after the *Nakba*. I remember my mom laughingly recounting the time she and her sisters shortened their skirts by hand after buying "acceptable"-length skirts of the sort my beloved maternal grandmother Sittee Um-Ahmad (Allah yirhama), approved. As I think about the stories of Sittee Um-Ahmad that my mom shared with me, I wonder at the ways Sittee Um-Ahmad negotiated gendered norms and expectations at a time when the opinions she held in relation to girls' education, travel, and professional aspirations were not at all commonplace.

When my mom describes her early family life with Sittee Um-Ahmad, Jiddee Abu-Ahmad, two older brothers, and three sisters, she usually mentions the steady stream of people who would visit her dad, a well-respected activist in Bar-Elias's Palestinian refugee community. Beaming whenever she tells this part of her story, my mom says that she and her siblings were always at the very top of their class. She notes that the eldest child in her family, Khalee Ahmad (Allah yirhamu), was actively courted by several post-secondary institutions in Lebanon before he eventually decided to travel to Russia. She says Khalee made the difficult decision to move because, unlike Lebanon, Russia did not stipulate employment options or areas of professional specialization for Palestinian refugees. In Lebanon, my mom and her siblings were still considered Palestinian refugees regardless of the fact that they were born in Lebanon. Khalee was in the process of earning a PhD in physics after several years of study; however, he died when my mom was eleven years old, just as he was completing graduate studies. Mom says that although they wholeheartedly believe that life and death are in Allah's (SWT) hands, the pain of Khalee's untimely passing likely contributed to Jiddee's death approximately two years after his eldest son passed away.

Mom says their deaths changed everything. Accustomed to a full house throughout her childhood, the steady stream of visitors slowly waned and then stopped almost completely the year after Jiddee's passing. Mom says that because Sittee now needed other sources of income to pay for her children's school tuition, everyone agreed to help. Still a middle school student, Mom secured weekend and summer jobs working nearby fields, helping seamstresses, and whatever other odd jobs she could to save enough money to pay for her own tuition. Mom said this was her routine for several years, saving enough money for her tuition during weekends and holidays, before she married my dad and joined him in Canada in her final year of high school.

Travelling to Mama's Worlds

My relationship with my mother has shaped, and continues to shape, who I am, who I was, and who I am still becoming in indescribable ways. Our relationship, however, has shifted over the years as well as my perceptions of it. As a child, I remember feeling an overwhelming sense of love and attachment but also of confusion and longing. I knew without a doubt that my mom would give me anything and everything she could give, always so generous with her love, strength, and presence. But for the longest time, she withheld something I longed for—her stories of childhood. I wanted to know Mom beyond what I knew, to see her through her eyes, to extend "the possibility of life between us." I would get so confused when she would change the subject any time I tried to ask questions about her childhood experiences. With time, I have come to understand that her silence was protective, shielding her from very painful memories. Mom started to share her once-silenced experiences several years ago, at first in sparse, bare language, but then in increasing detail with every re-telling. Adrienne Rich beautifully discusses the possibilities when women begin telling one another that which they had previously silenced: "It isn't that to have an honorable relationship with you, I have to understand everything, or tell you everything at once, or that I can know, beforehand, everything I need to tell you. It means ... that we both know that we are trying, all the time, to extend the possibilities of truth between us. The possibility of life between us" (*On Lies* 193-194).

Reflecting upon my relationship with my Mom, I think of Maria Lugones—who in a beautifully written paper weaving together her "coming to consciousness as a daughter and ... as a woman of color" (3)—differentiates between loving and arrogant perception. For Lugones, loving perception entails an identification and an appreciation, and willful travel to another's worlds. A "world," she clarifies, "need not be a construction of a whole society. It may be a construction of a tiny portion of a particular society. It may be inhabited by just a few people. Some 'worlds' are bigger than others" (10). Lugones emphasizes that "worlds" are *constructions* created by and for each of us, by and for ourselves and others. She argues that we may or may not agree with the worlds others have constructed for us but that we may nonetheless "be *animating* such a construction" due to the limited space available for us to manoeuvre in certain times, places, and relationships (10).

However, it is possible to negotiate a multiplicity of worlds, Lugones asserts, because one "can 'travel' between these worlds and one can inhabit more than one of these 'worlds' at the very same time" (10-11). A playful, loving attitude, Lugones affirms, is what allows us to remember ourselves whilst appreciating others, is what "enable[s] us to *be*", in this back and forthing among and between our own—and each other's—worlds (8).

In contrast, arrogant perception entails an agonistic, colonizing attitude. Lugones stresses that it is impossible to world-travel with arrogant perception without attempting to colonize that "world," and, by extension, its inhabitants. Drawing upon her experiences as a woman of colour in the West and her relationship with her mother, Lugones illustrates how women are often both perpetrators and victims of arrogant perception depending on the situation.

I find myself reflecting upon my relationship with my mom every time I read Lugones' words because, similar to Lugones, I held several assumptions of my mom's worlds. I grumbled about the constant stream of guests and accompanying chores that night without considering that my mother genuinely loved this part of our familial curriculum-making. I assumed that, like me, she was privately annoyed with the continuous stream of visitors, but did not express her annoyance because of cultural norms and expectations. And I felt sorry for her. My arrogant perception, however, started to unravel that night. I now appreciate that I imposed my own preferences and ideals on what I believed my mother's worlds to be. As anyone who has ever witnessed my mother's life-making can attest, "there are 'worlds' where she shines as a creative being. Seeing myself in her through traveling to her 'world' has meant seeing how different I am from her in her 'world'" (Lugones 18). I feel that I have often imposed a reductionist view of my Mom's worlds and her unparalleled beauty and strength in travelling among and between myriad worlds without lovingly attending to who she is, who she is becoming, and how *she* views her worlds. Mom would always model gratitude for me and my siblings, saying 'Alhamdulillah' in instances that did not seem to warrant gratitude. That night, I began to understand that Mom was not saying 'Alhamdulillah' superfluously. As one of her most cherished stories to live by, one planted in me, her gratitude for Allah's (SWT) blessings is authentic. When she says 'Alhamdulillah,' she means it.

As I prepared to come alongside co-inquirers in this research, I thought about the stories I knew first and how familial stories have been so integral to my being and becoming. The most profound stories that I live and that live in me are those composed alongside my mother. Through travelling to her worlds, I have learned to recognize the loving and arrogant perceiver within myself. I wondered about the familial stories that co-inquirers live *by*, *with*, and *in*. Do they, too, involve world-travelling between and amongst the worlds of mother and daughter? Is their world-travel accompanied by, at turns, loving and arrogant perception? I wondered what stories have been planted in the mothers and daughters, what stories they are planting in each other, and what stories are being relationally shifted and shaped as they continue to compose their lives over time in different places and relationships?

Planting Seeds of Home

tap tap tap tap tap tap ... **Smack**

The scene is so familiar, so vivid. Stirring from a deep sleep to the sounds, smells (the absolutely glorious smells), and emotions inspired by early-morning ka3k-making. The trek out of the bedroom to follow the tantalizing aroma, the comforting sounds of Mama and the Aunties chatting rhythmically in Arabic, and—of course— the sounds of ka3k dough being pressed into, and then forced out of, the mould...

tap tap tap tap tap tap ... **Smack**

The race to the kitchen to see if any ka3k had come out of the oven yet. The sheer joy if there were warm and fluffy ones waiting for me. The giddy anticipation if they were still baking. Carefully biting into a fluffy and warm ka3k followed by a sip of my sweetened, milky shai. Savouring this delicious breakfast alongside my siblings, soothed by the voices of the women we love in the background.

This is what I knew first.

This is home.

(revisiting) What I Knew First

People talk to you a great deal about your education, but some good, sacred memory, preserved from childhood, is perhaps the best education. If one carries many such memories into life, one is safe to the end of one's days, and if one has only one good memory left in one's heart, even that may be the means of saving us.

(Dostoevsky 868)

I was born on a cool Edmonton evening in the fall of 1980. My parents, alongside my Aunt and Uncle (my Dad's only two siblings in Canada at the time), had just saved a sizeable down payment to secure the home that we would live in for the next eleven years. Just like our bodies tell a story (Caine), so does my childhood home. A place I still dream about, I return to it every so often to remind me of important stories, and I remember ...

I remember my mom and the aunties and early-morning *ka3k* making. I remember planting trees and raking leaves with my mom, dad, and siblings. I remember celebrating birthdays, Eids, Christmases, Halloweens, and get-togethers with our wonderful neighbourhood community. I remember playing soccer, tag, and water games with my beloved cousins Billal (Allah yirhamu), Marina, Monzer, Cristina, Mohammed, and Yehia (Allah yirhamu) in the back yard. I remember sledding down the side hill that bordered the street. I remember the time a bird flew into the window my mom just cleaned. I remember trying to nurse the poor bluebird back to health but, alongside Suha and Marina, laying it to rest under a tree next to our home as we read the verses that we knew from the Qur'an. I remember teaching my brother Mohamed to skate in the community rink about a block down the road. I remember my sweet little sister Fatima yelling for us to wait up when we rode our bikes down the back alleyway searching for crab apples. I remember my adventurous baby brother Walid always being bruised, scratched up, or worse because he loved to jump off anything even remotely above ground. I remember Sittee (Allah yirhama) patting the floral-upholstered loveseat and asking me to sit and share *shai* and stories with her. I remember Jiddee (Allah yirhamu) laughing his unforgettable belly laugh and telling me to go outside and make some mischief. I remember all of this, and I think of my youngest sister, intelligent and beautiful Eman, who was born the year after we moved out of what still seems to be a place brimming with magic.

It is not my intention to gloss over the difficult moments in my life or to create an idealized story of my childhood. While that home nurtured so many beautiful and sustaining stories, tension-filled stories were also being lived. These too are stories that live in me. However, these are not the stories that flood my senses when I revisit my childhood home. The stories I hold close and nurture, the ones that hold and nurture me, are those that make my blood hum and my legs long to run or bike down the street. Alongside more tension-filled stories, I (re)tell and (re)live these sustaining childhood stories alongside my children, co-inquirers, and others to both help them travel to my worlds and to help me travel to theirs.

Reflecting on the stories I have shared thus far of my early experiences, many wonderings emerged. I wondered about co-inquirers and the stories they knew first. I wondered how these stories have shaped, and continue to shape, their experiences. I wondered about the stories that sustain and nurture the mothers and daughters as girl co-inquirers travel(led) the spaces between girlhood and womanhood. And I wondered about the ways they experience multilayered cultural, temporal, familial, intergenerational, social, and personal stories that they live.

Keeping It All in Perspective(s)

Sittee: I can see her smiling as her eyes follow the words across the page and my heart smiles with her. I feel bad that she hides away in her room to read; I think she is afraid that someone will tell her to put the book away. I tell her to never mind their worrying but I think she does anyways. I am so grateful that she has the opportunity to go to school and to learn, Alhamdulillah. Habibty, she looks so intent on what she's reading. I will ask her to sit and have shai later and tell me about the story.

Mama: Look at my little reader. I am so proud of her, but I worry about her too. Even though I am happy that she loves reading, I worry that she is closeting herself away from her family and friends far too often. Imagine! Just yesterday a group of children came to the door to ask her to join them in play outside and she says, "Thanks, but maybe tomorrow." I love that she loves to read but I do wish she would be more balanced about it.

Me: Yes – I can finally get back to the story! Evening chores took forever after a loooong day of school. I so want to and out what happens next ... but there is way too much noise here. Sigh. They will get upset with me if I sneak away to read. They will say that I need to be more involved with the family. But I get so overwhelmed with all the noise and chores and people and hmmm, maybe they won't notice if I slipped away this time.

Things Are Not Always What They Seem

I think of Greg Sarris as Mom and I sit side by side in my parents' living room in a familiar potato peeling and prepping process. Narrating a potato-peeling story, Sarris details how Mabel McKay, a well-respected Cache Creek Pomo elder, taught him that "things aren't always what they seem" (3). I had called my mom about an hour earlier, "Salam Mom, I just bought a rotisserie chicken … wanna share?" That's how we came to be sitting together, preparing a side of mashed potatoes. I am peeling the potatoes with a vegetable peeler (I had given up trying to shed the skin as thinly as Mom expected with a plain old knife), and Mom is cutting them into large cubes so they can be easily boiled and mashed. Pausing to look at the play of light shining through the designs in the draperies, I ask Mom for a story of me as an elementary school student and, without hesitation, she says, "You were always reading your books! You would just read and read all the time. Even in very poor light. I used to really worry about your eyesight." I chuckle a bit at her worry, an old habit not easily suppressed, and Mom looks unimpressed as she focuses on her task. But, peeking at her side profile, I could tell she was having a difficult time trying to force the corners of her mouth all the way down.

Learning to Travel to (real and imagined) Worlds

Novels and stories are renderings of life; they can not only keep us company, but admonish us, point us in new directions, or give us the courage to stay a given course. They can offer us kinsmen, kinswomen, comrades, advisers—offer us other eyes through which we might see, other ears with which we might make soundings.

(Coles 159-160)

Reflecting on my Mom's words, I recalled the tensions caused by my book-wormish ways, often perceived by family members as an anti-social way to hide away from them. My love of reading was indeed partly related to stealing away for personal time, as, in the late 80s and early 90s, dozens of paternal relatives steadily joined us in Canada. By the time I was in grade six, our extended family had grown from just one Aunt and Uncle living in Canada to boast over thirty members. My parents lovingly opened our home to every family member joining us in this beautiful land.

For my siblings and I, however, these changes meant innumerable shifts in the way we lived alongside our parents and each other—innumerable shifts to the worlds we inhabited and the ways we travelled to, within, and between them. While my parents worked hard to secure lodgings for our relations, the entire family needed to extend space, time, and energy to the process as well. I recall sharing a tiny room with my sisters Suha and Fatima for several years, not to mention the sharing-a-single-bathroom-with-a-dozen-or-more-people part of growing up. While I loved my family and enjoyed playing with my cousins, I often found it challenging to negotiate the chores and the lack of privacy. Being among the elder children in our large extended family, I was also expected to help with the household chores and younger children. I cherished whatever stolen moments I could secure to learn, explore, and dream alongside the characters of my literary worlds.

Greg Sarris posits that "In understanding another person and culture you must simultaneously understand yourself" (6). For me, stories, whether narrated orally or unfolding through the written word, were much more than a way to escape the beautiful chaos of my childhood. Travelling alongside countless people, real and literary, learning about so many worlds helped me to know *myself*, to travel within and between *my* worlds. However, I know that real and textual stories are not external resources from which I can draw upon at will. Like the land, they live in me, rooting me, providing me with life-making sustenance and strength. From the moment I am drawn into a story, its imagined landscape intertwines with those that live in me, and those that I live by, shifting and shaping the real and imagined boundaries of both locales. For, I am also a part of the land—giving of myself, changing it irrevocably.

Thus far, I have literally and metaphorically laid my stories alongside those of my mom and Sittee (Allah yirhama) to illuminate the impossibility of attempting to attend to only one story or one perspective in my stories of being and becoming. Ruminating on coming alongside co-inquirers, I thought about the many familial, temporal, intergenerational, cultural, and social stories living in me and I wondered about the stories living in them. What are the stories that co-inquirers live *by*, *with*, and *in*, especially in an increasingly globalized (Smith) world? What stories do they draw upon as they imagine forward-looking stories? For, as the forthcoming sections illustrate, I have gratefully drawn upon the strength and sustenance of many of the stories planted in me in the process of composing my life.

Worlds Forever Changed

On the morning of September 11, 2001 (9/11), I woke up late following one too many slaps of the snooze button. The process of running around (where are my keys?) and of driving to the nearest transit station were pretty ingrained practices considering it was my fourth and final year of undergraduate studies. On the transit ride to campus, I overheard two women across from me discussing Osama Bin Laden. I thought the topic of their conversation was odd, but I also understood that terrorism was discussed with increasing frequency since the 1993 World Trade Center bombing by so-called Muslim extremists. I took pride in my Muslim heritage, but I did not wear the traditional Islamic headcovering, often referred to as the hijab, at that time, so the women did not seem at all awkward discussing Muslim extremists in front of me. As I stepped off the platform, I shook my head and mentally shrugged my shoulders and continued walking.

It was the first day of classes, and towards the end of my first class, the professor said something that really confused me; she said something along the lines of her family being really blessed but how afraid she was that some maniac would decide to target the oil rigs her husband worked on as an engineer. I puzzled over her comments, but mentally shrugging my shoulders again, I headed to the Students' Union Building for a quick break between classes. There, I saw students crowded around the TV sets in the cafeteria. I walked closer to see what it was that was captivating their attention, but felt my cellphone vibrating.

I answered and it was Mom on the line—she sounded frantic, "Muna! Where are you? I've been calling for over an hour!"

I had gotten married a few months ago and no longer lived at home, so I assumed Mom forgot that I had begun my fall term. I told her that I was at the university and that she had nothing to worry about, but, interrupting my words, she said she needed me to come home.

"Now?"

"Yes, NOW!"

Heart skipping, I asked if everything was okay? Was someone sick? She said that everyone was fine but that she needed me to come home right away. So I did. I literally ran to the transit station and then drove the last leg to my parents' place with a heavy heart, all the while thinking that someone had passed away but Mom did not want to tell me over the phone.

There was a sombre feel that I was not accustomed to as I walked into my parents' house, as it was usually filled with a lot of people and a lot of noise. My parents, Sittee, and my siblings, were all sitting in the family room watching unfolding coverage on CNN of what appeared to be an airplane hitting a tall building. But no, that could not happen, could it? Did the pilot fall asleep at the wheel? Did the plane lose the ability to navigate somehow? These thoughts whirled around in my head when Mom noticed me standing in the doorway. She jumped up and crushed me in a protective embrace, saying "Alhamdulillah," and started explaining that she heard that Muslims were being attacked on busses and even in their schools and places of work because of what was happening. That even people who were not Muslim were getting harassed because they looked like they may be.

At that point it all clicked—the women's conversation in the morning, my professor's seemingly random fears, the students crowded around the TV's, Mom's frantic call. I looked at the TV, and my entire being shook, "Oh my God. Oh no." My family all talked over and alongside one another, explaining the footage and all the horrifying details that were still emerging. I sat on the living room couch next to Sittee and held her hand as we tearfully watched the coverage that was replayed again and again in dismay, shock, and fear.

Later that evening, after the dinner table was cleared of mostly uneaten food, we sat dejectedly in front of the TV again, each of us in a sombre shock-induced reverie. And I silently prayed. I prayed for the victims. I prayed for the survivors. I prayed for the families and loved ones of those who lost their lives or were injured. I prayed for those who witnessed the attack. I prayed for the emergency responders. I prayed and I wondered what would happen next.

I went to the university the next morning to visit the professor for the class I missed the day before. I wanted to introduce myself and to pick up course materials. When I approached his office, I noticed the door was open and that he was bent over reading something on his desk. I knocked on his door quietly, introduced myself, and was about to explain why I had come by when he motioned for me to come inside, and gestured to the paper he had been reading while asking, "What does this word mean? Do you know?"

I do not recall what exact word he was pointing to, but it was a derivative of the word "Jihad," a beautiful Arabic word that means "to struggle" that has sadly become associated with terrorism. I was somewhat taken aback and wondered how he knew that I understood Arabic. I responded uncomfortably to his question and then awkwardly tried to explain that I was hoping to get the syllabus and any other course materials I had missed from the day before. He asked me why I had not attended the first day of class, and I answered truthfully, explaining a little about my mom's worry. He responded by saying something about how I couldn't afford to miss class because it was very challenging to get a good grade, even with proper attendance. I thanked him for the material, but left his office feeling incredibly judged.

I did not miss another class, and studied a little more diligently for his class than the rest of my courses that semester. I think it was because I wanted to prove that whatever assumptions he held about me based on that one missed class and/or my cultural/religious heritage were unfair. By chance, I happened to run into this professor at the beginning of the winter semester, and he stopped to ask me how I had done it. I asked what he meant. He said that most students complained that his tests were overly challenging, but that I was able to achieve near-perfect grades. Was I a straight-9 student? I chuckled and said I did all right, but that his class was actually the one and only class in which I ever achieved a 9 standing. But how? Why? What was different about his class? He seemed genuinely confused. I then explained how I felt that day in his office and how I had resolved to change whatever perceptions he had of me. He apologized for inadvertently making me feel that way and even offered me a letter of reference. I accepted his offer, and we made arrangements to meet for coffee a few days later. When we met, he apologized again and said that he reflected on what I had said and felt awful about the whole situation. I smiled and said that it had not been a completely negative experience after all. I gained a good mark, a letter of reference, and a new friend in the process.

Over fifteen years later, that tragic day's horrific events continue to shape so many lives around the world, innocent victims of the attacks and their families and communities, innocent victims in the so-called War on Terror, and everyday lived experiences of Muslims—or those who look to be Muslim—around the globe. All of whom continue to pay the price for the actions of deranged individuals and groups claiming Islam as their banner.

Disrupting Single Stories

> I've always felt that it is impossible to engage properly with a place
> or a person without engaging with all of the stories of that place
> and that person. The consequence of the single story is this: It robs
> people of dignity. It makes our recognition of our equal humanity
> difficult. It emphasizes how we are different rather than how we
> are similar.
>
> (Adichie, "Danger")

I sat and stared at my computer screen for what seemed like hours after I typed, read, and re-read the story of my experiences during, and immediately following, the horrific events of 9/11. I struggled with how to approach the story and its unpacking with nuance and fidelity. What could I possibly write that could approach its profundity? How can I ever come close to portraying the infinite ways that people's worlds all over the globe changed that day? This feeling of enormity is all the more difficult because I type these words at a time when the so-called Islamic State[13] is continuing to commit unimaginable atrocities in a region that is, all too often, ravaged by violence.

My doctoral supervisor Dr. D. Jean Clandinin, however, reminded me that I need to begin with, and stay close to, experience. I need to attend to lives composed over time in different places, and in relation, because pulled though I may be to engage in generalizations about 'the Muslim experience' post-9/11, "people are never only ... any particular set of isolated theoretical notions, categories, or terms. They are people in all their complexity. They are people living storied lives on storied landscapes" (Clandinin and Connelly, *Narrative* 145). Individuals who identify as Muslim are linguistically, racially, culturally, politically, and even theologically diverse (Ali; Aslan; Niyozov; Ramji "Creating", "A Variable"). I am trying to be wakeful (Greene) and honour this diversity by sharing my experiences in a way that does not attempt to generalize my personal experiences to the over 1.8 billion people who

---

13 My family refers to this group as *Daesh*, a derogatory Arabic word for "those who trample and crush." This treacherous group is known by many different names, such as IS (Islamic State), ISIS (the Islamic State of Iraq and Syria), and ISIL (the Islamic State of Iraq and the Levant).

identify as Muslim ("The Changing"). While undeniably shaped by larger social (dominant) narratives, my experiences are mine, rooted in specific times, places, and relationships. Drawing inspiration from Maxine Greene's concept of wide-awakeness, however, I think about how she discussed the concept of wide-awakeness as an "awareness of what it is to be in the world" (35). She also highlights that through purposeful and elevated consciousness that uncovers and critiques life's taken-for-grantedness, wide-awakeness simultaneously entails an awareness of what *ought* to be (35).

Chimamanda Ngozi Adichie also discusses the impossibility of generalizing lived experiences ("Danger"). Drawing upon her experiences in Nigeria, Mexico, and the United States, Adichie argues that a "single story" is created when places and/or people, in all their multiplicity, are repeatedly (mis)used to represent a singular construct. She asserts, "So that is how to create a single story, show a people as one thing, as only one thing, over and over again, and that is what they become." As I share stories of times I have, as a Muslim girl and woman, contended with single stories and discrimination in the pages to come, I stress, using Adichie's powerful words, "All of these stories make me who I am. But to insist on only these negative stories is to flatten my experience, and to overlook the many other stories that formed me. The single story creates stereotypes. And the problem with stereotypes is not that they are untrue, but that they are incomplete. They make one story become the only story" ("Danger").

In the next section, guided by the metaphoric three-dimensional narrative inquiry space of temporality, sociality, and place (Clandinin and Connelly, *Narrative*), I highlight some of the ways my personal stories of experiences with discrimination relate to some of the concepts in the literature I reviewed.

Salam ... Is So Hard to Live

Scrreeeech ... "Hey!!"

I was in grade eight, and Suha and I were crossing the busy street after purchasing lunch and a slurpee across the street from our junior high school when the car full of high-schoolers accosted us. The summer before my grade eight year, after attending Friday classes at the Masjid for over a year, we decided to don the veil.[14] *I had been so pumped! I knew it would not be easy, especially considering that we were basically the only girls wearing hijabs at our school, but I never imagined we would have to contend with several instances of overt discrimination.*

I turned around to see a car full of older boys. One of them had opened the window to stick his head out and shout, "Do you mind if I borrow that rag off your head to clean my car?"

Waves of mortification. Then, anger represented by a finger raised even as the boys drove away laughing. More mortification but mainly with myself this time. Suha cast a sideways look at me, trying to conceal her embarrassment and anger. "Why would you do that?" she asked.

"Because they deserved it." I stated with feigned confidence while my insides twisted. Why did I do that?

Word travels fast in school. People approached me to say "Good for you!" but I was so embarrassed and unhappy, not only to have been the target of derision but because my reaction was contrary to what my hijab signified for me—Salam, or translated into English, peace.

On (mis)Representation and Community

> A community does not make sense of the world through statistic,
> but stories.
> And bigots are painfully unimaginative.
>
> (Gonzales)

---

14 The head covering that some Muslim women don is also referred to as the hijab or headscarf. Although many scholars are careful to differentiate between the terms headscarf/veil and hijab, arguing that the concept of hijab is infinitely broader than a piece of fabric meant to cover a woman's hair, I use the terms headscarf/veil and hijab interchangeably. I do this because this is the term many veiled Muslim women use to refer to their headscarf/veil. However, the concept of hijab includes a requirement for men and women to observe modesty in demeanour and dress. The headscarf/veil is considered a form of hijab, and Islamic scholars from diverse Muslim communities differ in their opinions as to whether it is required to fulfill hijab for women.

Although the reverberations of 9/11 continue to be felt, anti-Muslim and/or Islamophobic[15] sentiment and rhetoric is not a new phenomenon (Aslan; Mattson; Said). However, the days, weeks, months, and years following that tragic day involved increasingly salient and disturbing narratives (mis)representing Islam and Muslims in mainstream media and literature. For me, some of the most jarring stories and images have been those related to Muslim girls and women. One of my most striking post-9/11 memories is listening to U.S. First Lady Laura Bush's radio address in November 2001, a month after the U.S., along with several allies, launched Operation Enduring Freedom in Afghanistan:

> Because of our recent military gains in much of Afghanistan, women are no longer imprisoned in their homes. They can listen to music and teach their daughters without fear of punishment. Yet the terrorists who helped rule that country now plot and plan in many countries. And they must be stopped. The fight against terrorism is also a fight for the rights and dignity of women.

While her words were intended to bolster a grieving nation at war, I recall feeling a heady sense of indignation. I struggled to understand how raining bombs upon people—the vast majority of whom were innocents—can ever be equated with rights and dignity. Alongside the damaging narratives, images of, at turns, mysterious, suspicious, exotic, and wounded girls and women filled television screens and book shelves—images of girls and women who looked like my mom and Sittee and friends and family ... and me.

Leila Ahmed highlights how Mrs. Bush's words, and the inundation of rhetoric surrounding the so-called War on Terror, were used to spin a story of the need to rescue "oppressed" Muslim girls and women, ironically serving to simultaneously legitimize the violence sometimes forced upon them. Muslim women—especially veiled Muslim women—are often storied by the media and in literature as any combination of the following: poor, uncivilized, oppressed, meek,

---

15 Islamophobia is described as "prejudice towards or discrimination against Muslims due to their religion, or perceived religious, national, or ethnic identity associated with Islam" ("What Is").

exotic, suspicious, less-than, and primitive.[16] These narratives ignore the very real historical, cultural, and imperial contexts that have sown and grown conflict, distrust, and extremism in the Middle East, Africa, and other areas with sizable Muslim populations (Mattson, "Fences"). They also ignore vast national, linguistic, cultural, racial, political, and theological diversity within Muslim communities (Aslan; Esposito and Mogahed; Niyozov; Ramji, "Creating", "Variable"). Further, based on a large multi-year Gallup study between the years 2001 and 2007 (and tens of thousands of hour-long, face-to-face interviews with Muslims from more than thirty-five nations), John Esposito and Dalia Mogahed assert that the "clash of civilizations" narrative that has been perpetuated about Islam in relation to the West is "far from inevitable. It is more about policy than principles" (xi). Regardless of these facts, a single story has been perpetuated about a global community of 1.8 billion people, comprising approximately a quarter of the world's population ("The Changing").

The (mis)representation of Muslim girls and women as oppressed victims in need of rescue is damaging on multiple personal and social levels. While Muslim girls and women in different parts of the globe have unfortunately been forced to cover, it is deleterious to deny that, like me and the females in my family, many girls and women *choose* to cover. Some Muslims believe that girls are required to practice hijab at the onset of puberty; others believe it is a personal matter of deciding when one is prepared to practice hijab, while still others do not believe that physically donning hijab is required (Abo-Lughod; Ahmed; Ali). Furthermore, the practice of hijab, and the extent to which Muslim women choose to cover different parts of their bodies, varies greatly. Muslim girls and women practice hijab in a multiplicity of ways and for reasons as diverse as the girls and women themselves (Abo-Lughod; Ahmed; Ali; Aslan; Barlas; Bullock and Jaffri; Khan; Ramji, "Creating", "Variable"). Leila Ahmed contends that, contrary to stereotypes, Muslim women have sometimes decided to don the veil to assert gender equality and control over their bodies. She also discussed the ways that this empowering narrative has all too often been

---

16 See: Abo-Lughod; Ahmed; Aslan; Bullock and Jaffri; Eid and Karim; Keddie; Khan; Nagra; Ramji "Creating", "Variable"; Sensoy and Marshall "Save", "Missionary."

co-opted by others, particularly by men and mainstream media. Rubina Ramji highlights how, for many of her veiled Muslim participants, hijab has helped them to "negotiate their private religious identities in the public sphere" ("Variable" 120). Farheen Khan illuminates some of the complex ways and diverse reasons that Canadian Muslim girls and women in particular conceptualize and practice hijab.

My profoundly spiritual, continually unfolding relationship with my hijab has been tension-filled. I chose to don hijab for the first time when I was in grade six, only to remove it a couple of weeks later because I was not comfortable with the decision. I thought I was ready to try again in the summer before grade eight, but I removed it again in the summer before grade nine. I struggled to come to terms with a practice I knew was viewed with varying degrees of suspicion, curiosity, and sometimes outright contempt by others with the meaning and esteem it held for me and my family. For me, veiling is symbolic of my faith—a visible manifestation of my jihad. The word jihad itself, a beautiful concept so integral to my faith, has often been coopted. It means to strive or struggle in the way of the Creator,[17] including the struggle against turning away from the Creator as well as the struggle against oppression and injustice (Aslan).

Born in the early 1930s, Sittee (Allah yirhama) veiled according to the local custom of her family's Palestinian village; my mom decided to veil when she was in her early 30s, after more than a decade of living in Canada; and my sisters Suha, Fatima, and Eman, all second-generation Canadian Muslim girls, donned the veil when they were in junior high school. Following my failed attempts at veiling, I was content to practice my Islam as a mostly private matter, one between me and Allah (SWT), until, shaken by the events of, and narratives following, 9/11, I decided to veil shortly before my twenty-second birthday, the month after I discovered I was pregnant with Noor. I resolved to live my Islam more publicly, with sincerity, and in peace. I sometimes struggle with this resolve, however, as it is often tested in many different ways.

Reflecting on some of my experiences with discrimination, I think

---

17 Allah (SWT) is referred to by ninety-nine sacred names in Islam. The Creator (Al-Khaliq) is one such sacred name.

about how I have often tried to respond with an "I-couldn't-care-less-what-you-think" cover story (Clandinin and Connelly, "Teachers'"). I confronted my doubts and my pain in private, supported and nurtured by family and friends. I still struggle to negotiate what it means to live as a veiled Muslim woman alongside others. Elsewhere (Saleh et al.), I have written of my struggles with silence and to allow for vulnerability in public settings:

> While deeply personal, my decision to wear the hijab is also extremely visible and public, carrying with it a myriad of stories—stories that shift depending upon the eye of the beholder. Some of these stories hearten and sustain me, some confuse and irritate me, and some intimidate and frighten me. Although the stories shift depending upon the beholder, I often feel the weight of each beholder's single story (Adichie, "Danger") of who/what I am and who/what I should be like in their stories of a woman who wears a hijab. I often feel their stories of me bumping up against my stories to live by, stories that are multiple, multifaceted, experiential, contextual, and always shifting. Feeling this weightiness and the bumping up of, at times, conflicting stories caused me, over time, to construct a defensive wall of silence. (Connelly and Clandinin, *Shaping* 274)

Later in the article, I write "I sense that I will continue to struggle against the urge to hide behind silence as I work to co-compose spaces of belonging ... I am aware of the ethical *necessity* of struggling against silence, for how can I be fully present in a caring, open, and reciprocal relationship if vulnerability is a one-sided expectation?" (Saleh et al. 274-275). Indeed, regardless of the discrimination and misrepresentations I have experienced and will likely continue to experience, I continue to struggle against silence, to try to "wage beauty" (Gonzales) in my everyday interactions and live my Islam with peace and integrity for myself, for my children, family and friends, and for all the worlds I inhabit and communities to which I belong.

Continuing to deepen my understandings of my research puzzle as I prepared to inquire alongside co-inquirers, I wondered what personal, familial, cultural, social, and institutional stories they might bump up against (Clandinin et al., *Composing*) as they compose their lives. Do they disrupt single stories with their stories of being and becoming?

Do they at times feel the need to animate constructions (Lugones) others have of them? As I considered the time period of this inquiry— amid daughter co-inquirers' transitions into adolescence—I was reminded that this time of transition may be spiritually profound as well. Sana Ali discusses the significance of secondary school as a time when most Muslim girls become *baligh,* "a term used in Islam to refer to one's coming of age, signified by reaching puberty. Once an individual is *baligh,* they are responsible and held accountable for observing religious practices. Though the exact age varies between Islamic sects, it is usually during their teenage years that Muslim girls are expected to actively observe their faith" (8). For Muslim girls in the process of transitioning to adolescence, this active observance may include expectations to fulfill, to the best of their ability, the five pillars of Islam[18] and some form of hijab. I wondered if/how co-inquirers have experienced these expectations and if/how they have already shaped some of their experiences.

Go Home (???)

Breathing deeply, I check the time on my phone. Why does it seem to be moving backward? It's Mother's Day. I should be sitting and getting pampered in some spa somewhere, not in a noisy overfilled amusement park, but there was no way I could have escaped bringing the kids when they knew their cousins were here. Thinking about grabbing a much-needed coffee on the way home, I turn to see Suha coming up the steps of the latest ride, tears rimming her eyes. Concerned, I ask her what happened. She gestures to a man standing with two small children at a nearby ride and says that he had pointed at her and shouted, "Shoot Bin Laden!" and "Go home!" while she and the children, seven in total, were playing a laser tag game. The children seem confused and disturbed, unsure why their mom and aunt was attacked, or, even more heartbreaking, somewhat familiar with the hate lobbed their way.

I breathe deeply again, this time out of anger. The man is looking at us at that point and, at turns, is shouting for us to go home or about terrorists.

---

18 These pillars include the following: the belief in one God and that Muhammed, Peace Be Upon Him, is His final messenger, five daily prayers, giving whatever one is able to give in charity, fasting the month of Ramadan, and performing Hajj (pilgrimage to the *Ka'ba* in Mecca) if one is physically and financially able.

Without much thought, I physically bridge the space between us. Feeling for the children beside him and extra cautious with my language for fear my rage would spill over into my words, I ask him, "So, who is the terrorist in this situation?" He pauses for a few moments but then shouts, "You! Look at how you look! Look at what's on your head!" Recognizing the futility of engaging any further with him I say, "I feel sorry for you, and especially for these innocent children, for the hate you are living."

I turn, ready to walk away as he continues spewing vitriol, when I see security guards approaching us. They ask what is going on and the man shouts something about terrorists causing trouble. When I am finally able to speak, I explain what happened, all the while embarrassed by the crowd of onlookers that had formed. The four guards seem to be visibly upset at the words and hate still being shouted, one even has tears in her eyes. Finally, a guard shouts, "Enough! I'm Muslim. Do you have a problem with me too?" The man finally stops shouting. The same guard guides us to a quieter area in the park and apologizes profusely to us for being attacked like that. After escorting the man to their office, the guard tells us to please try and forget about the incident and enjoy the rest of our day.

Suha and I are too upset to continue playing, so, emotionally drained, we leave the park. Noor and Yehia, seven and five years old at the time, ask why the mean man kept shouting at us, and why the police took him away. I try to explain a little about people who could be mean just because of how you look, but that seemed to only confuse them more. "But why Mama?" I do not know what else to say, so I tell them that some people are just unhappy in life and attack others just because. They are uncharacteristically quiet, and I wonder how they are making sense of everything. Knowing we will talk about this again, when we all have had more time to process, I think about the man's children and wonder if they too are asking questions and how they are making sense of the day's events. I wonder what stories were planted in Noor and Yehia and in the other children who witnessed the events that day.

The guard who had said he was Muslim called later that night and told me that the man was banned for a year from the mall that housed the park. He said that he isn't actually Muslim, but said so because he was so disturbed for us and for the children who witnessed the man's rage. He said he was really sorry that we were attacked so unfairly. It was only then, after thanking him and disconnecting the call, that I finally allowed some tears to fall. They were shed, however, not because of one man's hate but because of another's kindness.

Home Is Where the Heart (and soil) Is

> I am turtle, wherever I go I carry "home" on my back.
>
> (Anzaldúa 21)

"Go home!" is, unfortunately, a directive I have heard several times in my life. I know the same is true for many family and friends. The first time I was actively aware of the perception of some that I was not home was in grade six when a running child shouted it at me in passing near our school's playground. After that, however, it seemed to be hurled in my direction or the direction of those I love, with increasing frequency. In grade seven, I remember my mom coming home one day, visibly shaken, saying that a woman swore at her in the supermarket parking lot and shouted at her to "go home".

Ingrid Mattson, reflecting on the concept of "home," discusses how home is a place where you have nurtured the soil, where you have dug and planted and watered, where you have lived a give-and-take relationship with the land ("Rooting"). She asserts, "If you know your water, your land, your woods, you are going to feel at home." Vera Caine describes home as embodied and ontological, existing "somewhere between my memory and nostalgia for the past, my present and my future dreams and fears ... Home is also tied to people I have come to know and to significant events that are inscribed in the landscape" (1305). Home, then, is where the heart (and soil) is. Like the land, it lives in us.[19]

As I contemplated my research puzzle, I thought about my experiences with discrimination and the roots that held me to the lands of my birth and ancestors. I thought of the arbitrary lines drawn upon flat representations of topographical terrain, of places sacred and embodied. I thought of what the word "home" signifies for me and for my mom and Sittee, and I wondered what it means for my daughter Noor and other Canadian Muslim girls and their mothers, for

---

19 However, as an intergenerational survivor of Palestinian displacement and as a woman profoundly committed to fulfilling my obligations as a Treaty person living within Treaty 6 territory for "as long as that sun shines and yonder river flows", I think about how complex home-making can be within lands that Indigenous peoples called home long before European sailors arrived in North America (Taylor).

co-inquirers in particular. I thought of the multiple studies in literature related to Muslim children, youth, and families I have come across, and how many writers situate their studies around research questions related to "belonging" as though it was assumed a priori that Muslim children, youth, and families would feel a *lack* of this general, all-encompassing concept. I thought about some of my experiences with discrimination and I wondered if co-inquirers have contended with similar experiences, especially in the wake of recent worldwide terror attacks and the horrific exploits of IS/ISIS/ISIL/*Daesh*. I wondered what home places and spaces may look like for co-inquirers and if/how these spaces are being composed/found within familial and school landscapes. I wondered about daughter co-inquirers' experiences in particular, as the scarce literature around the diverse experiences of Canadian Muslim females usually revolve around older youth and women ...what interior and exterior locales are the girls tied to, heart and soil?

Prayers through the Storm

Grief and shame and fear
Wash over
A vast ocean of bewildering tides
From the East and the West
Moments of lucidity
Within cyclical storms of horror and hate
Torrential showers of grief
And shame
Because one thought was
Please Allah, please don't let them be Muslim
Amidst prayers
That this is not true, not really happening
That loved ones can return home to their beloveds
That humanity can survive and rise above
Storms of horror and hate
Butchers who invoke God's name as they slaughter
Leaders who invoke security as they rain bombs
Terrorists shouting 'terrorist' at one another
Treacherous currents that threaten all

......

When the most powerful waves recede
I am washed ashore
lost
pained
weary

And I force myself to rise up once again
To cleanse myself in calming waters
Offer another prayer for the day

and ask Allah

To rain love on the victims, their loved ones, and us all
To shower peace and blessings upon them, their loved ones, and us all
To pour strength and mercy on us all

to resist, I pray

That I will continue to be blessed with the strength and courage
To leave my house
To smile at strangers
To project peace
And love
And prayers
Without shame or guilt or suspicion or fear.

Growing (maternal) Stories of Uncertainty

Leaving the theatre's party room smiling, I join the birthday girl, my niece Rana, and her friends in the ladies' washroom. The fourteen girls, ranging in age from five to twelve years old, had just finished eating pizza and birthday cake, interspersed with musical chairs and freeze-dancing games. Remembering how I used to dream of going to the movies when I was a child, and not having stepped into a theatre until I was 14 years old, always makes movie theatre parties extra special for me.

Before we move from the party room into the theatre, my sister Suha and I think it would be a good idea to partner each older girl with a younger girl to visit the washroom. I walk the short distance to the washroom and see that most of the girls are now washing or drying their hands and preparing to leave. I lift one of my younger nieces, Reanne, so she can wash her hands at the rather high sink when I hear a voice shouting with annoyance lacing her words, "Move out of the way girls!" I turn to see my daughter Noor squeeze herself between two hand dryers to make room as a woman shoves past her. The woman catches my eye, glares at me, and shakes her head disapprovingly. Ignoring her, I proceed to move with Reanne to the drying area when I notice Noor looking at me with a mixture of confusion and surprise. I understand her look, one that questions why I did not say anything in response to the woman's rudeness. I shake my head slightly and, without thinking, bite the bottom part of my lip in a gesture my mom always used to signify the need to hold myself and my words, not to say or do anything rash. Noor stares at me, obviously unhappy and, then, looking away, walks out of the washroom a short distance behind the unimpressed woman.

No longer smiling as I hold Reanne's hand to return to the party room, I think about who I was in that moment in relation to the woman and to Noor. I wonder if the woman is having a bad day and had behaved in an uncharacteristic way. I wonder if she has a son or daughter and what she would have done in my situation as a mother. I wonder if she has ever felt the need to be extra cautious with her words and actions because of her gender, cultural or religious background, or because of different reasons altogether. I wonder if she would have yelled at the girls like that or shaken her head at me if she knew the context of why we were there, taking up more space than she felt appropriate. I wonder if it would have made a difference if she knew that, for me, the birthday party had been a brief reprieve from anxiety amidst so many uncertainties facing my family.

Sitting in the darkened theatre after the chaos of sorting seats and snacks, I think about Noor and how I used to dislike it when my mom used that lip-biting gesture with me—how often I felt upset at being silenced as a child and youth—although as a mother I now appreciate the overwhelming urge to protect my children and to try to slow down moments that could become even more ugly. I think about the infinite times Noor has witnessed me speak up yet try to remain calm and respectful even while incredibly upset when words or actions directed at me or my loved ones were not okay, and I understand her surprise at my silence. I think about so many of the stories I have not shared with Noor about some of my friends' experiences in the wake of several global terror attacks—like one friend being shouted at to "go home" by a man at the bus stop or how another friend was accosted while waiting in a fast-food drive-

through by a woman who got out of her car with the express purpose of pounding on my friend's window to yell, "Take that fucking rag off your head!" I think about these stories that anger and terrify me and make me extra protective, extra cautious. Stories that I haven't shared with her because I want her to love every part of herself without fear or disillusionment.

On the way home, I ask Noor if she liked the movie. She responds that it was okay, but then immediately asks me why I did not respond to the woman who, in her words, "Freaked out at us." Gathering my thoughts, and carefully choosing what to (not) share before answering, I tell her that, as a woman in hijab, I often feel the need to weigh my words and actions extra carefully. I talk about how uncertain I am in these types of situations—do I speak up or not? Is it worth a possible escalation? Will I be upset with myself if I do not say anything? Will I just be reinforcing stereotypes if I do? All of these thoughts and many stories, the woman's and mine, hovered in the spaces between us in that tense moment before I decided to turn away. I tell Noor that even though I really wanted to say something, in that situation, speaking up probably would not have been advisable because it may have ruined her cousin's birthday party. Noor seems to be listening intently and contemplating my words, but she does not really respond. We ride in silence for the remainder of our drive home.

On (not) Sharing (single) Stories

> my whole life
> i have
> ate my tongue.
> ate my tongue.
> ate my tongue.
> i am so full of my tongue
> you would think speaking is easy.
> but it is not.
> —for we who keep our lives in our mouths
>
> —Nayyirah Waheed

Reflecting upon the events at the movie theatre that day, I worry about the stories I am planting alongside Noor in our familial curriculum-making. I worry about how and when to share stories that may upset her—stories that have the potential to shift the stories she lives and tells as a Muslim girl alongside me and others, and I wonder if mother co-inquirers have experienced a similar urge to "eat their tongue" to protect their children? Do they too worry about how, when, and/or if they should share stories that could be painful to hear? Reconsidering the stories I have live(d) alongside my mom and alongside my children, I wonder about how other mothers negotiate the tensions of making their children aware of the existence of potentially painful stories ... without unintentionally foretelling foreboding (single) stories of what their experiences *will* be?

Growing Forward ... and Rooting a Narrative Inquiry

> All stories of the past are
> filtered
> through the circumstances of the present,
> looking ahead to the future.
>
> (Bateson, *Full* 50)

Through engaging in autobiographical narrative inquiry (Clandinin, "Engaging"; Saleh et al.), I tried to attend to and honour the stories and wonders living within me as I prepared to engage in narrative inquiry alongside three other Muslim mothers and daughters. Contemplating the layers of complexity in the stories I live *by*, *with*, and *in* (Clandinin, "Engaging"), I wondered what stories would be called forth as I engaged in inquiry alongside co-inquirers. Sitting with the stories I live as a second-generation Canadian Muslim woman, (grand)daughter, mother, wife, teacher, graduate student, researcher, sister, niece, cousin, and friend, I wondered about who I was, who I am, and who I will become as I come alongside co-inquirers. Looking forward to the next chapter, I will make visible the ways I tried to ethically attend to and honour the stories living within me and co-inquirers—the stories we have live(d) *by*, *with*, and *in*, as we engaged in this relational work alongside one another.

Chapter 2

Rooting and Growing (Chosen) Narrative Inquiry Communities

Narrative inquirers tell stories about the stories they and others live and tell, keeping in mind how their own stories shape how they understand and tell the stories of others. They understand story as the fundamental unit of experience; one that cannot be broken down into smaller pieces without a loss of the wholeness of the life that produced it.

(Downey and Clandinin 387)

I have tried, thus far, to make visible the interconnectedness of some of the stories I live(d) *by*, *with*, and *in*. I have also attempted to simultaneously illuminate my belief in the storied nature and educative[20] (Dewey) possibilities of life and experience. My deeply rooted belief that we live *by*, *with*, and *in* a multiplicity of stories called me to engage in narrative inquiry alongside other Muslim mothers and daughters to deepen our understandings of our experiences in relation, over time, in different places, and always in the multilayered midst of stories. Connelly and Clandinin help me to understand the following:

20 Dewey differentiates between "educative" and "miseducative" experiences; an experience can be miseducative if it "has the effect of arresting or distorting the growth of further experience" (25). An educative experience, in contrast, encourages the growth of further experience.

People shape their daily lives by stories of who they are and others are and as they interpret their past in terms of these stories. Story, in the current idiom, is a portal through which a person enters a world and by which their experience of the world is interpreted and made personally meaningful. Narrative inquiry, the study of experience as story, then, is first and foremost a way of thinking about experience. Narrative inquiry as methodology entails a view of the phenomenon. To use narrative inquiry methodology is to adopt a particular view of experience as phenomenon under study. ("*Narrative*" 375)

Narrative inquiry is philosophically grounded in John Dewey's view of life as education and education as experience. This conceptualization is built upon Dewey's two criteria of experience, *interaction* and *continuity*, enacted in *situations*. The first criteria, *continuity*, calls attention to how "experience both takes up something from those which have gone before and modifies it in some way" (35). Dewey's conceptualization of the second criteria of experience, *interaction*, "assigns equal rights to both factors in experience— objective and internal conditions. Any normal experience is an interplay of these two sets of conditions. Taken together, or in their interaction, they form what we call a *situation*" (42).

Working from Dewey's ideas, Clandinin and Connelly develop the three metaphoric dimensions of narrative inquiry: temporality, sociality, and place (*Narrative*). These authors remind me that it has been important to situate this inquiry from within the three-dimensional narrative inquiry space throughout the research. However, Clandinin emphasizes the following: "the three dimensions in the inquiry space are interconnected and interwoven. Temporality is threaded into place and into events and emotions. The dimensions are not separated from one another ... as we compose and co-compose interim research texts, we awaken to the interwovenness of life experience" (50). When I began writing some of my stories of experience as part of an extensive autobiographical narrative inquiry, I was awakened to the impossibility of placing my experiences into compartments independent of other experiences. My awareness that my stories were intimately connected to those of my mom and Sittee called me to attend to, and honour, familial and intergenerational stories planted in my living alongside them, and how these stories continue to live in me and shape who I am and who I am becoming. The interconnectedness of temporality, sociality, and place, and the interconnectedness of the myriad stories mother and daughter co-inquirers and I live *by*, *with*, and *in* lived at the forefront of my awareness as I engaged in this work. It also lived at the periphery of my awareness, for as Mary Catherine Bateson beautifully notes, "I know that if I look very narrowly and hard at anything I am likely to see something new—like the life between the grass stems that only becomes visible after moments of staring. Softening that concentration is also important—I've heard that the best way to catch the movements of falling stars is at the edge of vision" ("Peripheral" 103-104).

Growing Forward ...
Always *in relation* and in the Midst of Stories

> "Relationship is key to what it is that narrative inquirers do"
> (Clandinin and Connelly, *Narrative* 189)

As I prepared for and engaged in this study, Clandinin reminded me that *thinking* narratively – honouring experience as an inherently storied and relational phenomenon – will help me to stay wakeful to the interconnected wholeness of lives lived in relation, over time and place ("Engaging"). Narrative inquirers view themselves as people in relation inquiring alongside others *in relation* (Huber). Co-inquirers and I live *in relation* to our past, present, and not-yet-lived future. We live *in relation* to others—to family, friends, and many others. We live *in relation* to, and in the midst of, personal, social, intergenerational, cultural, temporal, historical, political, linguistic, familial, and institutional narratives. In this view of life and research, 'I, the researcher' cannot be considered as somehow detached from '*Them*, the researched.' Inherent in this commitment to honouring life as profoundly relational is a commitment to honouring co-inquirers and our stories—stories that root and sustain us (Clandinin, "Engaging"; Lopez).

Winter 2015: Closing my eyes after tearfully lighting the memorial candle, I make duaa that Allah (SWT) has mercy on the souls of Deah, Razan, and Yusur.[21] I pray that their families and loved ones somehow feel the love and peace emanating from this gathering and that they be blessed with sabr. While it is a chilly February evening, there are a few hundred people taking part in tonight's vigil to honour Deah, Razan, and Yusur's lives. As I pray silently, I hear, "Assalamu Alaikum ... Muna?" I turn to see a woman and girl in hijab smiling at me. I had been in contact with Ayesha, a Muslim mother who contacted me and expressed an interest in participating in this research a few weeks ago. Talking about the vigil during our brief phone conversation, we agreed to meet here for the first time. Smiling back at them, I say, "Ayesha and Zahra? It's so good to meet you, but I wish it was under different circumstances."

Growing an Inquiry Rooted in Relational Ethics

> What ought to be interesting ... is the unfolding of a lived life rather than the confirmation such a chronicle provides for some theory.
>
> (Coles 22)

As I rooted and grew a story of engaging in inquiry that honours the stories mother and daughter co-inquirers and I (re)told and (re)lived, M. Huber et al. has helped me to understand that my relational responsibilities to co-inquirers are akin to the responsibilities of my friendships in an "ethics of life" (qtd. in Charon and Montello 218). Clandinin and Murphy similarly emphasize that although I must necessarily attend to the "so what?" and "who cares?" justifications for engaging in this inquiry, my uppermost consideration must be to honour those who are inquiring alongside me and the stories of experiences they have entrusted me with, since "the ethical stance of narrative inquirers is best characterized by a relational ethics" (600).

Turning to reconsider the stories I shared in Chapter 1, I think of how difficult it can be to inquire alongside others in ways that honour

---

21 The vigil was held in honour of Razan and Yusor Abu-Salha, and Deah Barakat, three Muslim American students killed by a neighbour in Chapel Hill in what many deemed to be a hate crime (Elliot; Talbot).

relational ethics. I experienced a great deal of uncertainty as I thought and rethought, considered and reconsidered some of the stories I (re) presented (Ely). Although I tried to be careful when inquiring alongside my mom and Sittee (Allah yirhama) into the stories of experience they shared with me, I understand that our conversations—and my representations—included memories of painful experiences. My loved ones approved of my writing and representations within these pages; however, my experiences inquiring alongside them emphasize for me the profound responsibility in honouring the stories co-inquirers entrust me with, for as Lopez reminds me, "the stories people tell have a way of taking care of them. If stories come to you, care for them."

Summer 2015: I re-read the three words in the report over and over again: "Displays Autistic tendencies"—three clinical words that carry a multiplicity of stories. While I requested the meeting with the community health nurse because I was worried about my youngest daughter's, Hannah's, speech development, I was not prepared for the life-altering import and uncertainty of these three words. As the nurse spoke of referring Hannah to the Autism Clinic, I try to steady my breath and racing thoughts by making duaa, "Insha'Allah khair" ...

Growing Forward ... Alongside Co-Inquirers

> And who are you that [wo]men should rend their bosom ...
> See first that you yourself deserve to be a giver,
> and an instrument of giving.

Khalil Gibran, *The Prophet*

Following ethics approval from the University of Alberta's Research Ethics Board in early January 2015, I contacted several friends, colleagues, and community liaisons from my work as a teacher and community volunteer to assist me in inviting co-inquirers to this research. A few weeks later, in mid-January 2015, a close friend passed my introductory letter to Zahra, a Muslim girl my friend knew from her work with Zahra's community. Zahra's mother, Ayesha, contacted me to express an interest in participating in this research. A week later, in late January 2015, another close friend called me to excitedly share the news that her friend, Safaa, and Safaa's daughter, Rayyan, were looking forward to a phone call from me to discuss possible participation in this research. In the summer of 2015, Layla and Maya were the third mother and daughter co-inquirer pair to come alongside me in this research. Layla reached out to me after she heard of my search for potential participants from her older sister, Sara, who is a very close friend of mine. In Chapters 3, 4, and 5, I give more detailed accounts of how Safaa and Rayyan, Ayesha and Zahra, and Layla and Maya and I came to live and inquire alongside one another.

In larger group gatherings with our families, conversations with mother and daughter pairs, and one-on-one conversations, we have frequented each other's homes, picnicked in community parks, dined out together, shared coffee and play dates, enjoyed movies and movie nights, and planned field trips and mosque visits/events together. Always in the midst of a multiplicity of stories, we engaged alongside each other in ways that blurred the (unclear and shifting) boundaries between our research and our living and growing as co-inquirers and as friends. However, as M. Huber et al. remind me, like the rhythms inherent in all life relationships, research relationships require continual care, nurturing, and wakefulness to not only honour relational responsibilities, but to make visible the possibilities of living our stories in different ways.

I iteratively collected, co-composed, and analyzed field texts (commonly referred to as "data") and simultaneously composed and negotiated interim and final research texts alongside co-inquirers throughout the inquiry—from February 2015 to February 2017 with Ayesha and Zahra, and Safaa and Rayyan, and from June 2015 to March 2017 with Layla and Maya. Part of negotiating participation with co-inquirers involved asking each mother and daughter if they would like to relationally co-compose field texts alongside me, and if so, what forms of field texts they would like to compose. Ayesha, Safaa, and Layla, three busy women and mothers, indicated that they would enjoy engaging in face-to-face, digital, and telephone conversations. Zahra, Rayyan, and Maya—three talented girls in the midst of transitioning to adolescence—were more varied in their responses to my question. As we began our conversations, I gifted all three girls with disposable cameras, sketchbooks, coloured gel pens, and journals as possible ways to co-compose field texts. While I engaged in multiple conversations and community excursions alongside Zahra, Maya, and Rayyan, only Maya decided to include her artistic and reflective compositions as field texts. Other field texts include recordings and transcriptions of multiple one-on-one and group conversations, field notes of all conversations and communications, including telephone and digital communications, co-composed and/or co-inquirer composed annals, and our reflective and creative writing. Memory box items (Clandinin and Connelly, *Narrative*), including photographs, home videos, letters, and other artifacts, were also used to help guide some of our conversations.

Thinking about the many different places co-inquirers and I engaged in inquiry, I am reminded of how Huber et al. were awakened to the curriculum continually composed by children, youth, and families within familial and community landscapes. Drawing upon Lugones' notion of world-travelling, Schwab's curriculum commonplaces of teacher, learner, subject matter, and milieu, and Connelly and Clandinin's (*Teachers*) conceptualization of curriculum as a living, evolving composition (a "course of life" rather than simply a course of study), Huber et al. reconceptualize curriculum-making as occurring within two worlds: familial and school curriculum-making worlds. Wondering about the world-travel children engage in as they live in, and move between, familial and school curriculum-making worlds, they write

> Given these two worlds, what seems important is to more clearly understand how both worlds are places of curriculum making and that, as parents, teachers, and societies, we ask children to move between two places and live in both worlds on a daily basis. It seems imperative then to keep asking about, and working towards, understanding how we might engage children, teachers, and families in playful world travel with loving perception. (Hubert et al. 141)

While this inquiry includes explorations of co-inquirers' in- and out-of-school experiences, it is situated within familial and community contexts. This involved coming alongside co-inquirers within the diverse array of contexts they chose to invite me to—including our homes, restaurants, playgrounds, theatres, sports arenas and centres, community functions, shopping malls, and mosques. I agree with Huber et al. that while both familial and school curriculum-making need to be regarded as valuable to the composition of lives, school curriculum-making has been prioritized in the study of curriculum. Through purposefully inquiring alongside co-inquirers into our familial curriculum-making practices, we value and make visible the curriculum-making that occurs within our familial and community contexts.

Fall 2015: Tearfully driving away from the Masjid, I make duaa for Maya and Layla and their loved ones. Being alongside them at Maya's grandmother's funeral (Allah yirhama) was incredibly hard. Sharing in their grief, I remember Yehia and Jiddee's funerals (Allah yirhamun) and I make duaa for Maya's grandmother and the souls of all our loved ones who have passed.

Rooting and Growing Relational Ethics ... within Communities of Choice

It may well be imaginative capacity that allows us also to experience empathy with different points of view, even with interests apparently at odds with ours. Imagination may be a new way of decentering ourselves, of breaking out of the confines of privatism and self-regard into a space where we can come face to face with others and call out, "Here we are"

(Greene 31)

Attempting to be mindful of the multiplicity of stories we live *by*, *with*, and *in*, I sought to live and inquire in relationally ethical (Clandinin et al., *Relational*) ways alongside mother and daughter co-inquirers. In Menon et al., I write about how "living ethically alongside one participant may mean giving her time and space to reach out to me when she feels ready to share her experiences rather than giving in to my urge to follow a pre-set conversation schedule" (86). For another participant, living ethically "may mean leaving my beloved audio recorder at home (!) so that she feels more comfortable sharing some of the more tension-filled experiences she has lived" (86). I continue:

These shifts to what I had originally imagined when planning this study are not simply for ensuring comfort; I make these often difficult decisions in the hopes of living in ethically relational ways with participants—girls and women who have agreed to live and inquire alongside me for deeper understandings of our often ignored/silenced/ misconstrued experiences as Canadian Muslim females. (Menon et al. 86-87)

As I reflect upon coming alongside Safaa and Rayyan, Ayesha and Zahra, and Layla and Maya, I think about how my view of living and inquiring in ethically relational ways has expanded over the two years since I typed those words. Clandinin et al. (*Relational*) assert, "It matters if, and how, we tell our stories and listen to others' stories in narrative inquiry. If, and how, we listen can influence, can shape, the lives of both listeners and tellers." In Chapter 7, I draw upon Hilde L. Nelson's conceptualization of communities of choice—wherein members create spaces to co-compose, live, and tell morally self-defining stories (28)—to illuminate the many ways that mother and daughter co-inquirers and I resisted taken-for-granted single stories (Adichie, "Danger") and arrogant perceptions (Lugones) alongside one another. I make visible how this involved co-composing conversational spaces (Clandinin, et al, "Reverberations") within in our (chosen) narrative inquiry communities to tell, listen to, and inquire into our stories and how this hard yet sustaining work was undergirded by an ethics of being *in relation.*

Winter 2015: As I prepare to leave Rayyan and Safaa's home, Safaa asks me when Hannah's appointment at the autism clinic is scheduled for. I sigh and say, "Not for another six months." Safaa shakes her head and says, "Muna, you have to keep calling them. They need to know that six months is too long to wait. You and Hannah need support." Grateful for her love and friendship, I smile at Safaa and say, "I will insha'Allah call them so much that they will be tired of hearing my voice." Hugging me tightly, Safaa makes duaa that everything works out in a good way, and I say, "Ameen."

Growing from Field Texts to Interim Research Texts

> Wherever lives overlap and flow together,
> there are depths of unknowing.
>
> (Bateson, "Full" 3)

Clandinin ("Engaging") reminds me that the move from collecting, composing, and co-composing field texts to writing research texts is a recursive, always relational, process oftentimes laced with tension and uncertainty. As I began to compose initial narrative accounts of inquiring alongside one another, I wondered how I could give a sense of our experiences that calls forth the gaze of loving perception (Lugones). How could I write of our experiences in ways that eschew sanitizing and colonizing our stories for voyeuristic consumption? Elsewhere (Menon et al.), I ruminate about inking words to paper in ways that honour co-inquirers and our ongoing life-making "without reducing our diverse and nuanced experiences to a single (stereotypical) story (Adichie, "Danger") of what it means to be a Canadian Muslim female" (88). I wondered, "How can I give a sense of the artistry and improvisation (Bateson, "Composing") with which we have composed our lives amidst myriad personal, familial, intergenerational, social, cultural, linguistic, institutional, and temporal plotlines" (88)?

As I slowly moved from composing field texts to interim research texts, to help root and sustain my work as a narrative inquirer, I carefully attended to the three-dimensional narrative inquiry space, and engaged in several conversations about my writing process alongside co-inquirers, my supervisor Jean, and my response community friends, Jinny Menon and Hiroko Kubota (Kubota et al.; Menon et al.; Saleh et al. "Naming"). Trying to be wakeful to the multiplicity of (ongoing) stories co-inquirers and I live *by*, *with*, and *in*, I approached the composition of interim texts with a profound ontological commitment to take care of our stories, and of the friends and co-inquirers who generously shared and lived them alongside me.

Spring 2016: I smile at my phone as I read the text from Ayesha offering help with my move. Having jokingly competed in the "who moves more?" game, Ayesha's text assures me that she knows of several tips and tricks to help with the tedious task of packing, moving, and unpacking boxes. I reply, "Almost there! Thank you so much for your kind offer my friend!" I think about how all three mother co-inquirers have offered to help with my family's move, and loading another box into the moving van, I say Alhamdulillah for wonderful friends.

Growing from Interim to Final Research Texts

> Wisdom comes not by the accumulation of more and more
> experiences but through discerning patterns in the deeper mystery of
> what is already there ... Wisdom, then, is born of the overlapping of
> lives, the resonance between stories.
>
> (Bateson, "Full" 243)

Planted in me over many seasons of inquiry, the stories mother and daughter co-inquirers and I lived and shared continue to live in me. The narrative accounts in Chapters 3, 4, and 5 are rooted in embodied, experiential living and inquiring alongside co-inquirers for approximately two years. Clandinin, et al. explained, "The term narrative account, or perhaps narrative accounting, allows us to give an account, an accounting, a representation, of the unfolding of lives, both participants and researchers, at least as they became visible in those times and places where our stories intersected and were shared" ("Reverberations" 9). Before, during, and after each conversation (as well as during the times between them), I composed detailed field notes, including my observations, wonderings, resonances, and tensions. I re-listened to our conversations and re-visited field notes often, adding new wonderings and considerations over time. Each time I transcribed our conversations—a process which would occur over a period of two to three days depending on the length of the recording—I travelled back to earlier times and places alongside co-inquirers, pausing often to make notes of wonderings, resonances, silences, continuities, discontinuities, tensions, and the emergence of possible threads in the margins of the transcript or in my nearby notebook. Every time I revisited the recorded and/or transcribed conversations, more notes would be added and more connections and disconnections would become visible. I carried these notes and wonderings with me to the next conversation and, as we discussed them, new wonderings and possibilities for future discussions and inquiry often emerged.

In the fall of 2016, I began an intense process of (re)turning to the field texts with the intent of discerning resonant threads for each pair of mother and daughter co-inquirers. I searched for "threads that echoed and reverberated across" (Clandinin, "Reverberations" 14) the stories of being and becoming that co-inquirers and I (re)told and (re)lived alongside one another over time. Feeling overwhelmed by the number of field texts we had composed and co-composed over two years of inquiring alongside one another, I resolved to somehow organize field texts for each pair of mother and daughter co-inquirers. I chronologically ordered transcribed conversations, field notes, and other field texts co-inquirers and I composed because I felt that this would help me in identifying the shifts in our (re)living and (re)telling over time.

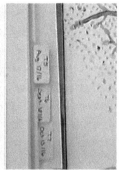

LtoR: Field texts organized in binders. Field texts organized chronologically.

Because research texts, including interim texts, are interpreted texts composed via the understandings co-inquirers and I have of the resonances, threads, "disruptions, interruptions, silences, gaps, and incoherences" (Clandinin, "Engaging" 50) of the stories we lived and shared, I then painstakingly and repeatedly (re)listened to our conversations and (re)read all of the newly organized field texts to identify continuities, discontinuities, silences, resonances, tensions, and wonders. I engaged in this intense process for all three pairs of mother and daughter co-inquirers, and composed detailed notes in the process.

This intense and iterative process of reading and re-reading field texts, and revisiting recorded conversations, involved identifying and then making visible the resonant threads and the connections among and between overlapping, deeply intertwined stories that co-inquirers and I (re)told and (re)lived over time. After identifying stories and threads that seemed particularly important to include in our narrative account, I met with co-inquirers to discuss their thoughts about my interpretations of our discussions and inquiry. I typed and printed out a page of emerging threads, as well as a few pages of initial writing about how we came to inquire alongside one another. As we read these pages aloud, I felt nervous and wondered if I had, in some way, reduced or misinterpreted our conversations and/or living alongside one another? I asked variations of the following questions: "Are you comfortable with this? Do you recognize yourself in this? Do you feel that it honours the stories we shared, lived, and inquired into alongside one another? Is anything missing? Does anything seem out of place or did I seem to misunderstand or misinterpret anything?"

As I began writing about my experiences inquiring alongside Safaa and Rayyan in November and December of 2016 (I later wrote narrative accounts of inquiring alongside Ayesha and Zahra in January and February of 2017, and Layla and Maya in February and March of 2017), I decided to organize my writing chronologically, by writing about our conversations in the order we engaged in them. I did this to show, rather than simply tell about, our coming alongside each another over time as co-inquirers. For, as Margot Ely notes, "our reports must glow with life. This not only to honor our stories but, more important, to support the ethic that undergirds them ... narrative researchers are obligated to present the stories of those people in ways that cleave as closely as possible to the essence of what and how they shared" (569). As I strove to "cleave as closely as possible to the essence" of the stories and experiences co-inquirers and I lived, shared, and inquired into alongside one another, I decided to restructure my writing by representing our conversations through the initial *telling* of our conversations in chronological order, then, following each telling section, unpacking our stories by drawing out resonant threads in *retellings* sections. To give a sense of the difference between the telling and retellings sections, I used the present tense in the *telling* of our conversations, and the past tense—as a way to indicate reflectively looking back—for *retellings* sections.

As I engaged in this work, I felt that referencing the specific dates of our conversations did not give a sense of the many months we engaged in this inquiry. Contemplating this, the idea to structure our conversations (and the times between them) around the seasons began to take root in my mind. Later composing narrative accounts of inquiring alongside Ayesha and Zahra, and Layla and Maya, I felt that continuing the representational form of tellings and retellings helped me to show rather than simply tell about how we relationally composed our inquiry over many seasons. I met with co-inquirers often during this process and we read over, and negotiated, interim texts, including initial drafts of our narrative accounts, together.

Following the co-composition and negotiation of narrative accounts, I began the process of looking across our narrative accounts for resonant threads in the stories Safaa, Rayyan, Ayesha, Zahra, Layla, Maya, and I (re)told and (re)lived in our inquiries. As I engaged in this recursive and reflexive process, many resonances, tensions, continuities, discontinuities, silences, and educative possibilities were made increasingly visible in our life-making as Canadian Muslim females. Holding our embodied, experiential stories of being and becoming close as I (re)visit ideas and concepts in the literature I reviewed, in chapters 6, 7, and 8, I draw attention to some of the threads echoing across our narrative accounts. In these ways, throughout our transition(s) from composing field texts to composing research texts, I sought to honour the ways co-inquirers and I relationally lived and inquired alongside one another over time.

Fall 2016: I watch Noor and Yehia playing with Hannah at the park, and I feel tears of gratitude well in my eyes. Incredibly moved and proud of the way Noor and Yehia have become even more loving and patient with Hannah after her diagnosis with Autism Spectrum Disorder (ASD) a few months ago, I say Alhamdulillah for countless blessings ... especially being blessed with the opportunity to mother and live alongside three awe-inspiring souls.

Rooting Stories to Grow By ... Together

We are fully dependent on each other for the possibility of being
understood
and without this understanding we are not intelligible,
we do not make sense,
we are not solid, visible, integrated;
we are lacking.
So travelling to each other's "worlds"
would enable us to *be*
through loving each other.

(my emphasis, Lugones 8)

Mary Catherine Bateson writes, "Wherever lives overlap and flow together, there are depths of unknowing" ("Full" 3). Although inquiring alongside co-inquirers has been an incredibly illuminating and fulfilling process, it has also been tension-filled work imbued with uncertainty. As our narrative accounts in the following chapters make visible, I have experienced "depths of unknowing" and have wondered about how to negotiate innumerable aspects of narratively inquiring and living alongside co-inquirers, as our lives met and continue to "overlap and flow together." I have frequently wondered who I am— and who I am always in the process of becoming—as a Canadian Muslim woman, mother, (grand)daughter, graduate student, teacher, scholar, and narrative inquirer alongside co-inquirers. However, as I reflect upon the many wisdoms Safaa, Rayyan, Ayesha, Zahra, Layla, and Maya have planted in me, I am grateful for the opportunity to live and inquire alongside six girls and women who taught me so much about composing lives *in relation* to personal, familial, social, cultural, temporal, institutional, linguistic, faith-based/religious, and other narratives ... for, as the following chapters make visible, depths of knowing grew within me in the process.

Chapter 3

A Narrative Account of Living and Growing Alongside Rayyan and Safaa

> But in your thought you must measure time into seasons,
> let each season encircle all the other seasons.
> And let today embrace the past with remembrance and the future
> with longing.
> —Khalil Gibran, *The Prophet*

Rayyan and Safaa's Family

Safaa—Mom

Ahmad—Dad

Children by Birth Order

Leila

Ali

Sadia

Rayyan

Marwa

Amina

Thinking Back ... and Growing Forward

I am sitting with many thoughts after Safaa, Rayyan, Marwa, and Amina's visit tonight. We spent the last two hours reviewing transcripts and interim research texts and discussing possible ways forward in the writing of our narrative account. I reflect on composing a relationship alongside them, and I think about time. I think about how the meaning and measure of time changes for me, over time of course, but also in relation to different periods and moments in my life. How many times have I been impatient to begin or end something, and how often have I wished for time to go slower, to find moments and spaces to think, reflect, savour, and just be? I have been blessed to live and inquire alongside Rayyan and Safaa over many seasons, getting to know them and some of their stories slowly. I have been blessed with time to co-create spaces to share our stories, and the hopes, fears, resonances, and struggles we have had and continue to have moving forward.

Our relationship has undoubtedly shifted over time, and I felt I needed to show these shifts through telling the story of our co-composed inquiry over the many seasons we spent together. However, the rhythm of our relationship cannot be quantified or measured by the seasons or with a calendar. Composing our lives alongside one another has been a process of learning to travel to one another's worlds with loving perception. While this study will soon be drawing to a close, I know that time is not over for our relationship, for we have become friends for all seasons.

Rooting a (research) Relationship—Winter 2015

The smell of buttered popcorn, along with sporadic wafts of chlorine and the splashing and hollering from the nearby pool, overwhelm my senses as I wait to meet with Safaa and Rayyan at the YMCA café area. A close friend called me a few weeks ago to tell me that her friend is interested in participating in this study alongside her daughter. Ecstatic at this news, I thanked her for helping to connect us. She said, "Safaa remembers you Muna; she said you used to teach one of her older kids." Surprised, I asked her for my former student's name. She replied, "I think that her children's last name is different than hers, but the child you taught could have been Ali, or Leila, or maybe even Sadia?" I had taught many youth with those names in the past and was so curious and excited to find out just who I would be getting (re)acquainted with. I wondered what stories they have of me as a former teacher, what stories I (may) have of them, and how these stories could shape our living alongside one another as co-inquirers.

I once again look around the busy YMCA café nearby entrance and pool areas. Rayyan and Safaa will be joining me at any moment, and I am feeling acutely aware of just how many familiar faces I have already glimpsed in this always bustling community place. Safaa suggested meeting here because Rayyan has a swimming lesson this evening, and she thought it would give us a good opportunity to reconnect before Rayyan joined us. A week ago, after playing phone tag for a few days, Safaa and I spoke on the phone for a little over half an hour, and she helped me to fondly recall teaching her eldest daughter, Leila, several years ago. Having taught hundreds of students in my teaching of youth in grades six to nine, there are many parents and caregivers who I have never met face to face. Safaa, however, is a parent I have met with on more than one occasion, and I vividly remember the sense of warmth she exuded each time we engaged in conversation.

I am nudged awake from my reverie at the realization that Safaa is walking towards me. Walking behind her are three beautiful girls; two of the girls look to be around the same age and are wearing hijab, and the third is very young and extremely cute. All three girls and Safaa are wearing bright colours that tease of summer under the winter chill still clinging to their coats. With a wide smile and hug, Safaa breathlessly apologizes for being late, turns to the girls behind her, and directs them towards the doors of the swimming pool, calling out to them in the Somali language as they rush away. Safaa turns back to me, apologizes again, and sits down with another wide smile while gesturing for me to please sit too. I smile back at Safaa and laughingly say that there is no need to apologize—as a mother of three, I totally understand. She chuckles and asks me about my children. What are their names and ages? How are they doing? Do they know that their Mama is in school too? I share a few details about Noor, Yehia, and Hannah and then ask how Leila is doing. Safaa smiles and says that I probably would not recognize Leila anymore. She is a grown woman now about to finish her university degree! Safaa tells me that Leila is a wonderful role model to her younger sister, Rayyan, who is in grade six, and to her four other siblings: Ali, Sadia, Marwa, and Amina. I look at Safaa in amazement and tell her I did not recall that Leila has five siblings, mash'Allah! She smiles widely again and says, "Yes,

Alhamdulillah, we were blessed with six kids." In response to my incredulous look and to my question of "How do you do it?", Safaa says that life is, indeed, busy for them, but that Allah (SWT) makes it easy. She is able to balance family life and her work as a full-time medical practitioner and as a multicultural consultant with the help of God and with the support of her husband and children.

Safaa asks me what led to my interest in studying the experiences of Muslim girls and mothers in particular—"Why girls, Muna?" I explain that my daughter Noor is currently in grade six, and I have a lot of wonders about her experiences transitioning into adolescence, especially because she is coming of age in the current sociopolitical climate. I also share some concerns I have after reading the literature in relation to the experiences of Muslim girls and women. Safaa begins talking about how, in her experience, raising her only son, Ali, during his transitions through adolescence and young adulthood was more tension-filled than raising her two eldest daughters, Leila and Sadia. I do not have the opportunity to ask Safaa any more questions about this comment as Rayyan, Marwa, and Amina join us, all fresh-faced from swimming.

I greet each of the girls and say how wonderful it is to meet them as Safaa formally introduces us. Rayyan quietly responds that she has met me before, she was with her mom once when they visited my classroom. I laughingly reply, "Then, it's wonderful to see you again!" We talk about the study, and I try to emphasize that I am not asking for their commitment tonight; I want them to talk about it with each other before signing any of the consent forms, since it is a longer-term commitment. Safaa responds by saying that they are already committed because, turning to look at Rayyan, "It's important to help others, right?" Rayyan smiles back and nods, and I get the sense that this is a familiar familial refrain. We hug each other goodbye, talk about connecting again soon, and walk out into the cold February night and towards our cars, together.

Rooting Stories of Being and Becoming Alongside Safaa—Spring 2015

The continuous whirring of multiple caffeine machines along with the nearby caffeinated conversations usually would not give me pause. Anyone who knows me (or has seen the ever-present coffee cup in my hand) knows that I thoroughly enjoy coffee and the establishments that specialize in it. However, as I wait for Safaa, I look around and wonder if it would be okay to ask her if we might sit on the outdoor patio. It has been a few months since we have been able to meet in person, and I was really hoping that we would be able to talk in a place that would allow for an intelligible voice recording. Safaa called me a little over a week ago to ask if I would be free to meet with her and Rayyan over the weekend, but I was in Chicago for a conference at that time. I asked if it would be possible to meet during the week instead. She said that she would be able to meet during a break from work, but that Rayyan would be in school. We eventually agreed to meet alone for this first research conversation and try for a second meeting with Rayyan when things were less busy. It is not how we initially hoped to begin out conversations, but we soon discover that some of our expectations needed to be continually negotiated in the midst of busy work, school, and family schedules that were often beyond our control.

Safaa texts me to tell me that she was running about ten minutes late, so I reply that it is not a problem and ask what I can order for her while I wait. Sitting with our beverages and pastries, I jot down a few observations and test my voice recorder as I wait. I look up, as I sense an approaching figure and stand up to greet Safaa. She greets me with a warm hug and an enthusiastic "Muna! Assalamu Alaikum!" Before I can suggest it, Safaa asks me if it would be okay if we sit outside. It's a beautiful sunny day, she explains, and the winter seems extra long this year. I laughingly tell her she read my mind, and we take our things and head outside.

We exchange pleasantries as we get settled, and in my typical awkward fashion, I ask Safaa if it would be okay to record this conversation. She laughs and says, "Of course!" As Safaa speaks, I begin sketching a timeline to help me understand Safaa's stories chronologically. I am struck not only by her words, but by the incredibly rhythmic way she recounts her experiences. Her manner of speech is poetic, drawing my attention again and again to her melodic storytelling and turns of phrase.

For this reason, below, I have arranged some of the stories Safaa shared that day using her words, only shifting words or sentences for temporal clarity.

Safaa in Her Words

My dad and mum got divorced when I was little, so I was raised in a very big extended family, aunties, uncles, grandma.

I started school in Somalia when I was five, and when I was six we moved to Kenya.

It was a really big transition for me.

I came to [live with] my father and his wife, and it was totally different in Kenya. The school was run in English, and the language of the community was Swahili.

Language was an issue. I think that's where I get the passion for helping people with language.

When I was younger, I would look forward to going to high school.

I said I liked math, so after I finished high school, I went to college for accounting.

I didn't finish, you know, that's when the Somali civil war broke, and then we got so many people coming to us, I don't know what happened. I got distracted.

The refugees came, and my dad rented a big house near our home, and that was his siblings and their children that were coming.

So I stopped going to school.

That was one of the things my grandma was upset about. She came to live with us when the civil war broke.

When the refugees came to Kenya, I was volunteering my own time, you know helping people, interpreting for them.

I found I had a passion for that. It was something that I enjoyed doing, and I would go out of my way. And at that time I think I was sixteen, so that's how I started the work in the community.

I was sometimes not around at home, and my grandma always wanted me to be around with her.

I know my rights with my grandma, and the rights that they have on us.

And my grandma actually gave me a name ... my name is Shirko, something that is shared.

And she used to complain to my dad and say, "Your daughter? She is shared. She belongs to everyone" [laughing].

She was a powerful woman. She was strong. She was an amazing woman.

One of the things my grandma told me before I left was "Is this how you're going to behave when you are with your husband? Being shirko [shared]? Your marriage is not going to work out if you are going to be behaving this way, I'm telling you" [laughing].

Coming to Canada, I didn't stop. I like to help people and go out of my way.

I got married to my husband in 1994 and came to BC. It was just me and him.

It wasn't good. I got pregnant right away. I got sick—you know new husband, new to the country, new to everything, body changing.

I wasn't even here for nine months when I had Leila. I had pregnancy-induced hypertension so they had to induce me before nine months.

It was a rough time actually, but I managed Alhamdulillah.

I used to go out, walk around you know, because language wasn't a barrier for me.

We lived a little bit far from where everybody in the community lived, so my husband would take me on the weekends, on Saturdays and Sundays, to the madrasa, and that's how I would get to know women in the community.

At around seven months [pregnant], I moved from where I was. I came to live at the centre of the community. I said, "No I'm not going to be alone here."

We moved, and it was really a great neighbourhood; the women would help each other with childcare and all that.

Ali was born about two years later, and Sadia was born in 2000, so by five years I had three children.

And then I moved to Alberta in 2002, and Rayyan was the first born here in 2003.

Before we moved here, I was going to school. I was doing accounting in BC.

I also applied for the medical practitioner program, and they put me on the waiting list there.

I always like to keep myself busy [laughing].

Marwa was born when Rayyan was two, and I decided to apply to the medical practitioner program.

I got in when Marwa was two.

I love people. I love numbers, but I like to work with people. I don't want to be isolated with papers. The reason I think I was doing financial management in BC was because my husband was self-employed; he had a business, and I was just doing that for [its] sake.

When I came here to Alberta, I was just looking around at organizations that support immigrants.

I directly approached an organization and visited with the director and had a talk with her, and a few months later they said, "Are you interested to work with us?"

And I enjoy it. I work with immigrant and refugee newcomers, you know, interpreting for them.

Actually, I started school here in Alberta in 2007 when I was with the organization. I finished my medical practitioner program in 2011.

I always loved school; it was my grandma's inspiration actually. She would always tell me "go to medical school."

You know back home, when someone is sick, they always put up IVs at home and give the fluids, like nobody goes to the hospital, so if a family has a medical practitioner they have a treasure.

My grandma always used to tell me, "You are smart, you can do it, go for it."

By the time I was finishing my program, I was pregnant with my little one, Amina.

I finished the program in April and then actually got the job as a casual at the time, sometime in June, and Amina was due sometime in July.

So I didn't even go. I didn't start the job; I just went to the orientation.

By the time Amina was four, I started as a casual, once a week kind of thing at the hospital. Amina was my number six [child] [laughing].

Many people asked, "We thought you were going to quit when you [got a full-time job]" but even if I leave the job [as a multicultural consultant], I would still work with the community [laughing]. That's who I am.

With the help of God, I didn't do it myself. I had very good family support as well. My husband was supportive. I wouldn't have done it by myself. He did it with me.

Actually, I am telling my children, "I'm thinking of doing my master's" and they all say, "Mama, please no!" [laughing]

But it's just about the timing.

Retellings
"I *made* a family" (Safaa, Spring 2015)

As I re-read Safaa's words from that first conversation, I am once again in awe of her strength and improvisation through so many discontinuities across her life. I think about how five-year-old Safaa—raised by her paternal grandmother and large extended family in Somalia following her parents' divorce as a baby—might have experienced learning that she would be moving to another country to live with her father. I imagine how she might have felt the first time she attended her new school in Kenya and tried to understand the language of the community (Swahili) and the language of instruction at school (English). I wonder at sixteen-year-old Safaa's decision to put her studies on hold to help translate for and otherwise support the influx of Somali refugees in Kenya. I envision twenty-three-year-old Safaa moving away from her extended family yet again and settling in Canada as a new bride, pregnant and far away from the beloved people and places that helped raise her. I listen to the recording of that first conversation and am once again transported to different times and places, attending to so many parts of our conversation that I now realize were likely painful for Safaa to share. I read our words with more knowing eyes and hear our inflections with more discerning ears for we have lived several months and seasons alongside each other since that time.

I sit with Safaa's early life stories, stories of family and community and taking care of one another. I wonder if moving to Kenya, away from Somalia and the only family she knew, was as difficult for her as her later move across the globe and away from her family and community in Kenya to join her new husband in Canada. Although I later learned that Safaa regularly reconnects with her mother, half-siblings, and extended family in America (sometimes referred to by Safaa and Rayyan as "the States") and her father and half-siblings in Kenya (not to mention cousins, aunts, uncles, nieces, and nephews in many different places around the world), I am reminded of the multiple times in our conversations in which Safaa has talked about *building* familial and community relationships in the various places she has lived, not necessarily composed of blood connections, but those of the heart: "I have a good support network, lots of friends ... I *made* a family." I am also reminded of how often Safaa has said that she has "managed, Alhamdulillah" ... that while she was challenged during different periods in her life, her faith and her family helped her to negotiate these times and sustain her: "With the help of God, I didn't do it myself. I had very good family support as well."

The Two R's

As I read over Safaa's words, my attention (re)turns to when Safaa said: "One of the things my grandma told me before I left was, 'Is this how you're going to behave when you are with your husband? Being shirko [shared]? Your marriage is not going to work out if you are going to be behaving this way, I'm telling you' [laughing]." Although she laughed as she shared her grandmother's words, Safaa understands her grandmother's warnings about not giving so much of her time to others that she would not be able to fulfill familial responsibilities: "I know my rights with my grandma, and the rights that they [grandparents/ elders] have on us."

I think of the many conversations in which Safaa has talked about rights and responsibilities. One conversation in particular from the winter of 2016 elucidates the importance of rights and responsibilities— the "Two R's"—in Safaa's familial curriculum-making (Huber et al., *Places*). We had been enjoying tea in my home when Safaa shared that she tells her children, "Everybody has rights and responsibilities. If we are careful with those Two R's, then you are going to survive ... you have rights *and* responsibilities ... I tell them, 'You don't allow anybody ever to take your rights away. *Anybody.* But make sure you also fulfill your own responsibilities. If you are careful with those Two R's, then you will be okay.'" For Safaa, The Two R's of rights and responsibilities are inherently communal. She believes that personal and interpersonal responsibilities are intricately intertwined with personal and interpersonal *rights*. This deeply rooted belief is one that reverberates throughout the stories Safaa shared with me and, as will be elucidated, is a thread woven throughout her familial curriculum-making.

Trying to (slowly) Plant Seeds of Trust—Spring 2015

I am sitting under a tree, on an orange- and white-checkered park mat to the side of the main YMCA outdoor playground and splash park, as I write field notes before Rayyan and Safaa join me. It is Victoria Day, a late May holiday, and many children, youth, and families are at the park enjoying the beautiful spring day close to the end of the long weekend. The squeals of joy make me smile, and I vow to come back soon with my children. Last weekend, after weeks of trying to connect, Safaa invited me over to their home for tea, but I suggested meeting at the park this weekend instead. I knew that she had just gotten off of an unexpected night shift at the hospital and I did not want her to feel like we needed to stick to our original plan regardless of whether she was tired or not. I am glad we agreed to meet today instead. With the food and drinks spread around the mat, we should be able to enjoy a lovely picnic as we engage in conversation. I'm so excited to begin conversations with Rayyan and I make duaa that she will feel safe and comfortable sharing her stories with me.

I soon spot Safaa, Rayyan, Marwa, and Amina to the side of the main playground, and I walk over to greet them. Safaa and I hug, and I turn to the girls as Safaa smilingly urges, "Say Assalamu Alaikum!" I immediately reply with "Assalamu Alaikum!" We all laugh because it is clear that I was not who Safaa intended the reminder for. After Safaa says a few words in Somali, Marwa and Amina run off to play while Rayyan, Safaa, and I walk back towards the picnic area. We sit in a way that allows us to watch Marwa and Amina play as we engage in conversation. Turning my phone's voice recorder on, I start by asking Rayyan a few questions related to some of her earliest memories and begin sketching a timeline of the stories and details she shares. Just as with Safaa, it is important to highlight what Rayyan shares with me using her own words to give a sense of how she stories herself in that first recorded conversation.

Rayyan in Her Words

So my birthday is in June.

I remember every year when we would go to [large indoor playground] when I was a baby with my mom and dad and sisters and brother.

I remember being sad when [my siblings] leave [for school] and being happy when they came home.

I didn't like that they were gone.

Oh, on my first day of preschool my mom was teaching me!

They taught us four different languages; they taught us in Somali, Arabic, English and Kurdish, and I'm good at Somali and Arabic.

I went to [an Islamic School] for kindergarten, and I still go there.

I didn't like it when we would have to wake up early because my mom had school, but I didn't understand, I was little

I regret saying it.

My teacher's name was Ms. [Teacher] and my best friend was [name of friend], and I remember going to the zoo that year.

I liked snack and lunch time best [laughing].

When I ended school early, Leila would let me go to her locker.

School was cool, but then after a couple of years it got boring.

Ms. [grade five teacher] is my favourite teacher because she's kind and she made everything fun

Like in social [studies], we did plays and stuff and everything,

I love Islamic Studies because we can learn the Qu'ran.

I remember there was a girl who would call me names in grade one and two but then it stopped.

I told the teacher.

Actually, my teacher sometimes has to call parents because people are saying mean things to each other.

Me and my friends like to play Red Rover and soccer.

I like soccer a lot; I play for my community team.

I like going to visit our family in Seattle and when we go to [the] Family Fun Centre.

We're going there this summer.

We text with them all the time.

I like riding my bike and going places with my mom. I like swimming.

I like eating [laughing].

I really like writing poems.

I will bring you my poetry book for next time.

Retellings
"I'm quiet sometimes, but not shy"
(Rayyan, Winter 2016)

From the above word images, it is clear that Rayyan did not offer very many details about herself in that first recorded conversation. This is partly because we talked for approximately forty minutes before Rayyan's longing looks in the direction of the playground prompted me to say that we could continue our conversation at another time so that she could join her sisters in play. I vividly recall her smile of appreciation at my words. Another conversation we shared in the winter of 2016 gives added insight into why Rayyan, who I originally assumed was shy, spoke sparingly that day. Sitting at a halal foods restaurant with Rayyan and her sister Marwa several months after that first conversation, I asked Rayyan how she would describe herself to someone she was meeting for the first time. I intended the question to be a different way of asking her to describe herself. She responded by saying, "I would tell them my name, my age, my hobbies, like how we go swimming on Sundays, and that I like to read books, um... and play on my iPad ... And maybe that I like soccer ... if I didn't know them and didn't trust them, I wouldn't tell them very much." During that same conversation, Rayyan explained that she is "quiet sometimes but not shy":

Marwa: When I'm around other people I don't know ... I get shy.

Me: Me too ... how about you Rayyan? Do you get shy too?

Rayyan: Sometimes ...

Marwa: No! When she met our cousin for the first time she was like, "So!" [said confidently], and she just kept talking [laughing].

Me: Okay, so there are times you're shy and others where you aren't shy?

Rayyan: Like, I'm quiet sometimes but not shy ... and it depends on if they're talkative. If they're talkative, then I'm talkative. But if they're not talkative, then I'm not either.

In her quiet but profound way, Rayyan drew my attention to the importance of reciprocity in every interaction, every relationship. As she spoke, I recalled our first conversation and inwardly cringed because, in that moment, I realized that I had not really shared much about myself in the beginning, yet I had asked Rayyan to share a lot about herself.

I now recognize that Rayyan shared what she felt were safe stories at first because we had not yet built a trusting relationship. All she knew of me was that I was a former teacher to her eldest sister Leila and that her mom felt it was important to participate in this research. Over the course of this inquiry, Rayyan has repeatedly helped me to appreciate that while she may be quiet at times, she is not shy ... and that she will take her time deciding if she will share. She, too, knows the value of building relationships and communities carefully.

"She learned that your language is not only at home" (Safaa, Spring 2015)

As we enjoyed our picnic at the park, I was surprised when Rayyan exclaimed, "On my first day of preschool, my mom was teaching me!" Perhaps reading the look of surprise on my face, Safaa explained, "It was a pilot program for a cultural preschool. They were in groups, so four different languages, and for each language group, they had to have somebody that speaks that language. I worked with them that year." Safaa and Rayyan explained that Rayyan's preschool program had been designed to encourage the home languages of students and families of their community school. They discussed with excitement that four languages were taught at the preschool that year: English, Somali, Arabic, and Kurdish. Safaa spoke fondly about working at the school as a Somali language consultant and teacher, and about how this approach "made a difference for the whole family, and the other kids too. Rayyan going to school and speaking her own language ... she got a strong base for the language and she would bring new words to the house ... she learned that your language is not only at home." While she lamented that this pilot program was discontinued shortly after that trial run, Safaa said she loved how Rayyan learned that her home language as well as the rich oral storytelling traditions of the Somali language were valued alongside other languages.

"Why Girls?" (revisited)—Summer 2015

Parking my car, I reach into my glove compartment and retrieve the running arm band to house my phone. I am not a runner. I purchased the arm band this morning because I am meeting Safaa for a walk around a community lake that we both love. I am hoping that the arm band will allow me to walk and talk alongside Safaa as my phone (hopefully!) records our conversation. Stepping outside, I once again appreciate the beautiful sunny afternoon and think about how long it has been since I have seen Safaa. We have been in contact over the last few months via texts and phone calls—most recently to wish each other Eid Mubarak after long spring and summer days in Ramadan fast. A week ago, after Safaa, Rayyan and her siblings returned from visiting family in Seattle, we talked on the phone about how peaceful Ramadan was this year, including the familiar refrain, "Oh, the days were long for sure, but it was actually much easier than I thought it would be." My family, friends, and I say a version of this comment almost every year, and we somehow still find ourselves surprised the following Ramadan that the approximately nineteen-hour fast (no, not even water) is not as hard as we feared it would be.

I am just about to text Safaa to let her know where I am when I glimpse her driving in. We wave and she exclaims, in what I recognize as her habitual way of greeting me, "Muna! Assalamu Alaikum!" We hug before we agree on the route our walk would take and venture off. We begin by revisiting one of her comments from our first conversation. I ask Safaa, "Can you say more about your comment of 'why girls?'" I remind her that she said that raising Ali during his transitions into adolescence and young adulthood had been more tension-filled than raising Leila and Sadia. She says the following:

> Well, Leila is in university, and Sadia is in grade eleven now ... and I think the reason why I said this is that my kids stayed in Islamic school until grade nine and then left [to public school] in grade ten ... but now that I think about the focus of your research, going from elementary to junior high, I think that's when most students have biological changes happening in their body .... I think that with high school, I think that's the age when they decide where they want to go, where they can be influenced, where they want to be and feel independent, you know, they're growing to be a woman kind of thing.

Safaa explains that she feels fortunate that her two eldest daughters, Leila and Sadia, negotiated their transitions into adolescence and womanhood with great poise: "And I do find that I haven't had a problem with my daughters, Alhamdulillah, they are amazing ... I was very lucky." She believes that their attendance in a community-based Islamic school throughout their elementary and junior high school years, the same school Rayyan now attends, helped guide them during these significant life transitions. Safaa discusses the changes her children experienced leaving the comfort of a school that "was like home to them" to large public high schools where they felt they needed to ask for special accommodations:

> With the high school that Ali went to, they give support to Muslim kids ... and actually the kids are the ones that fight for that. I always tell my kids, "Nobody knows what you want', you have to ask." They give them a room to pray in on Friday, but they say, "I want to pray *Dhuhr*" [one of five daily prayers interspersed throughout the day; *Dhuhr* is the afternoon prayer]. I say, "Go to the office and get it. Ask!" I think that when we bring our need out and talk about it, the majority of people listen to you, especially in this Canadian culture whereby the laws are written to be multicultural and people are equal. They don't want to seem like they are not supporting this ... they may not be, but they cannot plainly say "No!" you know?

Safaa believes that for her children and for the children, youth, and families she supports as a multicultural consultant it is important to feel represented in schools: "Our kids want to see someone who looks like them in the school system." She discusses how she views her work as "a link to the system." She elaborates:

> And it feels good, you know, I work with and have a partnership with [the public school district] .... It makes a difference when you have an Egyptian teacher, or a Falasteeni (Palestinian) teacher, or a Somali teacher, a Muslim teacher in the school system, you know? It changes children's self-esteem and confidence ... Our children need to see people like us everywhere, right?

Retellings
"A mother's conversation is always there"
(Safaa, Winter 2016)

In responding to my query of why she had initially asked "why girls?", Safaa centered her response on her experiences with raising her eldest daughters, Leila and Sadia, through their transitions into adolescence and young adulthood. She also spoke about her concerns and fears about the tragic number of deaths of young men in the Canadian Somali Muslim community in recent years. Safaa worries about families who have lost loved ones to drugs and/or violence, families she knows through her work with Muslim and Somali community organizations or through ties of friendship. Safaa has expressed her concern, anger, and fear at the rising number of deaths in the Somali community over the course of our inquiry. In the winter of 2016, she spoke of worrying about her son Ali:

> There were so many boys his age who were not doing great in our community, ended up doing drugs, you always talk with them about that. That's the worry you have, you know? .... I give them stories, give them a heads up, and when Ali was growing up, we always talked about this ... so there is always a fear when you are raising kids. And the fear is even about their surroundings, what is surrounding you and what is happening to you in these surroundings, you know?

Safaa emphasized the importance of open conversations alongside her children on an everyday basis, not primarily because an event or issue necessitates it. She said that her husband also engages in discussions with their children, but not in the same ongoing way that she does. She stressed, "I will always talk to them, *always* give them a heads up .... A mother's conversation is always there; it never, never, ends."

"I always tell my kids, 'Nobody knows what you want, you have to ask'" (Summer 2015)

Safaa has shared many stories with me about the importance of encouraging her children to advocate for themselves and others. For Safaa, this story to live by is intricately connected to another that I discussed in a previous section—the Two R's of rights and responsibilities. She teaches her children, family, friends, colleagues, and those she supports as a multicultural consultant that everyone has the right and the responsibility to resist injustice.

During our conversation in the summer of 2015, Safaa shared the story of how Sadia, Rayyan's older sister who was in high school at the time, challenged a teacher who she felt had been making unfair comments related to Islam and Muslims. Safaa said that she was already worried about Sadia because her teachers had been telling her that her daughter should participate more in class:

> The issue that I had with my Sadia in Islamic school is that teachers would tell me, "She won't stop talking! She chats so much, being social is more important to her" and when she went to public school, the teachers would tell me, "She needs to ask questions; she needs to speak up." It was so unexpected. I asked her, 'What's wrong with you? Why don't you speak up?" And she says, "I can't. I'm shy in front of all these people" [I would say,] "But teachers used to complain about you talking too much!" [She would respond,] "That was my home!"

Safaa could not understand how Sadia, usually outgoing and talkative, seemed to be getting more and more reluctant to share her opinions and questions in class; instead, she would approach teachers during break times or after school. However, Safaa was proud that Sadia was able to overcome this reluctance during a class discussion about terrorism. Safaa explained that the teacher had been making remarks in relation to Islam and Muslims that were painful for Sadia to hear: "She confronted that teacher, and she was upset ... she told him, 'That hurts me; you can't say that' ... and I think at the end he apologized." While Safaa was proud that Sadia challenged the teacher's remarks, she felt it was important to also speak up as a parent:

I talked to him. I said that it's not fair for our kids to be exposed to that kind of talk, you know? Because this teacher was consistent, you know, he would say who did 9/11, and other things. So I went to him and said, "I believe it's not only her who feels like that; you have more [students] than her who are of the Muslim faith … and they don't feel good about what you're saying. Sometimes your words can be really sensitive to others" … but he was understanding actually.

Other stories Safaa and Rayyan shared with me highlight the many times Safaa taught Rayyan and her siblings the importance of speaking up and advocating for themselves. A deeply troubling story was shared by Rayyan and Safaa in the winter of 2015. I had voiced my concerns about how my daughter Noor was feeling excluded by a group of friends. Rayyan responded by telling me about her younger sister Marwa's experience in school:

Rayyan: She left them because they were being racist.

Me: What do you mean habibty? How were they being racist?

Rayyan: The girls were saying, "Oh, you're dark chocolate." Sadia was with her too [they went to tell the teacher], and the teacher said, "But she *is* dark chocolate," and Sadia slammed her hand [on the desk] and said, "You have *no* right to say that!"

Safaa: I went to the teacher, and Sadia was with me at the time, and we said that Marwa is having issues with these girls, and one of the things they are saying to her is "[in an angry tone] Stay away from us; you look like the *darkest* chocolate!" And then he said, "Of course, you are dark chocolate!"

Me: And that's so not okay.

Safaa: And Sadia took the lead, and what grade was she? I think grade nine at that time. She said, "It's not what they said; it's *how* they are saying it."

Me: Yes.

Safaa: It's *how* it is being said. Of course, we are proud; her skin is like beautiful dark chocolate, but it's not about the colour. It's about what they *mean.*

Me: He was so uncomfortable probably with what was happening, but that was so insensitive.

Safaa: Sadia said it before I even spoke! [Rayyan laughing].

Me: Mash'Allah. Good for her.

Safaa: And he apologized to us after that and said he will talk to the girls, and he did.

Deeply troubled by this story when I returned home that day, I wrote the following in my research notebook:

> Sitting with the stories Rayyan and Safaa shared today, I'm so troubled and disgusted at how lip service is paid to Muslims being one Ummah while racism and discrimination within Muslim communities is an often unacknowledged, silenced story. Friends and former students have shared countless stories of feeling discriminated against by other Muslims because of their race or cultural heritage or how "pious" (or not) others deem them to be, and in so many other ways.

In challenging the racism Marwa experienced, Safaa, Marwa, and Sadia resisted the teacher's attempt to smooth over the racist intent behind the words "dark chocolate," for, as Sadia eloquently stressed, "It's not what they said, it's *how* they are saying it." They resisted the invitation to gloss over racism and asserted their right to speak up in the face of injustice.

Safaa has also repeatedly encouraged me to advocate for my children. I am reminded of how, upon hearing news of my youngest daughter Hannah's diagnosis with Autism Spectrum Disorder (ASD) in the summer of 2016, Safaa immediately began asking who I have been in contact with and advised, "You can't be shy asking for supports Muna." Every time we meet, Safaa always askes me, "How are you and Hannah doing?" and "Are you feeling supported?" Through sharing their stories and through responding to mine, Safaa and Rayyan have repeatedly taught me about how important it is for me to live a life of speaking up and advocating alongside my children ... because teaching them about rights and responsibilities necessitates *living* the Two R's alongside them.

Growing into Grade Seven ... and in Comfort Alongside One Another—Fall 2015

I survey the veritable snack feast spread across my kitchen table and know I probably overdid it. Okay, not probably. I overdid it. I really want Rayyan, Safaa, Marwa, and Amina to have a good time tonight. I am also starting to worry about having already engaged in three one-on-one conversations with Safaa but none with Rayyan so far. I am trying to be patient and to go slow. I have not yet asked Rayyan if she would like to have a conversation with just the two of us, as I wanted to slowly build more comfort and trust in our relationship. But time has definitely not been supportive over the last few months. We have already rescheduled this shared conversation two times over the last few weeks because of our conflicting schedules. Safaa has been working night shifts at the hospital, and I have been busy with back-to-school activities and with Hannah's many appointments, and Rayyan's time has been busily spent with school, soccer team commitments, and other extracurricular activities at school. Looking out into the autumn evening, I make duaa that our conversation goes well and that we will be able to share our stories within co-composed spaces of mutual trust and vulnerability.

The doorbell rings, and I rush to the door to find Hannah and Yehia already there, waiting to greet our guests. Noor is upstairs getting ready for her aunt to pick her up for a fundraising event they had purchased tickets for weeks ago. I open the door and embrace Safaa, Rayyan, Marwa, and Amina as they walk in. Noor joins us as I am greeting them, and I make the introductions. Safaa and I are surprised and excited to discover that Noor and Rayyan already know each other, and we remark at what an incredibly small world it is. Closing the door after Noor leaves, I invite everyone to have a seat at the nearby kitchen table. Wissam comes home from work almost as soon as Noor leaves, and I laughingly introduce everyone again. After filling our plates and laughing at Hannah's at-the-top-of-her-lungs singing in the next room, Safaa, Rayyan, Marwa, I sit down and begin, as always, with "Bismillah."

Rayyan begins by sharing some of her experiences over the last three months. While she still attends the same K-9 Islamic school, Rayyan has already experienced many shifts and changes in her transition to grade seven. She talks about enjoying her grade six graduation celebration (especially the throwing their caps in the air part), the year-end field trip, their recent trip to visit family in Seattle, and school supply shopping. Rayyan says she was glad that she could go home after her year-end exams because she was fasting for Ramadan— "it was pretty good."

I ask Rayyan what she had been most looking forward to at the end of grade six, and she immediately exclaims, "Getting a locker!" Rayyan explains that "getting a locker" is something she "waited so long for." Rayyan continues, "It was so hard to use a lock! I was practicing for a week!" Safaa explains that she purchased the combination lock for Rayyan the week before school, and I told her, "You need to practice every day." The conversation continues:

Safaa: Yeah, I couldn't imagine giving her a lock the day of or the night before school.

Me: Oh that makes so much sense because that's what we did [with Noor] [laughing].

Safaa: Because she's your oldest, I think I have experience!

Our conversation shifts to the upcoming federal election—including the disturbing rhetoric of the so-called "niqab issue" and the proposed "barbaric cultural practices hotline" (see Macdonald). Safaa incredulously says, "Can you imagine that? What they are saying in the news? ... They are playing their mind games. It's very sad." I express my fears that this rhetoric may embolden people in their xenophobia, and I share a recent experience of being made to feel invisible and uncomfortable at a public lecture. I was the only woman wearing hijab in the room as several attendees debated how to respond to the call for a ban on the niqab during Canadian citizenship ceremonies. One woman said something akin to "Let's not forget that the niqab itself can be seen as a way of oppressing women." I share how, body and voice shaking, I responded to this woman's comment with the assertion that "we have to be very careful of imposing an arrogant understanding of the reasons Muslim women often *choose* to cover." Safaa says, "Good for you!" and Rayyan shares a recent grocery store experience:

Rayyan: I was going like this [fanning herself] because I was really, really, really hot and then a lady came.

Safaa: She was really hot because we just came from Friday prayer and it was crowded.

Rayyan: And the lady said, "Don't worry, when you're eighteen you won't have to wear that [points to her hijab] anymore."

Safaa: Because you're in Canada now [rueful laughter].

Rayyan: Yeah, she said, "Don't worry, when you're 18."

Safaa: Yeah, when you're older you can take it off and nobody can force you.

Me: Nobody is forcing her *now*.

Safaa: Yes, that's what I told her, that nobody forced her to wear it ... but that's what she thought, that we are forcing the little ones to wear that .... make inquiries don't make assumptions. And, of course you are mad, but you don't want to be seen as being mad ...

Rayyan: And you don't want to hurt someone's feelings.

Troubled that the woman at the grocery store assumed that her hijab was symbolic of coercion/oppression, Rayyan explains that inspired by her mom and older sisters, she chose to don the hijab in grade three. She says she has never considered taking it off and considers her hijab an integral part of her faith: "I will never take it off ... it's important to me as a Muslim." Safaa states that she is so proud of her daughters for choosing their hijabs at young ages and shares that she was inspired by her close friends' and neighbours' example to don hijab when she was around sixteen years old. As we talk, I wonder about our children, and so many others, growing up in the midst of what feels like ever-increasing suspicion, misunderstanding, and vitriol. But I also marvel at the compassion Safaa and Rayyan demonstrated in their responses to what must have felt like an attack on their agency and familial practices.

Retellings
"That's how we learn; it's through living"
(Safaa, Winter 2016)

In the midst of our conversation, Safaa reminded me not to feel guilty for not thinking of encouraging Noor to practice opening her combination lock before school began: "Because she's your oldest, I think I have experience!" At the time, I thought she was mainly trying to reassure me as a fellow parent. However, I have come to appreciate that, while she was indeed being kind and supportive, Safaa also strongly believes that we learn from experience. In the winter of 2016, Safaa reflected, "As parents, we like everything to be perfect ... and it's not." In this same conversation, reminiscent of Dewey's view of education as life and life as experience, Safaa stressed that parenting

> is a process. They learn through modelling, every day. It's not something we can give them with a spoon. I don't know how to explain other than this—they live it. It's something they will be learning every day, right now, step by step, daily reminder, conversations. That's how I grew up; nobody ever told me, "Do this, and do that." It was through lived examples ... that's how we learn; it's through living.

Safaa believes that she has learned much from living alongside her children. In the summer of 2015, and again in the winter of 2016, she discussed how her children help her to learn about new technologies, social media, and, perhaps most profoundly, about kindness and patience. She shared this story with me in the winter of 2016:

> Something I can never forget is when Leila was four or five [years old]. I had gotten them Eid clothes and they had tried them on and put them away. Then Sadia comes into the kitchen and I was busy cooking and she has her Eid clothes on. She says, "Mama look, don't I look pretty?" and I said [in annoyed tone], "Go put your clothes away!" and then Leila said [in a gentle tone], "*Abayo*, sister, you look so beautiful but it is not time to wear these clothes. They are for Eid." I felt so bad! She pulled my heart so much! It was so sweet, but I felt so bad. You know sometimes your kids teach you a lesson.

"Not every Muslim is like what you see in the news" (Rayyan, Winter 2016)

Sadly, Rayyan and Safaa shared several other experiences related to discrimination. Similar to the way Rayyan shared her story of being arrogantly perceived (Lugones) by a woman at the grocery store after I shared my fears and experience related to the "niqab issue," some of our stories were in response to the rhetoric of 2015 Canadian federal election cycle. During a discussion at Dairy Queen in the fall of 2015, Rayyan said that she feared that the incumbent Conservative government would be re-elected because "Harper doesn't like Muslims." Hearing this statement troubled me as I realized that Rayyan believed this about the only prime minister she had known at that point in time. Later, in the winter of 2015, Rayyan talked about the reactions of her family, friends, and classmates to the election of Justin Trudeau and how "everyone is happy Harper didn't win."

At different times, Rayyan and Safaa shared a story related to discrimination that Leila, Rayyan's eldest sister, had experienced. During our conversation in the winter of 2016, Rayyan and Marwa told this story in the following way:

Marwa: Leila was on the bus, and a guy said, "Go back to your country! You don't belong here!" to her and ....

Me: Sorry? To Leila?

Rayyan: Yeah, on the bus ...

Me: And this was recent?

Rayyan: Last week. He said, "Go back to your country!" and ...

Marwa: She called Ali and talked to him in our language, so the guy wouldn't understand.

Rayyan: Because she was scared he would hurt her. So she never answered him and kept talking to my brother and ignoring him.

Me: Oh, so sad ... and that's the first time something like that's happened to her?

Rayyan: Yeah.

Me: And how was she doing when she got home?

Rayyan: She was afraid of that man. When she walked in, she said, "Guess what happened to me today?" and told us about it ... that's the first time that's happened to anybody in my family.

Me: I'm so sorry that happened to her.

Rayyan: Yeah, because not every Muslim is like what you see in the news.

Me: And how many people were on the bus?

Rayyan: She said it was full but that nobody said anything.

Me: Why do you think they didn't say anything?

Rayyan: They were probably scared of him too ... but even if you're not Muslim, you should always stand up for people.

Safaa shared the story in the spring of 2016 with me as we sat at a neighbourhood park:

Leila was on the bus, and there was this man who was yelling at her about her hijab, "Go back to your place!" and all of that. So Leila ignored him, but what surprised her is that nobody on that bus said anything about it. She was shocked ... so she had to call Ali and was talking to him to feel safe. But she said, "It wasn't him that was the problem, Mama, there might be a mental health issue or something going on with him. What surprised me most was that nobody on the bus said anything about it."

Safaa thinks that anti-Muslim rhetoric during the Canadian and American election cycles along with terrorist attacks contribute to people being increasingly fearful or suspicious of Muslims: "It happened after the France attacks ... and can you imagine the things Trump is saying?" However, she cautioned, "But we cannot say all society acts like that." Rayyan attributed the bystanders' silence to their fear of the man on the bus. My heart hurting as I listened to her, Rayyan said that she wishes people would realize that "not every Muslim is like what you see in the news" and that "even if you're not Muslim, you should always stand up for people."

Continuing to Grow and Nurture Trust—Fall 2015

Parking my car in front of Safaa and Rayyan's house, I take a deep breath and recite the duaa my mom taught me to recite when I feel unsettled: *Rabbi ishrah lee sadri, wa yasr lee amree, wahl al3kdata min leesanni, yafkahhu kawwli* [O my Lord! Expand for me my chest (grant me self-confidence and contentment); Ease my task for me; And remove the impediment from my speech, so others may understand what I say] (Qu'ran 20, 25-28). I am fifteen minutes late in picking Rayyan and Marwa up. Hannah had been upset all morning and I did not want to leave the house until I settled her down for her afternoon nap, but it had taken a lot longer than usual. I message Safaa to let her know that I am running late and she responds, "Salam sister, the girls are ready. Drive safe dear." I smile and as I walk to their door, I think about how Safaa always begins her text messages to me with "Salam sister ..." The warm thought helps put me at ease.

I knock on the door, and, almost immediately, Rayyan opens it. Marwa is standing behind her and we smilingly exchange Salams and hugs. Safaa is standing at the top of the stairs and says, "Muna! Assalamu Alaikum!" She is wearing an apron, and I can smell delicious home cooking being prepared. I take my shoes off to jog up the stairs and embrace Safaa, and she tells me that she has just woken up after a night shift to take a meal to a niece who recently had a baby. I tell her, "Mash'Allah, I don't know how you do it." She laughs and says, "Alhamdulillah, Allah makes it easy for me." As I head back down the stairs to put my shoes back on, Safaa speaks a few words to Rayyan and Marwa in Somali, and wishes us all a good time.

With Rayyan in the passenger seat and Marwa in the seat behind her, we decide to go to a nearby Dairy Queen for ice cream. Although it is October, the weather is unseasonably warm, and we agree that it would be a good idea to take advantage of the beautiful weather. As I drive out of their neighbourhood, with Rayyan and Marwa guiding me, I remark about the beautiful tall trees flanking the streets that still have a few colourful leaves on them and tell them that what I miss most about my childhood home is the mature trees. They tell me that they love their neighbourhood; they have lived and played there for as long as they can remember and cannot imagine living anywhere else. Marwa remarks about the election signs littering the yards in front of many homes, and Rayyan tells me that their Islamic school staged a mock federal election. She laughingly shares that she does not think anyone voted for the Progressive Conservative Party after all their talk about Muslims, and Marwa laughingly agrees.

We order Blizzards when we get to the Dairy Queen counter and choose to sit on the outdoor patio to enjoy the beautiful sunny day. Rayyan has a plastic bag with her and tells me that she brought the poetry book she told me about and a few of her favourite photographs. We read through some of her poems, and I am touched at the love she often expresses for her mom in the collection. In response to some of her poems, we talk at length about friendships and how they change over time. Rayyan shares a story about a friend she has distanced herself from because she talks about others behind her back: "I don't like that …. but I don't give her the evil eye or anything. We still say Salam, we still talk, but we don't really hang out anymore." Rayyan describes negotiating a way to remain friendly with this girl because she's "friends with almost everyone in class," and believes it is important to be kind to everyone. Rayyan laughs as she talks about her best friends, "They're all really, really tall, much taller than me, some are even taller than my Mom!" Rayyan and Marwa laugh when I say that I was shorter than most of the people in my class too but that I prefer to describe myself as "short and sweet."

We laugh a lot during our conversation, especially at their playful explanations of Rayyan's photographs and at the following story shared by Rayyan and Marwa about their brother Ali growing up as the only boy among five sisters:

Marwa: Ali went to Seattle when he was fourteen by himself after Amina was born.

Rayyan: He told my mom, "If it's a girl then I'm leaving," and when she was born he left [all laughing].

Marwa: He came back, and Amina was big! [laughing].

Rayyan: When I was born, he was like, "I'm sick of girls!" and then when Marwa was born, he said, "I'm sick of girls!" [laughing].

Marwa: And then he cut Sadia's hair bald and then he put shorts on her [laughing].

Rayyan: He tried to make Sadia a boy and named her Hassan [laughing].

Me: [laughing] Oh my goodness ... I can't imagine how your mom reacted to that!

Rayyan: Sadia was crying, but we all laugh at it now [laughing].

On the drive back home, Rayyan shares her excitement about an upcoming play she will be performing in. She says she has been practicing with her cast mates all week and even into the weekend. Hearing her passion and joy, I smile and tell her that I am so glad she is able to nurture her love of the theatre. She smiles and says, "Alhamdulillah!" On my drive home, as I reflect on the stories we shared, I too am smiling and saying "Alhamdulillah."

Retellings
"Me and Marwa are always together"(Rayyan, Fall 2015)

As I type this, I think of the last time I saw Rayyan and Marwa. They had visited with me at my home, alongside Safaa and Amina, in the fall of 2016. We looked over some of our conversation transcripts and identified resonant threads we felt were most important to include in the interim research texts. I asked Marwa and Rayyan if I could include a piece in the interim research text about how special their relationship is. I said that considering how Marwa was usually alongside us in our conversations, it would be a way of honouring and representing our inquiry process. Rayyan thought this made a lot of sense, and Marwa smiled and said she felt like a part of this research journey alongside us. I said that she *has* been a part of it.

Rayyan and Marwa were born two years apart, but they have an incredibly close relationship. In the fall of 2015, Rayyan shared, "Me and Marwa are always together." In coming alongside them, I witnessed this closeness and the many ways they support, encourage, and laugh with/at each other. In the spring of 2016, Safaa and I were talking about their relationship:

Me: They really remind me of me and my sister Suha ... we seemed to bring things out of each other that almost isn't noticeable when the other person isn't there.

Safaa: Yes ... and every night, they discuss their day and their thoughts .... that's just a routine they made for each other by themselves.

Me: Me and my sister did that too.

Safaa: They are very close, and they are both very gentle with each other. Even when they were little, if someone gave one of them candy, the other would say, "What about Rayyan or Marwa? What about my sister?" They were always like that, even when they were two or three [years old]. Mash'Allah people would think they were twins.

There are many stories I could share to give a sense of their special bond, but the one that calls to me most is when we were eating together at a halal restaurant in the winter of 2016. After Rayyan had made it clear that she would not tell someone she does not know or trust much about herself, I reframed my original question to get more of a sense of how she stories herself:

Me: How would you describe yourself to someone you really trust [laughing]?

Rayyan: Well ...

Marwa: Maybe that you are fun, beautiful ...

Rayyan: That's conceited!

Me: I know how hard it is to talk about yourself, but no pressure, and we will never judge you or think that you sound conceited.

Rayyan: Well, I already know I'm pretty, I'm kind ... I'm generous.

Marwa: She really is.

Me: Can you tell me about a time where you were being really generous?

Marwa: [After long pause] I have one. I lost my iPod, and I tell Rayyan. She says, "Until you find your iPod, for the time being, I will let you share mine." That was so nice.

As they spoke, I travelled back in time to my memories of growing up with Suha, my older sister and best friend. I shared a few stories of my childhood adventures with Suha and how we even grew up sharing a bedroom like they do. I said that the only thing I didn't like about being so close was when teachers or relatives (negatively) compared us. Marwa agreed and said that teachers sometimes tell her to be more like Rayyan: "My teacher said, 'You have to be more like Rayyan, more *open*, more drama-ish.'" But both girls agreed that they are fortunate to have each other because, as Marwa said, "We're best friends."

"She really makes us laugh, she has a great sense of humour" (Safaa, Spring 2016)

Once Rayyan started to feel more at ease with me, I was impressed with her ability to joke, quip, and play with puns in a way that made everyone around her laugh but never in hurtful ways. Rayyan and Marwa often played off of each other's words, engaging in sisterly banter that reminded me of my relationships with my sisters. We often laughed at Rayyan's witty responses and stories. One that made us laugh the longest was shared by Rayyan and Safaa in the spring of 2016:

Safaa: She really makes us laugh. She has a great sense of humour ... you know what she did one time? Did I ever tell you? She went to a website called nikah.com ["nikah" is an Arabic word for marriage] and ...

Me: No way? [laughing] ... I'm already laughing!

Safaa: [laughing] Yeah, she went there and she put their names like Leila's names and all their names ... [Everyone laughing]. [To Rayyan] Tell her about it ... I still don't remember how you did it!

Rayyan: I was reading the Qu'ran on Qu'ran Explorer; it's an app I have on the iPad, and a message pops up about this website called nikah.com, and I thought it would be funny to register Leila ... so I put all her information in and went and showed her [laughing].

Safaa: Leila was saying, "People will think I am so desperate!" It was a year ago?

Rayyan: It was when I was ten.

Safaa: When you were ten, my goodness ... and she said to Leila the other day, "If you don't find a man in two years, I'm going to go back to nikah.com and find you one!" [laughing] ... it was so funny! ... to that extent, she's just very mature, *very* mature ... and very fun [laughing].

Sowing Seeds (and filling buckets) with Kindness— Winter 2015

Parking in front of Safaa and Rayyan's home, I pause in my warm car to make duaa before I walk up the snowy sidewalk towards their house. I am happily surprised to see Safaa drive into their driveway; we walk out of our cars at around the same time, and Safaa says that she will be joining me inside as soon as she brings the groceries in. I say that I had just done the same thing that morning, and despite her protests, I begin hauling the boxes and bags inside with her. We are soon joined by Rayyan and Marwa, and within minutes Safaa's trunk is emptied of its contents. Safaa asks me to please sit at the table she has already set with homemade pastries while they quickly put the groceries away. In the meantime, she has asked little Amina to show me some family photographs. Amina takes her task seriously, pausing at each picture and looking at me intently to ensure I have time to appreciate it. I ask her questions about the photographs and struggle to suppress my smiles at her adorable responses.

We are soon joined at the table by Rayyan and Safaa, who embraces and thanks Amina profusely for helping to make their guest feel welcome. Amina smilingly walks away, and Leila walks into the room to greet me. It has been a while since I have seen her, and I ask how she is doing and how are her studies going. We reminisce a bit about when I was her teacher, and she updates me about some of her former classmates who she is still in contact with. As I sit back down at the table, Rayyan's dad, Ahmad, comes into the room, and Safaa introduces us: "This is Muna ... [to me]. He's heard a lot about you!" We exchange Salams before he leaves with Leila. I am feeling extremely welcome and cared for as we begin to engage in conversation.

Safaa and Rayyan update me about some of their experiences in the last few months. Rayyan happily talks about a play she has recently starred in, and Safaa tells me about how impressed she is that Rayyan manages to do so well in school while also being involved in theatre, soccer, and a few other extracurricular activities. She shares that she never feels the need to remind Rayyan about her responsibilities: "She will never give up and quit. With all of them growing up, I have never seen anybody like Rayyan; she tries hard mash'Allah." However, Safaa expresses worry that sometimes Rayyan expects too much of herself, often working or studying *too* hard: "She sometimes pressures herself too much ... *a lot*." Rayyan listens quietly and smiles at her mom, seeming to silently reassure her.

We talk about the Canadian federal elections that took place a few months ago, and Safaa says that our new prime minister is "a good man." She continues, "He talks about justice and all of that; you know, I was surprised when the Syrian refugees started coming, [and] he went to the airport! Who does that, especially at his level?"

After I ask about how the school year is going so far, Rayyan shares a recent experience she had with another girl in her class. Safaa and Rayyan explain that the girl became agitated at a perceived slight from Rayyan and responded by being very aggressive and by physically intimidating Rayyan and verbally threatening her:

Rayyan: I didn't say anything. I slowly moved her back away and just walked away.

Safaa: And then what did you do?

Rayyan: And then when she was walking out, she said the B-word to me.

Safaa: And then what did you do?

Rayyan: And then I told the teacher.

Me: Good for you.

Safaa: And then what happened to her?

Rayyan: She got suspended.

Safaa prompted Rayyan to remember that it was her action of telling a teacher about the intimidation that helped to prevent against any further harassment. Despite this experience, Rayyan stresses that she usually gets along with everyone in class and is "friends with everyone."

As we continue talking, more stories about bullying are shared. Safaa tells me about how a mother she works with recently expressed her love for Rayyan and Marwa because, unbeknownst to Safaa, they had helped the woman's daughter to feel cared for at school. The woman explained that a few years ago, Rayyan had noticed her daughter sitting by herself at recess and invited her to play with her and her friends:

> Her daughter started school, and you know when you are new to school sometimes the kids will push her far away ... Rayyan and Marwa were younger than her, but they really helped her make friends. And until now the mum says, "Oh I love your daughters; they are so sweet!" because even if they couldn't find someone to play with her, they would leave their friends and play with her ... so amazing. I was really happy mash'Allah.

The girl later became friends with her classmates, and her mother said she will never forget Rayyan and Marwa's kindness. I ask Rayyan how she noticed that the girl was by herself that day:

Rayyan: Maybe because when I was in kindergarten [turning to Safaa] you gave me meat for lunch and the girls moved away from me.

Safaa: Because of the food that you were eating?

Rayyan: Mmm hmm.

Safaa: And then you felt it, and that's why maybe you don't like anyone to feel that way?

Rayyan: Yeah.

Me: And you remember that still ... Subhan Allah.

Rayyan: Yeah.

Safaa: Because she has experienced it and doesn't want any child to experience what she has. That's where it's coming from mash'Allah.

Safaa and I are deeply moved at the quiet but profound way Rayyan explains why she notices when others are excluded—she still remembers the feeling of being excluded in kindergarten and actively supports others going through similar experiences.

Later, Rayyan reminds Safaa about another experience with bullying at school:

Rayyan: Do you remember what happened in grade two?

Safaa: What happened in grade two?

Rayyan: With Ms. Teacher?

Safaa: Oh! What was the story? ... I remember we got that book.

Rayyan: Yeah.

Safaa: What did they do to you? ... I think it was a similar experience to Marwa's whereby some of the children in class didn't want to play with you.

Rayyan: No, they were fake-friending me.

Safaa: There was that book I took to your teacher. What was the name of it?

Rayyan: *How Full is Your Bucket?*

Safaa: I gave it to the teacher ... actually I even wrote a paper on that book when I was in school ... it was like when you insult me, my bucket gets empty.

Me: And you took the book because you said that somebody was fake-friending you. I'm sorry, I'm not sure what that means?

Rayyan: They were faking being friends.

Me: Oh okay, and how did you figure out that was what they were doing?

Rayyan: Because some of the other girls in my class told me.

Me: And what did you do when they told you that they were fake-friending you?

Rayyan: I told my teacher, but she said, "Okay," and then she didn't really do anything, so I told my mom, and she went to school.

Safaa explains that she took the book *How Full is Your Bucket?* (Rath and Clifton) to Rayyan's teacher to suggest reading it to the class. Rayyan searches for a nearby laptop for a YouTube video of the book being read. We watch the video together, and I learn that the book uses the metaphor of an imaginary bucket atop someone's head as a way to describe emotions. When the imaginary bucket is full, the person is feeling happy, and when it is empty, the person is feeling sad. The main lesson of the story is to encourage people to add to one another's buckets when possible and to avoid taking away from others' buckets. The story ends with the main character realizing that by filling others' buckets, he is also filling his own.

Retellings
Travelling Across Familial and School Curriculum-Making Worlds

I sit with the stories Safaa and Marwa shared with me that day. As I read through the transcript and listen to the audio recording of our conversation, I am reminded that I asked Safaa, "How did you think to share curriculum materials with Rayyan's teacher?" She responded, "I used to read it to the kids, and they really enjoyed it. We always used to say when someone would do something between the siblings, 'Oh imagine what happened to Rayyan's bucket?'" She said that she thought it would be a good idea to share the book and metaphor with the class and that the teacher thanked her for doing so. As I think of Rayyan's "fake-friending" experience, I am in awe of the courage it must have taken for Safaa to suggest a familial curriculum-making (Huber et al., *Places*) resource to Rayyan's teacher. But I also recall that Safaa had been a teacher in Rayyan's preschool and that through this experience, she might have learned to travel between familial and school worlds with greater ease (Lugones).

As I reconsider these stories of bullying and discrimination, I once again turn to Safaa's belief in the Two R's of rights and responsibilities and her interconnected belief that everyone has a responsibility to speak up in the face of injustice. These stories to live by seem to be foregrounded in the stories Rayyan and Safaa shared that day. I think of Rayyan's experience of being excluded in kindergarten and her ability to notice others experiencing exclusion—to travel to their worlds. When Rayyan and Safaa shared the *How Full is Your Bucket* story, I started to get a sense that this familial metaphor of filling each other's buckets—alongside Safaa's teaching of the Two R's and speaking up in her familial curriculum-making—helped guide Rayyan and Marwa in travelling to that girl's world and then *act* to try to fill her bucket ... and theirs in the process.

Rooting Stories of Motherhood—Winter 2016

I am excitedly setting the side tables in my family room with snacks and traditional tea as I prepare for Safaa's visit this afternoon. Hannah has just fallen asleep for her afternoon nap, Wissam is at work, and Noor and Yehia are at school. It is one of the rare times that the house is quiet. I am really looking forward to spending time with Safaa, as it has been almost three months since our last conversation, and I have missed her. I rush to the door at the sound of someone knocking, and I open it to find Safaa smiling. After I invite her in, and out of the cold February weather, we exchange Salams and hugs, and I say how happy I am to see her. She laughingly replies that she is happy to see me too—it has been way too long!

After we get settled on the living room couches, sitting kitty-corner to one another, we talk about some of the recent developments in our lives. I tell her that it has been a very hard few weeks for my family as we recently learned that my cousin Billal (Allah yirhamu), who is like an older brother to me, was diagnosed with cancer (Billal, Allah yirhamu, passed away in the summer of 2017). Safaa immediately makes duaa that Allah (SWT) will grant him health and a long life. I respond to her duaa with "Ameen ya Rubb," and Safaa reminds me, "Make duaa Muna, that is all that we can do ... everything happens for a reason."

Moved and thankful for Safaa's duaa and counsel, I say, "Yes, Subhan Allah." After a few moments, I ask, "How are the kids? I'm so excited to see Rayyan and Marwa next week." Safaa shares that she is extremely proud of Rayyan because if she didn't try hard, she wouldn't be doing as well as she does. Even Mr. Teacher says, 'I have never seen a student like Rayyan' ... Alhamdulillah she cares. She is that kid that will always check her marks. She is my first kid to be like that, the rest of them I have to chase after them, but she does it on her own." Safaa muses, "And you know, in my culture, we have a saying, 'We learn discrimination from our mothers' wombs' ... everyone is different, Subhan Allah." Safaa describes how each of her children is different in their personalities: "It's so funny. In the family, you have a mixture of people.... My children are all different Alhamdulillah."

I wonder aloud if Safaa thinks one of her children is most like her, and Safaa responds, "I think they all have different sides ... Leila has one side of me. Sadia has another; Rayyan has some sides of me, and Marwa also has some sides of me." She continues:

> For example, Rayyan, mash'Allah, is very kind. Today, her and Sadia were not on good terms. Rayyan was trying to tell her a joke, and Sadia [said], "I don't care!" [in a grumpy tone], and Rayyan got very upset. But then Sadia was telling us something, and Rayyan was laughing and I asked her, "Rayyan why are you laughing? She was mean to you," and she said, "Mummy, I don't want to be unkind. Whatever she does, I am not going to be unkind." Can you imagine that? So I said, "Sadia, look at that, this is your younger sister" you know? "I don't want to be unkind" That's the answer she gave me.

Pausing to consider her words, I ask Safaa, "As you were talking, I was thinking about some of our other conversations, and I wonder if you find that raising a boy is different than raising a girl? Does gender matter as much as personality?" Safaa contemplates my question and then says, "Actually I don't see a difference. Alhamdulillah, Ali was never trouble ... Even with my daughters, I see families who struggle, and I thank Allah for this, Alhamdulillah, I haven't gone through a tough time with them."

After talking about how important it is for her children to understand the Two R's of rights and responsibilities, and of learning to view life experience as education, both of our phones announce the call to prayer (we both have a prayer app on our phone that alerts us when it is time for one of the five daily prayers). After we pray, Safaa shares that she has learned a great deal about parenting from two important women in her life:

> There are two people that I admire in my life—my aunties. One is in Australia and one passed away three or four years ago in Seattle. They were very great examples in my life. So amazing, each of them had their own unique characteristics ... I remember one day, I think I was a teenager, and I admired my aunt and said, "Oh my God, I love you so much. I wish I could be like you." She was amazing, just very kind, leading with example; she raised great kids. She said, "You know what I made sure of in life? That they would be good people ... because Allah, when he asks me about my life, is not going to ask me what university they went to, or any of that. Allah will ask me about their manners and behaviour ... for them to be good human beings is what I care for."

Her words resonate with me, and I share some of my recent worries as a parent. Safaa reminds me that "when we plant a seed in the ground, it won't go shooting straight up. Sometimes, it wants to go over here [gesturing to the right with her hands], and we have to say, 'No, not that way' and we nudge it over, away from that area that harms them. We need to be patient and help our children to grow in the right way insha'Allah." Admiring her eloquence, I say, "Insha'Allah." I share that in my writing, I have been playing with the metaphors of planting and growing, and I am amazed at her beautiful words. She has made me reconsider my worries in a new way. She laughs and asks, "So did we achieve anything today?" I laughingly tell her, "Safaa, you are amazing and your stories always help me to think at a deeper level." She again says, "Insha'Allah." After Safaa leaves, my head and heart are incredibly full, and I am so thankful for the blessing of being alongside her.

Retellings
"Everybody is different" (Safaa, multiple conversations)

Throughout our conversations, Safaa has repeatedly called my attention to how "everybody is different." In the fall of 2015, as we discussed how negotiating household chores can be difficult, Safaa laughingly said that her children are very different when it comes to doing their chores: "But they say you learn discrimination from your mother's womb ... they all come out as different people!" A few months later, in the winter of 2015, Safaa and Rayyan shared the story of Rayyan and Marwa befriending a girl who they noticed was being excluded, and Safaa shared, "Actually, when they were young, Rayyan would always say, 'Mama, that person is by herself, she doesn't have a friend' and she would always look for those people ... she is different."

In the spring of 2016, I shared a story with Safaa about feeling judged as a mother. After months of pleading and negotiations, Noor purchased a cellphone with money she had saved up, and I was told by a few female acquaintances that I was making a poor parenting decision. They asserted they would never allow their children to own cellphones until they were in high school, and could not imagine what I was thinking. Safaa was indignant on my behalf:

Safaa: But everybody's different!

Me: Exactly. And I actually thought of you and how you told me about how different Leila and Sadia were when it came to wanting cellphones.

Safaa: And these are sisters!

Me: Yeah, I know.

Safaa: Everybody is different, you can't compare anybody to anybody else ... and you don't want to hear aunties comparing you to anybody; it's not nice. She is unique and is a different person.

Through sharing her stories of mothering, and through responding to mine, Safaa often reminded me of the importance of recognizing and honouring my children's unique personalities, needs, talents, and abilities because "everybody is different."

Growing Forward (and looking back) with Rayyan and Marwa—Winter 2016

I knock quietly on Safaa and Rayyan's door, hoping that it's loud enough to hear but not loud enough to wake Safaa up. Safaa responded to my text last night asking if Rayyan and Marwa are still okay to come for lunch with me today: "Salam sister, the girls are excited to go with you. I will be catching up on sleep when you come, but they will be ready insha'Allah." I know that Safaa likely worked the night shift at the hospital, and I was worried that I would have to knock again when Rayyan answers the door. Her hijab is not yet pinned in place, and she quietly says that she and Marwa would be ready in a few minutes. I whisper that I will wait in the car for them, and they join me a few minutes later. Marwa sits in the front seat this time, and I know from our last trip that they take turns sitting up front with me. Their passenger seat negotiations remind me of similar negotiations with my siblings, and I smile.

As I drive, we debate about where to go for lunch and eventually decide on a large restaurant near their home that offers halal food options. Rayyan and Marwa share their excitement about an upcoming science fair. We are still talking about their projects as we are seated at a corner booth at the restaurant. Saying "Bismillah" as my phone begins recording our conversation, I ask Rayyan and Marwa how the last few months have been. Rayyan and Marwa say that they had a good time going to the zoo with their family a few weeks ago. Rayyan explains that the whole family went to the zoo, except for Laila, who travelled to Seattle to visit their maternal grandmother. As they talk about their extended family, the rhythm of their sisterly discussion holds my attention:

Rayyan: We love to go to Seattle, we have fun when we're here too, but we go almost every year ...

Marwa: Because it's good to see your family ...

Rayyan: And we might still go in the summer ...

Marwa: My dad wants to go but my mom isn't too sure ...

Rayyan: And we have lots of family in Texas too now, so we now have two summer spots ...

Marwa: Yeah, my dad's sister and all her kids are there and my mom's first cousin too.

Me: So both sides of your family live in Seattle and in Texas?

Marwa: Yeah and some family in Kenya because my mom's dad had kids after my mom left Kenya ...

Rayyan: The last time my mom saw her dad was ...

[Rayyan and Marwa in unison]: in 2009

Me: And you guys remember when your mom went to Kenya in 2009?

Marwa: Yeah.

Rayyan: We stayed in Seattle with my grandma.

Rayyan and Marwa continue talking about their extended family and how their maternal grandmother recently visited them in Alberta. Rayyan says that they were so happy that their grandma could visit them because their mom "was so happy to have her here."

After Rayyan makes it clear she would not share details about herself with someone she does not know or trust, our conversation shifts to Rayyan and Marwa sharing their older sister Leila's recent experience with being yelled at and told to "go home" on the bus. Although Rayyan believes that "even if you're not Muslim you should always stand up for people," she says that she does not know what she would do if she witnessed something similar happening to someone else:

Rayyan: If I wasn't wearing hijab maybe I would speak up because then people wouldn't know who I am.

Marwa: It's easier for men because nobody can tell if they're Muslim or not.

Me: Well, I guess it depends on what they're wearing ... and I guess if they look Muslim in some way to others ... and even their name.

Rayyan: Yeah.

Me: But I did notice a difference in how people treated me after I wore hijab, especially now.

Rayyan: After all the attacks.

Me: Yes.

I then ask Rayyan to say more about why she thought she would be more likely to speak up if she were not wearing hijab:

Rayyan: Well, because of all the stuff that's happening, even Donald Trump and that stuff ... saying, "Oh Muslims this and Muslims that."

Me: And you feel like that's made a difference in the way people treat you? Or see you?

Rayyan: Yeah.

Marwa: He's crazy.

Rayyan: Because he says things he doesn't think about it ... and even Stephen Harper!

Me: I just think it's so sad.

Marwa: I am so happy about Justin Trudeau. You know that video of the Syrian refugees coming to Canada ... he went to the airport and was even helping them.

As we prepare to leave, just before I turn the phone recorder off, Marwa and Rayyan lighten the mood and make me laugh as they share how much they are looking forward to the renovations planned for their home because they will be moving into a bigger room:

Marwa: Ali and Leila have *huge* rooms!

Rayyan: Even bigger than my mom and dad.

Marwa: Leila is my dad's princess.

Rayyan: Because she's graduating ...

Marwa: And he never argues with her; he always takes her side ... but my dad always calls us his princesses and queens.

Rayyan: And he says Ali is his favourite son even though he's his only son!

We are still laughing as Rayyan sits in the passenger seat on our way home.

Retellings
"It's good to see your family" (Marwa, Winter 2016)

As I revisited our conversation, my attention turned to when Rayyan and Marwa talked about visiting their extended families and how, as Marwa elucidated, "It's good to see your family." The importance of reconnecting with family is a strong thread running across the stories Safaa and Rayyan have shared with me. In the spring of 2015, during our first shared conversation, Rayyan talked about looking forward to visiting with family in Seattle. She said that they stay connected via FaceTime and text, and Safaa reflected, "It's interesting. I watch them and for the first five or six months they stay in touch and then you see them detaching as time goes by. So I say, 'Okay, it's summertime, time to get that relationship again!'"

As time went on, Safaa and Rayyan shared more stories of staying connected with their extended family. In the summer of 2015, a few weeks after returning from their family trip to Seattle, Safaa shared with me that she started using Facebook as a way to reconnect with family: "We went to the States, and we saw how they used Facebook to connect with our family in Australia and everywhere; we are spread out all across the world, and I brought Facebook into the house, and I said, 'We need to get in touch with our families.'" Later, in the winter of 2015, Safaa said, "Insha'Allah I have to go back [to Kenya] and see my dad again if he can't come to us ... I'm trying to have him come visit, and I hope he can come." Rayyan responded with excitement upon hearing her mom say this and fondly remembered when her grandma came to Alberta to visit with them. During our last recorded conversation in the summer of 2016, Rayyan and Marwa expressed disappointment that for the first summer in a long time, they could not visit with family in Seattle. But then Rayyan, reassuring herself and Marwa, said, "We will probably go next year, insha'Allah."

"Muslims this and Muslims that" (Rayyan, Winter, 2016)

My heart tightens every time I re-read Rayyan's words about how she would be more likely to speak up if she ever witnessed an incident similar to her sister Leila's bus experience if she were not wearing a hijab: "Well, because of all the stuff that's happening, even Donald Trump and that stuff ... saying, 'Oh Muslims this and Muslims that.'" As a mother, and as a woman who wears hijab, I found it deeply troubling to realize that Rayyan and Marwa are acutely aware of the dominant story of Muslims told via mainstream, disturbingly normalized, rhetoric and that being an identifiable Muslim sometimes limits Rayyan's options of how/when/if to speak up. I thought of the countless times Noor or Yehia have asked me about something they have seen on the news or have heard through various sources ... and I wondered yet again about how I can teach my children to be very aware and cautious of dominant stories without succumbing to fear, cynicism, and/or insularity.

Continuing to Grow Our Relationship and Inquiry— Spring 2016

Shielding my eyes from the early May sun, I search the crowded picnic areas at the YMCA park for a shaded area. I quickly realize that all the available spaces are too close to other picnickers. I'm not surprised. It is a beautiful Saturday afternoon, and this park is typically packed on the weekend. Resigned, I settle for a park bench that is mostly shaded and faces the playground. I barely settle myself on the bench before I hear, "Muna! Assalamu Alaikum!" I turn with a smile and embrace Safaa, and then Rayyan, Marwa, and Amina. Safaa says a few words to Marwa in Somali while Marwa holds Amina's hand and leads her to the swings.

I express how much I have missed them, and Safaa says that they have missed me, too. She shares that the last few weeks have been very busy. Their days and nights have been full with school, work, and also with spending time with extended family members who fled the Fort McMurray wildfire (see CBC News, "Wildfire"). Safaa says that although her family members have been provided with comfortable lodgings while they are here, they have spent most of their time with Safaa and her husband in their home. Safaa shares how distressing watching the videos of the Fort McMurray fire and evacuation has been for her:

> Safaa: Just watching the people running away and having no water, it just reminds me so much of the civil war in Somalia ... but at least that was something where you can hide. But a fire? You cannot hide anywhere ... it just is so swift. You know it's really stressing me out ... it's not because I'm afraid of it coming here, but because I am afraid for what people are going through ... who predicted this will happen? You know, this is a big country, a strong country, we are helping others out ... 25,000 refugees.

> Me: Yeah, I see what you mean. They are calling them evacuees, but ...

> Safaa: But they are like refugees for now. You know, they lost their home and their jobs, so many things.

> Rayyan: Yeah, a girl in my class came from there, and her house burnt down and even her school too.

> Safaa: And what's amazing is how everyone is welcoming them and helping them, right? [My family has our] own rooms, and even cards to buy food and things they need. Can you imagine that? They were invited to a big hotel, and so last night, they were going out for dinner—can you imagine? We live in the best country, Alhamdulillah. Even when they were driving, youth were helping and making sure they have gas and water.

> Me: Alhamdulillah, so much help.

> Safaa: Yeah, it's not self-interest ... or self whatever, that's the value of giving and community you see over here, right?

Rayyan talks about her school's fundraising response to the Fort McMurray wildfire. Safaa says that she loves and admires the community response to the crisis and to the recent Syrian refugee efforts in Canada: "It's just amazing."

Later in our conversation, as I scan the playground looking for Marwa and Amina to offer them snacks, I realize that it has been almost a full year since we had our first shared conversation at this very park. I tell this to Rayyan and Safaa, and Safaa replies, "Can you imagine? Time flies!" While we talk about time, a little girl who looks to be about five or six years old approaches us and asks, "Why is Rayyan sad?" Rayyan responds, "I'm not sad." But the little girl is not convinced. She asks, "But why aren't you playing?" Rayyan reassures her by saying, "I'll play with you in a bit!" Safaa laughingly explains that the girl is the daughter of one of her close friends and is not used to seeing Rayyan sitting at the park. I feel bad and tell Rayyan that we can catch up at a later time and to please go ahead and enjoy the playground! Rayyan smilingly says that she will go play with the girls and will come back soon. As we watch her leave, Safaa laughs and says, "She is a mother to Amina and the little ones my Rayyan."

Still laughing, I ask Safaa if she has noticed changes in Rayyan over the last year. She replies, "Yeah actually, she is more confident I think. If I look even from September to now, it's totally different. She is more confident and even more mature. She's ready to be a woman; that's what I see." Rayyan returns to sit with us, and Safaa and Rayyan then share the nikah.com story. We are laughing uncontrollably as Marwa and Amina join us for juice and snacks. Marwa looks at us with curiosity, and the story is shared again. Our laughter continues for a long time.

Later in our conversation, I share my frustration at feeling judged as a parent for allowing Noor to save her money to buy a cellphone. Safaa shares her indignation with me and says, "Yeah, and with aunties, culturally, we sometimes say things that we don't think is going to be hurtful, but the kids who are raised here think differently. They are completely different actually." Safaa reminds me, "You know your daughter, and what is best for your family."

Retellings
"The kids who are raised here think differently" (Safaa, Spring 2016)

Safaa has shared in different ways and at different times with me her belief that "the kids who are raised here think differently." In the winter of 2015, as we enjoyed tea and homemade pastries in her home, Safaa said that she sometimes compares the way that she was raised with the ways she is raising her children:

There, we say it takes a community to raise a child, so there was minimal interaction between the parents and the child because the child belongs to *all* the community, right? Whereby here you have long interactions, one-on-one interactions ... We grew up in a *rich* community whereby we learned from everybody, but for them, it's just you, and how much teaching can you give them by yourself to grow as you grew? It's very difficult.

In the winter of 2016, Safaa shared her response to a female relative advising her, "You really have to take your kids somewhere where they can learn their culture," saying, "But, Alhamdulillah, I feel like they are rich. They have enough culture. And, you know, Canadian culture has so many things that are good; like they are honest, polite and my kids have that too." Safaa shared that, while she sometimes worries about her children, she knows they have been raised in a "family where they are loved," and also feels blessed that she and her husband have been able to take them for almost yearly trips to visit with extended family. She also feels that attending a community-based Islamic school, which "is like home to them," has helped her raise her children in a community of people who care for them.

"She is more confident" (Safaa, Spring 2016)

As I think back to our conversation at the park that day, I once again think about our first shared conversation. I remember originally assuming that Rayyan was really shy and slowly realizing that her reluctance to share intimate details about herself was not shyness. Rather, it was a way of asserting her right to speak when/where/if and to whom she wants. It was Rayyan's way of coming alongside me carefully over time. This realization humbled me. It also made me appreciate Rayyan's keen sense of self-knowledge; she quietly but confidently began to share more when she felt more comfortable with me.

I admit that I was surprised at how Rayyan's confidence in her knowing seemed to be rooted so beautifully at such an early age ... and that, as Safaa reflected, Rayyan seems to have become even "more confident" over time. During my review of the literature before commencing this research, I became familiar with the work of Brown and Gilligan. They contend that girls transitioning into adolescence seem to believe that to speak about their experiences hold "the reluctance to know what one knows and the fear of one's experience, if spoken, will endanger relationships and threaten survival" (Brown and Gilligan 41). After reading their work, I had assumed that girls transitioning into adolescence would become more uncertain over time. However, I wonder at how Rayyan seems to have *grown* in confidence and self-awareness during her transition into adolescence.

Growing into Grade Eight—Summer 2016

The sun is glaring as I park my car in front of Rayyan and Marwa's favourite halal restaurant. Inside, we excitedly talk about our favourite dishes and what we will order as we walk into the (thankfully) air-conditioned seating area. It is a summer afternoon, and we are the only customers in the restaurant. We happily choose our own booth and head to the front to order. We already know what we want. As we sit back down with our drinks and wait for our food, we talk about Ramadan and how it was not as difficult as we feared it would be to fast during the last month of school and into the first week of July. Rayyan says, "It was actually nice because after exams, we could go home."

Marwa and Rayyan then tell me about staying in the city this summer rather than visiting with family in Seattle like they usually do. Rayyan says, "My mom said, 'We'll have fun in [the city]; we'll go around to the areas that we don't go that much and just have fun there.' So we went to a lot of the parks." Marwa adds, "And the lakes." They are excited over their plans for the weekend to go swimming, jet-skiing, and hiking with family and friends. They also talk about some of the new renovations taking place in their home and how nice everything looks so far. They love that they will have a bigger room to share. Marwa says, "We get to move into Leila's old room which is *huge*, and she will take our old room, which is medium-sized."

Our conversation shifts to talking about the last month of Rayyan's grade seven school year. Rayyan says that it was mostly "okay," but that she feels bad for some of her classmates who "don't get their work done and then regret it." I ask Rayyan, "Why do you think they don't get their work done?" She replies, "Maybe they spend a lot of time on their phones, on Snapchat ... even when I'm studying, I get so many snaps from my friends saying, 'I'm bored' so I'm like, 'Well do your homework,' and they'll be like, 'Stop being annoying' [laughing]." Rayyan also thinks that her classmates are sometimes distracted by their cellphones during class: "People text other people in the class or school ... Like some people will message and ask, 'Are you understanding any of this?' and stuff like that ... And lots of people skip class too." I ask Rayyan why she thinks people skip classes: "Sometimes their friends are skipping and they just go along with them," she says.

Later in our conversation, as we enjoy our donairs and fries, I ask Rayyan if she is still friends with the same group of girls she told me about when we first started having conversations:

> Yeah ... mostly. Some of them started to slack in school, like I had a friend who was being influenced in doing bad stuff. Like, I understand listening to music, but some of the songs have *bad* swears and stuff in them. And she would be like, "Rayyan, listen to this," and I would be like, "Sorry, I can't listen to that." And she would be like [teasing voice], "Aww, you can't listen to music? Aww ..." and I was like, "Well I listen to music but not that song" ... it was stuff that even an adult shouldn't listen to.

I ask Rayyan if she noticed any other changes in her classmates in the transition from grade six to grade seven: "Well, definitely people matured and were more responsible. In grade six, they would be more kid-ish like laughing if someone said 'doody' or something, but now they'll say, 'Stop acting like a kid.'" Rayyan later clarifies her understanding of the concept of maturity:

Marwa: I feel like Rayyan got more mature.

Me: Do you agree with that Rayyan?

Rayyan: [smiling] Yeah.

Marwa: Like one day, I was asking Rayyan to play this silly game we sometimes play, and she was like, "Umm, I don't want to play that."

Rayyan: Some people think that they're more mature, but they don't really know what mature means. Like if I'm staying inside rather than outside, and I'm on my phone, then I'm a big girl, you know what I mean? Being mature means being responsible; you have more responsibilities.

Me: So being mature doesn't necessarily mean acting like you're an adult. Being mature means taking your responsibilities seriously.

Rayyan: Yeah people think mature is, "When I was in grade six, I used to play inside, but now that I'm a teen, I go inside and am on my phone all day." No, that's not mature.

Rayyan talks about how social media, especially Snapchat and Instagram, have "lots of fun stuff on there," and her mom "uses Instagram for a lot of Islamic stuff." Yet these apps sometimes contribute to and escalate conflicts. She shares the story of friends who had a very public rift: "Some girls will fight about pictures on Instagram. They'll take pictures of stuff and post it. Like, a girl posted a picture of her and her ex-best friend, who wasn't wearing her hijab in the picture. The girl who posted it was like, 'Well she deserved it!' ... and she even wrote about who her crush was." Appalled, I ask Rayyan if anything like that has happened to her: "No, I usually go on my mom's Instagram to see pictures, but I don't have Instagram. I only have Snapchat, and only have a few people on it [who can see my pictures]."

Before we clean our booth and end our conversation, Rayyan says she is looking forward to starting grade eight in a few weeks, saying, "I like school, so I'm excited."

Retellings
"Being mature means being responsible"
(Rayyan, Summer 2016)

I re-read Rayyan's words— "Being mature means being responsible"— and I think about the many times Rayyan and Safaa have talked about responsibility. A few months after Safaa shared her deeply rooted belief in the Two R's of rights and responsibilities, she shared, in the spring of 2016, that Rayyan had "been growing and improving, working hard ... she's always worked hard, but is taking even more responsibility." Our discussions over several months and seasons have shown that for both Rayyan and Safaa, maturity and growth are intricately connected with fulfilling their rights and responsibilities, including the right and responsibility to nurture relationships and to be nurtured with kindness.

I am reminded of the conversation with Rayyan and Marwa at Dairy Queen in the fall of 2015, in which Rayyan shared a story about a friend she had distanced herself from because she would talk about others behind their backs: "I don't like that .... but I don't give her the evil eye or anything. We still say Salam, we still talk, but we don't really hang out anymore." After I remarked that her response was "such a mature way of looking at it," Rayyan stressed that it is important to be kind to everyone. Her view of maturity entails rights and responsibilities towards herself and others; it is profoundly rooted in her belief that kindness is essential to growing herself and her relationships. For Rayyan, kindness is a way of being, and of becoming, in relation with others.

Epilogue: Tending to Each Other (with love and care) – Winter 2017

Walking the halls of the children's wing of the hospital, I am reminded of the many nights I slept by Yehia's bedside in this area when he was just months old. Saying "Alhamdulillah" for his health and for his remarkable growth over the last eleven years, I turn the corner and my thoughts turn to Rayyan and Safaa. I make duaa that Allah (SWT) grants Rayyan a quick recovery. On the phone earlier today, Safaa assured me that Rayyan was in the hospital because of her dehydration following a vicious influenza bug that lasted longer than it should have. However, from my own experience, I know that it is hard to be in the hospital and constantly waiting for updates from doctors and medical staff. Safaa and Rayyan have been here for three days, and I have brought some gifts and treats in the hopes to brighten their day.

I ask a nearby nurse if she can guide me to Rayyan's room, and she laughingly points to the one behind me. Smiling sheepishly, I thank her and make my way to the room. Walking into the room, I could not see who is behind the curtains drawn around the first bed, so I walk past it to the second one. Spotting a sleeping infant in a crib with no one else around, I silently make duaa for the baby for a long, healthy life as I turn and see that the curtain is not fully drawn on this side of the room. I suddenly hear, "Muna! Assalamu Alaikum!" and I rush forward to hug Safaa and then Rayyan, who is resting on the hospital bed. After thanking me for coming, Safaa tells me that she tries to keep a watchful eye on the baby next to them as her mother has other little ones at home and cannot be here as often as she wants. My heart constricts a little at her kindness and I say, "Jazakum Allahu Khairan [May Allah reward you with all that is good] Safaa; you are always so thoughtful." Smilingly waving my words away, Safaa asks me how I am doing: "How are the kids? How's Hannah?" I smile again at her questions and am not surprised that she is asking about me and my family even as she and Rayyan are spending their time in the hospital.

I tell Safaa that I have just left a funeral service for a dear, beloved friend, Dr. Joy Ruth Michelson (may she rest in peace) and that I already miss her. Safaa reminds me that "Inna li'Allah wa Inna Ilayhi Raj'oon [We belong to Allah and to Him we are destined to return]" and says that death is a right that life has upon us. I nod somberly and ask Rayyan how she is feeling. She quickly responds, "Bored. I miss school." I take out the bag of goodies I have brought with me. Rayyan excitedly reaches for the hijabs I picked out for her while Safaa exclaims at the bag of fresh, homemade *ka3k* and asks if I made them myself. I say, "No, but I watched my mom and Sittee make them and served as a taste-tester." We laugh and continue to catch up on each other's lives.

Eventually, we venture into a topic that has been often discussed in mainstream news and media and by family and friends—the recent announcement by the American government of the travel ban on all refugees and passport holders from seven Muslim-majority countries. As Donald Trump had repeatedly called for a "Muslim Ban" during his (ultimately successful) presidential campaign, many are of the mind that the "Travel Ban" from seven Muslim-majority countries (Iran, Iraq, Libya, Somalia, Sudan, Syria and Yemen) is a less direct version of his previous calls for a "Muslim Ban" (Yuhas and Sidahmed). While the Canadian government assured worried Canadians that this ban will not affect them, I shared with Safaa how worried I was that my cousin Billal (Allah yirhamu) will not be able to travel to see a cancer specialist he has been consulting with in America because he was born in Libya. Safaa says that she also worries, especially when the ban was first announced and there were reports that Canadian dual citizenship holders with ties to one of the seven countries would not be allowed to enter the United States. Born in Somalia, she worries that her almost yearly trips to visit with family in Seattle will probably not be possible anymore. We say, "Insha'Allah khair" but are interrupted by one of the machines beeping. Rayyan looks at her mom questioningly, and with experienced hands, Safaa quiets the machine manually as she softly explains why it is beeping. Reminded that Safaa works in a hospital setting, I ask her if she has taken this time off work, and she says she has cleared her schedule until Rayyan is better. I recognize her love and faith as she smiles and says, "Insha'Allah soon, we should be out in the next few days." I smile back at her and at Rayyan and say, "Insha'Allah very soon."

Chapter 4

A Narrative Account of Living and Growing Alongside Zahra and Ayesha

We are the seeds of the tenacious plant,
and it is in our ripeness and our fullness
of heart that we are given to the wind
and are scattered
—Khalil Gibran, *The Prophet*

Ayesha and Zahra's Family
Ayesha—Mom
Hassan—Dad

Children by Birth Order
Zahra
Sarah
Zainab

Growing Forward ... Amidst Uncertainty

I sit in front of my laptop with pages (and pages) of field texts spread across the kitchen table, and I contemplate how to begin writing this narrative account of the almost two years I have lived and inquired alongside Zahra and Ayesha. How do I give a sense of our coming alongside one another over time? How can I write about engaging as co-inquirers—and as friends—when our relationship and our inquiry have evolved so profoundly since we first met? How can I represent our conversations in ways that give a sense of our becoming without somehow constricting the complexity and fullness of our life-making and embodied experiences?

I think back to the conversation Ayesha, Zahra, and I shared two weeks ago. Indulging in tiramisu after enjoying supper at Zahra's favourite pasta restaurant, we talked about composing research texts. We had already reviewed threads and stories that might be included in our narrative account, and I asked them about some of the hard to tell stories they had shared or that we had lived alongside one another, "Are you sure you are comfortable with sharing that?" We talked for a long time about what to include and what to leave out of our writing. Before we left the restaurant, however, Zahra turned to me and said, "Don't worry Muna, we trust you." Ayesha and Zahra have expressed a variation of this sentiment every time we discuss the writing of research texts. Their trust heartens me ... and worries me. I worry that I will fall short of the trust they have placed in me.

Breathing deeply, I make duaa that I will be able to show how our inquiry and relationship(s) unfolded over time. Saying "Bismillah," I begin to type.

Will You Be My (research) Friend?—Winter 2015

Parking the car after a long drive, I check the message from Ayesha yet again to make sure I am at the right house. I try to calm my nerves as her text confirms that this is, indeed, where I am supposed to be. Making duaa as I gather my things and make my way to their door, I wonder if Ayesha and Zahra will want to participate in this study after we engage in this initial conversation. Ayesha and I have spoken a few times over the phone over the last few weeks and, yesterday, met for the first time at the Chapel Hill vigil. We communicated a few days before a planned candlelight vigil to honour the lives of Razan and Yusor Abu-Salha, and Deah Barakat. These three Muslim American students were killed by a neighbour in what many have called a hate crime (Elliot; Talbot). Taking one more deep breath and saying one more prayer, I knock tentatively at the door.

Ayesha answers the door without her hijab and envelops me in a warm hug, saying "Assalamu Alaikum!" Ushering me into their cozy and delicious smelling home, Ayesha asks me to have a seat at a nearby loveseat. I follow her request, but stand moments later as Zahra and her two younger sisters, Sarah and Zainab, approach me to greet me with "Assalamu Alaikum" and hugs. Ayesha then asks Sarah and Zainab to give us privacy as we talk. Zahra, in the meantime, brings out a tray of snacks of mixed nuts and dried fruit and the most delicious traditional tea with cardamom and cinnamon for us to enjoy as we chat. I smile widely as they talk about how happy they are that our mutual acquaintance has connected us to one another and how excited they are to participate in this research.

After over an hour of discussion, Ayesha walks me to the door. I thank her again for agreeing to participate and for making me feel so welcome. She hugs me goodbye and says that she looks forward to engaging in our inquiry; she thinks it will be lovely to think more deeply alongside Zahra about their experiences during this time. Alhamdulillah is in my mind, on my tongue, and reverberating throughout my body as we make plans for our first extended, shared conversation as co-inquirers. Insha'Allah Khair!

Planting Beginning Stories—Winter 2015

I am excited and nervous ahead of our first research conversation. I make duaa and knock on Zahra and Ayesha's door. It is cold outside, and I am grateful to be invited inside by Ayesha and Zahra with warm hugs and smiles. Sitting on the comfortable futons arranged so invitingly on the floor, Zahra, Ayesha, and I commence by sketching annals (Clandinin and Connelly, *Narrative*)—timelines of memorable dates and experiences around their early childhood experiences. Ayesha and I soon discover we were born a few months apart and also became mothers for the first time, to Zahra and Noor, months apart. Ayesha laughingly exclaims, "We were parallel!"

Later, as her mom prepares tea in the kitchen, Zahra says, "I was born in Afghanistan, the same place my mom and dad were born ... and I came here [to Canada] when I was six months old." I ask Zahra what the circumstances were that led them to leave Afghanistan: "I'm not really sure. My parents just tell me that we were there but that there was war again and stuff... and then we had to go to Pakistan for a little while and then we came here." Emerging from the kitchen and setting down the tray of tea and cups, Ayesha sits next to her daughter and talks about growing up in Afghanistan. She explains how her family decided to come to Canada by sharing several (hitherto untold) stories:

I was born in Kabul, Afghanistan. My father is a doctor, and my mother is a teacher. They both worked and were very busy. I grew up in a big family. There are six of us, three brothers and three sisters. I am the oldest.

I remember when we used to go to daycare; my mom used to drop us off. I didn't like the teacher there. I can remember her face still ... I was afraid of her I think.

Then when I went to school ... I don't know if it was the grade one teacher or grade two ... whenever I wouldn't pay attention or something like that, the teacher would say, "Oh you're the daughter of the doctor?" [sarcastic tone] and this and that, you know? But they did that to everybody there.

I moved schools for grade four and five because, at that time, the regime was run by Russians[22] ... and the Russians were imposing Russian ideologies there. My dad didn't like that so he moved me. In grade seven, I came back to this school because the regime changed, and there was no Russian teaching going on anymore.

When I came home from school, if they made something special, my grandma would keep it fresh for me and make it when I came ... I used to teach her. Actually, she was not literate ... so I used to teach her language, and she was such a brave woman. For the longest time, I didn't know that she was illiterate because she was so knowledgeable in everything ... and at that age, she wanted to learn, and I admire her for that ... she went through a lot too. They had a good life and house and everything, but during the war, they had to abandon their house, and they sold it for very little money and moved to Pakistan and they didn't have a very good life there ... and then my grandpa also died.

22 While the literature on history of colonialism and conflict in Afghanistan is extensive, I consulted with the Centre for Research on Globalization (Visalli) to help me understand more of Afghanistan's sociopolitical context.

Although Ayesha and Zahra were both born in Afghanistan and I understand that Ayesha's stories of childhood might contain stories of sociopolitical unrest, I was not wakeful to the ways that constructing annals alongside one another in our first research conversation could create spaces where some of our previously unspoken stories of childhood experiences could be voiced. As Ayesha continues to share, I notice Zahra is listening to her mom with wide-eyed, rapt attention.

I was about twelve years old, and I remember it was so scary. There were bomb blasts everywhere, rockets, and I remember it was so hard ... it was so scary we had to move from there. The Russians were out, but the government was still there, the Afghan government, and these Mujahideen [fighters opposed to the Afghan government] were attacking the capital. They were throwing the grenades, those rockets, from other places, outside the city ... so it would just drop anywhere ... and that was just so terrifying.

We were living in tall buildings, and the buildings had holes from the fighting and it was so terrifying ... At night we used to go to the underground basement of the building because it was dangerous to be in the house. Even when we were in the house, we would not go in the rooms. We would be in like a back kind of den because there [were] no windows, so if a rocket is coming in ...

Since I often struggle with voicing my doubts and fears, I have never been comfortable with silences. Perhaps because of my experiences and struggles with silences (from myself and others), I sometimes *feel* them in the spaces around me. I wonder if this embodied knowledge is why I have such a strong sense that Ayesha has not yet shared these stories of growing up in Afghanistan with Zahra.

It was horrific. I remember being so scared whenever you would hear the [making a long, high pitched whooooo sound of rockets being launched] and you don't even know if it's going to come to your house or if it goes to another.

It's horrific.

That's what we went through, all the children there. And what's happening is that my dad didn't have work. He couldn't go to work because there was fighting going on. And my mom wasn't working, and food was scarce and we had to, you know, be more careful, not to waste and stuff like that ... and we didn't have water running in the building, so we had to go and get water from a distance, and we had to go and walk and then bring buckets of water home [long pause].

Lots of people were injured, like in our building. So many times the rockets fell near the building, and people were injured ... upstairs in my building a guy was injured ... it was so hard to see all those things ... and I was also scared of those Mujahideen. They were always staring at you, you know? They did so many things, like forcing themselves and taking girls out of their families, and I was so scared.

It was just horrific.

How is Zahra experiencing hearing these stories? Should I somehow try to comfort her? Should I comfort Ayesha? Should I redirect the conversation (even with awareness that Ayesha *chose* to share these stories)? Is this conversation too intense, too soon? I continue to listen.

And for a while it was good, and I was still scared ... I remember sitting outside one day playing with my friends, and a guy walked by. He looked like one of the Mujahideen. I knew the other people in my building, and he was different. So he walked by, and then he turned back, and he came towards me, and he was looking at me, and I was terrified. I just got up and ran home ... whenever I remembered him, I thought he was going to come back and get me, and I was so scared. They could do anything, and there's no law or anything to protect you.

My grandpa really took it to heart ... losing all the life that they made ... they had to live off the money that was sent from my aunt from here [Canada] every month. And he had to live in our house in Pakistan, after we left Afghanistan, and my dad was good ... but still, living in his son-in-law's house was hard on him.

Sitting in that comfortable living room with the delicious aroma of traditional tea embracing us, we are transported, through Ayesha's stories, to earlier times and places of conflict. In this moment of profound disruption, I think of Sittee's stories of our family's exodus from Palestine. Although I am an intergenerational survivor of Palestinian displacement, I wonder how I can possibly compose thoughtful responses to Ayesha because having grown up in Canada, her stories are unfathomable for me.

My dad sent money here [to Canada] for my aunt to put in the bank ... they wanted to show that they had enough money for when you come here, but still the sponsorship was taking time. We were like, "It's probably not going to happen; it's probably rejected" ... but the embassy did contact us when it was time.

My father was always struggling to get us out of Pakistan because life wasn't very good there. There was no future there. We were not allowed to go to the Pakistan University [as Afghan refugees] ... I wanted to become a doctor, so I was in medical program in an Afghani University, but even that was closed, so that's why I couldn't pursue my career.

When we went back to Afghanistan I was around twenty-two years old ... it was a lot better. There was security, and you would not be afraid of any rockets being fired ... so, that was good.

We were living in Peshawar Pakistan when I got married; we got married there in 2002. And then we were working for nongovernmental organizations [NGOs] and at that time, when we got married, the Taliban were done in Afghanistan ... then, these nongovernmental organizations started going inside Afghanistan ... so that's how they moved in Afghanistan, and we had to move too because our jobs were in these NGOs.

We moved there, and Zahra was born there ... and then we came here because my aunt lives here and she had sponsored us. And then, during these three years that we were sponsored, it was just like we totally forgot about it. We thought it was not going to happen.

Unsure of how to respond, I continue to listen, asking a few questions for clarification or repeatedly stating, with sincerity, "I can't imagine." My main response, however, is to reach out to squeeze or hold Ayesha's hand as she shares.

And then I got married, and then finally after that, we heard from them [the Canadian Embassy]. I told them that I'm married now, and I have a daughter ... We never thought we would hear from you so we never told you anything, so they were kind enough to include my husband and my daughter in the sponsorship, so we all came together.

We came here.

I'm the oldest so I don't know, my brother and the second oldest sister probably remember ... I don't know about the others, but I remember that we were all trying to find stuff to do at home because we were always at home; you can't go outside to play ... I think they would remember ... but we don't talk about it.

I never talk about it. This is the first time I've talked about this.

Unspoken for so long, Ayesha's stories seem to flow out of her and reverberated for a long time in the spaces around and between us. Although Zahra and I are mostly silent in response to Ayesha's stories, we can articulate some of what we are thinking and feeling later in the conversation, with Ayesha and Zahra comforting each other:

Me: Wow. Subhan Allah. Thank you so much for sharing because, like I said ... I can't imagine. I can't imagine living like that.

Ayesha: Yeah, it's hard.

Me: I can't imagine. Is this the first time you've heard this Zahra?

Zahra: Yeah ... [reaching over to hug Ayesha]. You scared me to death Mama!

Ayesha: Really? I'm sorry baby!

Ayesha's vulnerability in sharing these never before told stories creates a space where Zahra and I can also share previously unspoken stories. As she recounts her earliest school memories, Zahra shares a story that Ayesha is surprised to hear for the first time. She talks about being bullied in grade one and two by a group of older boys in her school. Ayesha asks Zahra why she did not confide in her or a teacher at the time. Zahra tears up and does not answer Ayesha's question. Unsure of what to do, I steer the conversation away to give Zahra space, and for the first time, I voice how uncertain I am about Noor choosing the junior high school she wants to attend—what if she chooses to leave the Islamic school she has grown up in? Zahra responds by sharing why having the freedom to choose a junior high school for herself is so important to her, particularly after six years of attending a school with Islamic studies programming: "I want to go to public school because I hear there are going to be people who force you to do drugs and stuff, and I want to test and see if I ever experience it. I want to be like, 'Ok, I know how to say no to things.' I want to see if I'll be able to do that." Ayesha adds that "maybe we need to let them experience the things we're fearful of and let them try it. And it's not final, she can always go back."

We end our conversation with hugs and promises to see each other soon. Driving home, our conversation and stories are "working on [me]" (Basso 59). An Apache Elder shared the profound wisdom of sitting and thinking with stories: "That story is working on you now. You keep thinking about it. That story is making you want to replace yourself. You think only of what you did that was wrong, and you don't like it. So you want to live better" (qtd. in Basso 59). Thinking about the last part of our conversation, I resolve to compose more spaces for choices alongside my children. With their vulnerability and their courage, Ayesha and Zahra inspire me and make me want to live better alongside my children and loved ones.

Retellings
"At some point we need to let go and accept our children's choices" (Ayesha, Winter 2015)

Re-reading my field texts, I gain a renewed sense of the many wonderings that lived in me after that first research conversation alongside Zahra and Ayesha. In my field notes, I wrote about Ayesha's experiences of being unable to choose where she lived or attended school as well as the lack of choice in so many other areas of her life as a child and youth. Reflecting on Ayesha's words that "maybe we need to let them experience the things we're fearful of and let them try it," I wonder if experiencing a lack of choice(s) as a child and youth has shaped her stories to live by as a mother who creates spaces for her daughters to choose for themselves.

Ayesha has shared other stories that give a sense of her belief in the need to create spaces for choice(s) alongside her children. In the winter of 2015, Ayesha and I were enjoying dinner at one of my favourite restaurants when she talked about how she fell in love with her husband. She talked about how her parents, after initially opposing the relationship, came to accept her decision. She stressed, "At some point we need to let go and accept our children's choices; otherwise, you might ruin your relationship with them." Later, in the spring of 2016, as we enjoyed lunch, Ayesha reflected on the shifts in her parenting over the years. During this conversation, I started to get the sense that for Ayesha, creating spaces for her daughters to choose for themselves is intimately connected to listening to them. In relation to creating spaces for choice(s) alongside Zahra, she shared, "I try to *listen* more, and I try to tell her that it's her choice, and I don't mind whatever she chooses."

"We were parallel" (Ayesha, Winter 2015)

Reminiscent of my uncertainty about how to respond to Ayesha's stories during our first research conversation, I have experienced other moments and periods of uncertainty in how to move forward alongside Ayesha and Zahra. One such period of uncertainty was during the weeks and months following our first research conversation. Although Ayesha and I remained in contact through text and WhatsApp, coming alongside Ayesha and Zahra has been a slow process of negotiating our relationships and who we are, and are in the process of becoming, alongside one another. After several months of trying to connect face-to-face with Ayesha and Zahra after our first research conversation, I asked Ayesha if we could meet "off the record." We continued to use this phrase to signify times when we were meeting to discuss issues that might not be included in research texts. While many of our "off the record" conversations were later addressed by either Ayesha or Zahra in recorded conversations, I introduced the option of "off the record" conversations because I wanted Zahra and Ayesha to know that I would not share anything that they were not comfortable sharing.

I asked for an off the record conversation at that time because I was afraid that Ayesha was reconsidering participation in the research. I had a strong sense that Ayesha was hesitant to meet with me again, and I wondered if the intensity of our first research conversation contributed to her hesitancy. After three months of trying to meet, I messaged Ayesha and asked if we could discuss a few things off the record. I wanted to share that I would understand if she wanted to leave the research. I later learned that Ayesha was in the midst of many life changes. She had recently quit her job. She was moving into a new house and was experiencing many other changes and challenges. She later shared through a WhatsApp message in June 2015 that "I feel like everything is happening at the same time." In response, I wrote, "I completely understand! I just moved a month ago, and I can't imagine dealing with that and all the other things going on for you right now." Over the phone later that week, I offered to help her move because I have experience. I've moved three times in the last five years. She laughed and said that she has moved about seven times since coming to Canada twelve years ago. I laughingly conceded, "Okay, you win."

Experience with moving was not the only area of resonance I felt with Ayesha. We seemed to be "parallel," as Ayesha noted, in many other ways. Born a few months apart, we experienced the transition into adolescence at around the same time, although in very different contexts. Noor and Zahra were born a few months apart, and as we watched home videos in the summer of 2015 in their home, we discovered another similarity in our lives:

Ayesha: When Zahra was a year old, I remember, I started working in the summer.

Me: Yeah, I remember I started teaching, my very first year, when Noor was about five months old ... I felt so guilty, but I had to because of financial reasons.

Ayesha: Oh my goodness! Yeah, I know what you mean, us too.

Although our first research conversation mainly (and unexpectedly) focused on Ayesha's experiences, and although I mainly communicated with Ayesha at first, Zahra, Ayesha, and I creatively co-composed our research relationship over time. We engaged in conversations together, and then after several months as trust and comfort were taking root, I also met with either Zahra or Ayesha alone. Over time, through our inquiry, we became close friends. Our relationship is one of my sustaining stories, and I am incredibly grateful.

Planting Seeds of Trust—Summer 2015

I adjust the air conditioning in my car on the drive to Zahra and Ayesha's home, and I think about how wonderful a large Slurpee would be. I am not really a frozen beverage person, usually preferring a hot cup of coffee or water, but fasting the long, hot days of Ramadan this year has me yearning for a huge cup of frozen, sugary, caffeinated slush. Pulling up to their new house, I wonder how Zahra and Ayesha are experiencing Ramadan. Cradling their housewarming gift, a potted white calla lily in bloom, I make duaa and knock on their door.

Sarah opens the door with a smile and says that her mom and Zahra will be down in a minute. She invites me to sit on the living room couch to wait. I place the calla lily on the coffee table in front of me and am about to sit down when I notice Zahra and Ayesha walking towards me. We exchange Salams and hugs, and I compliment them on their new home. Ayesha smiles and tells me that there are still unopened moving boxes all around, and I laughingly tell her that my home has those nuisances all over the place too. We smile wryly at each other and then talk about Ramadan and how hot it is today.

I ask Zahra how the last few months of grade six were and she responds, "It was fun, minus the learning part." She then talks about attending an open house at the junior high school she chose to register in and how she is feeling about her transition there. She replies, "I'm nervous ... I'm going to school with a lot of people who are not that close. Before [in elementary school], I was close with everyone and now I don't know half of everybody." However, Zahra said she is glad because "most of my friends are coming, a lot of us Alhamdulillah."

Later in our conversation, we discuss Zahra's grade six graduation:

Zahra: It was nice. I told my friends, "Oh I'm going miss you guys!" and then half of them were like, "But I'm going see you again over the summer!" But I said, "I'm still going to miss you and it's not going to be the same."

Me: Yeah, I know what you mean. And how about you Ayesha? What did you think about Zahra's graduation?

Ayesha: It was nice, but I wasn't feeling sad [laughing]. Some of the parents were saying they cried at the graduation, but I was like, "I don't know, maybe I'm missing something?" I was not sad [laughing]. So people who have been here and have gone through it maybe know it's going to be harder, but I don't know, I'm not sad. I'm happy.

Me: I think some of it might be worry? Like, "What's going to happen next year? What's the transition going to be like?"

Zahra: How are they going to act [laughing] ... a lot of my friends changed over the year.

Me: Really? The ones who went on to junior high before you?

Zahra: No, my friends from my class the past year have changed *a lot.*

I ask Zahra to please say more about these changes: "One of them changed the way she dressed. Like before she picked up random things and put it on. Now, she takes more time and stuff like that .... and one of them who was so quiet became really talkative and people started saying, 'She talks too much!'" [laughing].

Trying to tread carefully, I later ask Ayesha about her experiences transitioning to junior high school, "Are there special friends or teachers who stand out for you?" She replies:

Well ... when we moved to Pakistan, I was supposed to be in grade seven, but I went to grade six again. I don't know why;

things were different there ... so there were Afghan schools funded by humanitarian organizations, and I attended one of them, and it was far from my house. I used to walk to school. But the school was just a yard with tents, and we would sit under the tents, and those were our classrooms, and the teachers would come and teach ... it was such a big change. I was not taking it seriously, and I was like, "I don't want to go here; I don't even want to go to school" ... and my mom was saying, "Okay, no, you have to go to school. It's okay whatever it is. You need to go."

Ayesha discusses her experiences transitioning to life in Pakistan and how there were many shifts for her and her family at that time: "I was thirteen when we moved, and because my mom was in the hospital with my brother, he got sick, and she was in the hospital for a few weeks. I was the eldest at home, and I had to do everything." Her story resonates with me, and I share how I had learned to shoulder more familial responsibilities in grade eight after my youngest sister Eman was born because my mom had gotten sick after giving birth to her. However, I continue, "I think my sister Suha would relate even more ... there's something about being the eldest." I turn to Zahra and ask if she has ever felt added responsibility because she is the eldest:

Zahra: All the time.

Me: Noor says so too, but in what ways? At what times do you feel that most strongly?

Zahra: When we have to do our chores. I have to do a little more than them.

Ayesha: One of my friends, she's also the eldest in her family, and she doesn't like the idea that you give more responsibility to the eldest, but I think that it makes sense. You count on them more, just like you will count on the younger ones too when it's time.

Zahra later talks about her relationship with her sisters Sarah and Zainab:

Zahra: We are pretty close sometimes ... depends on what time it is [laughing].

Me: When I was growing up, me and my sisters would argue or get annoyed with each other a lot, but it was also nice to have someone to talk to and laugh with.

Zahra: Yeah, me and Sarah, if one of us gets in trouble, even if we're not talking to each other, we make faces and start laughing.

Ayesha laughs and says Zahra and Sarah get annoyed watching home movies of Zainab as a baby because they say, "She's just sitting there and doing nothing!" We laugh as Zahra says, "It's true!" I ask if they would be comfortable watching some of their home movies with me at some point, and Ayesha invites me to visit next month right after Eid celebrations. We laugh wistfully as I say, "We won't be fasting then, so I volunteer to bring the popcorn!"

Retellings
(eldest) Sister Stories

Zahra's stories of who she is and who she is becoming alongside her younger sisters have profoundly shaped her life-making. Living alongside her for the last two years, I have repeatedly witnessed Zahra's love and care for her sisters. Born one year apart, she is closest in age to Sarah. I was reminded of my relationship with my sister Suha as I watched home movies with Ayesha, Zahra, Sarah, and Zainab in the summer of 2015:

Zahra: When we were younger, we [Sarah and I] always had identical clothes.

Me: That's exactly like me and my older sister [laughing].

Ayesha: And they would still fight over the dresses sometimes!

Several months later, as we enjoyed breakfast at my home in the winter of 2015, Zahra said her relationship with Sarah changed over the years, particularly as Sarah experienced her own transition into adolescence: "She goes through everything I went through, so she'll be like, 'I hate this!' and I will say, 'Ugh, I remember that, I hated it too.'" Zahra said she likes helping her sisters negotiate some of the challenges of growing older: "Now, when my sisters are going through everything,

I'm glad I can help and tell them how to go through it, although they might not always listen." While Zahra felt that she has extra responsibilities as the eldest, I also gained a sense of her as a proud older sister. I had asked Ayesha and Zahra to bring a few of their favourite photographs with them, and one of the photographs that Zahra brought was of Zainab sitting on a toilet as a toddler. Giving me a sense of her deep love and care for her younger sister, Zahra smilingly explained that she chose this photograph because she remembered how hard Sarah had worked to help potty-train Zainab.

In the fall of 2015, Ayesha said that she and Zahra "grew up completely different," but also highlighted the many ways that being the eldest (sister) among her siblings had shaped her life-making. Explaining that the responsibilities of eldest siblings cannot be simply reduced to more chores, Ayesha said, "There's other responsibilities too ... I think that my younger sister suffered even more than I did. She's so traumatized still; she's still haunted." I asked Ayesha to please say more about this: "After we left Afghanistan, she would cry and was sick all the time. I would feel so bad, and I would try to help her feel better." As the eldest (sister), Ayesha felt responsible for helping her younger siblings live and grow in sustaining ways. In the fall of 2016, Ayesha expressed excitement that she was helping her sister prepare for her upcoming wedding: "It feels good to see her so happy." In the many seasons we have inquired alongside one another, Ayesha has shared many stories of love and, sometimes, concern for her siblings that highlighted her sense of responsibility as the eldest (sister) and the many ways her siblings' happiness and sadness are interconnected with hers—stories that make me consider how the responsibilities of being the eldest sister can sometimes feel similar to the responsibilities accompanying motherhood.

Rooting Beginning (in Canada) Stories—Summer 2015

Excitedly carrying three bags of pre-popped, flavoured popcorn, I knock on Ayesha and Zahra's door. It is a beautiful summer afternoon, and we will be having a home movie viewing party. Zahra opens the door with a smile and says "Assalamu Alaikum!"; she looks beautiful in her flowy hijab. She leads me to the family room where Ayesha is adjusting the television. Ayesha turns to greet me with a hug, and we are getting settled as Sarah and Zainab come into the room and ask if they can join us. Ayesha asks me if that would be okay, and I say, "Of course!"

Settled with our bowls of popcorn and iced drinks, the first home movie we watch features two adorable toddlers playing dress-up:

Zahra: That's me and Sarah [laughing].

Me: *So* cute—I love your poncho! [laughing] How old were you here?

Zahra: I think I was two.

Ayesha: No, you were about two and a half.

Ayesha: This was a time when we had gone to visit my in-laws, and they speak Pashto, their language, and she had learned a few words there, and I'm just trying to speak that language with her and telling her, "Give me some raisins please."

Ayesha explains that there "are many cultures and languages in Afghanistan" and that her familial language is Farsi, whereas Zahra's father's familial language is Pashto. Zahra tells me that she knows both languages, and her parents also know both languages. Ayesha said that she also learned Urdu during her years in Pakistan. I express amazement, "Mash'Allah, so you know four languages and Zahra knows three." Ayesha says she tries to practice the other three languages when she can because she feels that she mostly communicates in English lately.

As we watch the film, I ask Ayesha if they still make home movies:

Ayesha: They can do it yeah, but they don't want to do it ... like they do funny things, but they don't want us to take videos.

Me: How come?

Zahra: It's embarrassing. You guys post it on Facebook!

Ayesha: No I don't [laughing].

Zahra: Daddy did that one time.

The second home movie begins playing, and I ask what year it was made in:

Ayesha: This was 2006. Sarah was about a year old.

Me: Oh okay, and you were home at this time?

Ayesha: Yeah. I stayed home with them for about one year ... then I worked at night when Hassan came home, and that's when I would go to work ... I would go to work three nights a week. I would come home at twelve [in the morning] and start at six [in the evening].

We laugh often, especially at the home movie of Zahra and Sarah opening Eid gifts with their parents, baby sister Zainab, maternal aunts, uncles, and grandparents:

[Zahra rubs baby Zainab's head in the home movie, and everyone laughs.]

Me: You're rubbing her head like a good luck charm [laughing].

Zahra: [laughing] I still do that sometimes.

Me: It looks like the gift wrapping are in Christmas colours. Was this in the winter?

Ayesha: Yes. It was during Christmas time. At that time, Eid was around Christmas, and Zahra would always say "magical Christmas."

Zahra: I wanted shiny wrappers that sparkle. I thought that was magical, so that's what they gave us.

[Hassan says "Eid" in a drawn-out way in the home movie, and everyone laughs.]

Ayesha: Eiiiddd!! [laughing].

Me: He sure knows how to set the mood! [laughing].

Ayesha: Yes. Zahra was talking about Christmas so much, and so her dad wanted to say Eid is good too [laughing].

Before I leave, our conversation turns to talking about school starting soon. I tell them that Noor has decided to continue attending the same school for grade seven because she wants to stay with her close friends, even though she is annoyed that she will be expected to wear a uniform:

Zahra: Ugh. I feel so bad for her.

Me: So Noor is already saying she doesn't feel like she's moving to junior high because they're also not sure about getting lockers this year.

Zahra: Oh! That's the one thing that makes it junior high. I feel so bad for her right now.

As I prepare to leave, we agree to try to meet again after school starts in September. I am smiling on my drive home, our earlier laughter echoing in my ears.

Retellings
"It's hard to go back to the way we used to be" (Ayesha, Fall 2016)

Listening to the recording, and reading the transcript, of our summer 2016 conversation, I realize how difficult it must have been for Ayesha to share not only previously untold stories of conflict and displacement, but also stories of familial experiences. Over the almost two years that we have lived and inquired alongside one another, Ayesha has repeatedly talked about how her familial relationships changed over time, as refugees in Pakistan after leaving Afghanistan and later as newcomers to Canada. In the fall of 2016, as we enjoyed breakfast in my home, Ayesha reflected on her relationship(s) with her family and said that she had been thinking a lot about "how our experiences growing up still affect us." Ayesha has expressed this thought in different ways throughout our conversations. During a dinner conversation in the winter of 2015, Ayesha discussed her family's experiences with making a life in Pakistan after fleeing violence in Afghanistan and then later making a life in Canada after Zahra was born. Thinking back to her family's transition to living in Pakistan, Ayesha spoke of her shifts in perspective over time: "I wasn't really paying attention to the challenges my parents were going through at that time."

Ayesha described her father's belief that Pakistan "could not be the final destination" for them, as there were limited school and career options for Afghan refugees in Pakistan. Ayesha remembers her father seeking opportunities to move to another place where they could be free to pursue a better life, even deciding to hire an English language tutor for them all to learn a language that might help them to leave Pakistan: "My father wanted to get us out from there in any way and was like, 'Take the TOEFL [Test of English as a Foreign Language] and maybe we can leave' ... I remember just struggling like that."

Earlier in our conversations, Ayesha discussed the many ways that her family had changed over the years. Although Ayesha said that arriving in Canada with her whole family was "like a dream come true," composing a life in the weeks, months, and years following their arrival was challenging. While Ayesha's comment that Hassan "wanted to say Eid is good too" in response to Zahra's childhood love of "magical Christmas" gives a sense of the challenges of adapting to a society and calendar centred around different beliefs and values, Ayesha said that living with Hassan and Zahra in the three-bedroom apartment they shared with her parents and five siblings was what made their early experiences in Canada "so hard." She recalled everyone feeling the pressure to contribute financially but finding it difficult to find jobs at first. Eventually, after securing employment, Ayesha, Hassan, and Zahra could move out and live on their own. However, even then, "We were constantly fighting, [and] I don't even remember about what." Ayesha reflected, "I've learned the hard way that it's hard to go back to the way we used to be."

A few months later, as we enjoyed dinner together, I was surprised when Ayesha shared that Hassan and her family had become estranged in recent years. Ayesha discussed some of the events that led to their estrangement and how difficult it had been for her to negotiate her relationships with her loved ones as a result. She shared her pain and anger as a result of this continued conflict: "I feel betrayed. My situation is that my family thinks I'm not of them and my husband thinks I'm not of him." Although she continued to visit with her parents and siblings alongside her children, she said they do not talk about her husband or the past. It is a deliberate, studied silence.

However, Ayesha said that Hassan sometimes brings the past up:

> I told Hassan to just leave it because he brings it back every once in a while. It's always there; it's never going to go away. I told him, "Don't bring this up anymore. It's not going to get solved. I'm not talking about this anymore." So hopefully, we'll see how it goes, but Alhamdulillah, we are still so blessed, and there's always going to be problems. I just think that it's not fair that you hold onto the past.

Reminding me of when she said "It's hard to go back to the way we used to be," she continues, "We just need to move away from it, or to move away from each other. Our religion says that, that if you forgive somebody, don't bring it up again; it's not fair ... and if you don't want to forgive, then you just need to leave ... Nobody can do anything about the past anymore. We need to keep going."

Taking a deep breath, as though she were drawing on her faith for sustenance, Ayesha said, "But Alhamdulillah, whatever Allah has planned, it's good."

"My parents signed The Parent Contract" (Zahra, Fall 2016)

I smile as I think about how Zahra explained why she refuses to make home movies anymore: "It's embarrassing ... you guys [her parents] post it on Facebook!" I am reminded of the many times Zahra laughed and covered her face in bemused embarrassment as we watched their home videos. I am also reminded of what she shared during our breakfast date in the winter of 2016: "I feel like before I was born my parents signed The Parent Contract, like, 'You embarrass your child. You wait five years before you get them a phone, and you make sure they go through a lot of trouble to get what they want.'"

Before jokingly sharing this thought, Zahra spoke about her parents' reluctance to allow her to buy a cell phone:

> Zahra: My dad, before he makes a decision, thinks about it for a long time and is like, "But you're so little!" And I'm like, "Daddy, I'm twelve." And he says, "Yeah, but you're still my baby."

Me: I still see Noor as my baby to be honest.

Zahra: My mom, she always says that, and I'm like "Mom, I'm twelve years old!" And, oh my God my mom, she'll be like, "I remember when you used to do this," and I'll be like, "Shhh, we're in public!" [laughing].

As I thought about how often Noor says I embarrass her in public, Zahra later talked about how Ayesha discussed menstruation with her for the first time during a mall trip: "It was the beginning of grade five, and I was like, 'Mom, I think you should tell me,' and she's like, 'You're so young!' But she ended up telling me, and we were in the mall, and she was like, 'And then [yelling],' and I was like, 'Oh my God Mom, shhhh!' ... and she was like "sorry!'" [exaggerated yelling voice]. Both of us laughed, and I ruefully responded, "I think I've signed The Parent Contract too!"

Growing Trust Alongside Zahra—Fall 2016

I excitedly knock on Zahra and Ayesha's door and appreciate the relatively mild November weather as I wait outside. Ayesha opens the door in her pajamas, greets me with a hug, and says that Zahra is ready and excited to go with me. As if on cue, Zahra approaches the door with her jacket on and sneakers in hand. We exchange hugs and Salams and are soon out the door, with Ayesha calling out to us to have fun.

Ayesha, Zahra, and I (alongside Sarah, Zainab, Noor, Yehia, and Hannah) have met several times over the last few months, enjoying breakfasts and brunches at each other's homes and a movie date. After I asked her what she would like to do for our next research conversation, Zahra said she would like for just the two of us to go somewhere. This will be the first research conversation we engage in alone. Directing me to a nearby coffee shop, Zahra is smiling as we talk about the movie we watched last week with Noor, Sarah, and my niece Hannan. Zahra makes me laugh often with her quirky observations as we wait for our drinks.

Settling down in a quiet, sunlit corner of the shop with our drinks, Zahra tells me she misses her old neighbourhood but likes her new house. She then talks about school and how she loves playing volleyball. She later shares an experience she had in gym class:

Zahra: In gym class, we have wrestling, and I was like, "Okay, I don't want to ruin my hijab," and you're not allowed to have straight pins on anyways, so I just took it off. And everyone was like, "Oh my God, you look so nice like this; your hair is so nice!" And I was like, "Okay, it's not going to hurt me; it's not going hurt me." But then one of my friends said, "She looks so nice with it on or off." And I was like, "*Thank you!*"

Me: Because you do mash'Allah, you're beautiful with and without it.

Zahra: Thank you too [laughing].

Me: I know what you mean though, getting compliments that don't really feel like compliments. So was it difficult going to a new school as someone wearing hijab?

Zahra: A little. Most of my old friends who were with me [in elementary school] still wear it so nothing changed with them, but I made new friends and most of them don't wear it. And they're sometimes like, "Oh I like your hair," and it's like, okay, stop.

I ask Zahra when she started wearing hijab:

Zahra: Well, it was kind of on and off, and then in grade six, it was like kind of at the beginning, I had to wear it ....

Me: So when you say you "had" to wear it, that was when you hit puberty?

Zahra: Yeah.

Me: Okay, so was that something that you felt strongly that you should do at that point?

Zahra: Well, sometimes I don't want to, but then I think, "I'm going to wear it eventually someday, so it's best to do it now."

I share my experience with donning and removing my hijab multiple times in upper elementary and junior high school: "It was a journey I had to go through ... actually it's an ongoing journey for me."

Backtracking a little, I ask Zahra what she meant when she said her "new friends" do not wear hijabs? She replied, "My old friends were not the best ... they say, 'It's your fault, you made new friends,' and I was like, 'The reason I made new friends is because you guys didn't treat me like a friend' ... I guess when I made new friends they kind of thought that I didn't need them anymore, so when I tried to show them that I did, then it kind of got better."

I ask Zahra if she turned to anyone for support during this challenging time: "Sometimes I talk to my mom, sometimes Sarah ... but sometimes I don't say anything." I ask Zahra why she sometimes chooses not to share:

> Zahra: Because my mom will sometimes get worried and start to say, "You need to do this or that," and I'm like, "Mom, I just want to tell you how I feel right now."

> Me: That sounds so familiar. I do that to Noor all the time.

> Zahra: I do it to Sarah too because there's a girl in her class who is so rude to her, and I'm like, "Sarah, why don't you do this?" and then I'm like, "Oh my God, I'm doing it!"

I share that I sometimes tell Noor it would be helpful if she tells me what kind of response she needs from me sometimes: "Does she need me to just listen or offer advice, you know?" Zahra replies, "I did, but my mom sometimes forgets, and I can't blame her anyways because she would never talk like that with her mom, well at least not openly, because it was different for them." I tell her that my relationship with my mom has been one of learning to be more open with each other over time. Zahra shares that her "mom is going through a hard time, like she has a new job and she's trying to adjust ... she doesn't have as much time to just sit down with us and she feels guilty. I feel bad for her, and I try not to give her too much trouble."

Later, our conversation turns to talking about the nightmares Zahra has been having after a group of attackers killed 130 people and injured hundreds in coordinated attacks in Paris, France on 13 November 2015:

> Zahra: I want to be a forensic scientist because it's cool. I love watching movies where there's like thrillers, and I always wanted

to be a spy and all that stuff. But my dad's like, "No, you'll have nightmares," and I was like, "I already have nightmares!"

Me: Aw, you've been having nightmares?

Zahra: Yeah. I recently had one that was really bad ... and it was because my dad told me about ISIS after what happened in Paris, and so my dream was that they came to our house, and they almost killed me and my sisters. Oh my God, it was so scary.

Me: That sounds terrifying. Have you ever discussed terrorism in school?

Zahra: My teacher, in social class, she talks about stereotyping, and how it affects us.... What happened in Paris made me so upset and so scared, and it didn't really affect anybody that much, like everyone was like, "Pray for Paris" and then left it, but I still think about it ... I'm so traumatized by it.

Zahra then connects the terror attacks to the recent rhetoric about accepting refugees from Syria by sharing how her social studies teacher talked about welcoming Syrian refugees: "Our teacher was like, 'Why are people doing this to Muslims? Like there's the KKK, and nobody blames all Christians.' She was saying, 'It's wrong,' and she asked, 'What do you think about Syrian refugees coming? What would you say?' and I was like, 'Come, let's be friends.' That's what I would do."

Our conversation later turns to Zahra reminiscing about hearing her mom's stories of growing up in Afghanistan and Pakistan in our first conversation:

Zahra: You and my mom are very alike, like the way you talk and can spill your guts, like I was surprised how my mom just met you and spilled everything.... She never told me half that, and I was like, "Wow."

Me: I was so worried about you because you were hearing so much for the first time.

Zahra: I was like, "Oh my God," but I could imagine it. I could imagine myself with her.... I love her so much. I always tell her, "Mom, I'm so happy you're my mom."

Zahra and I suddenly realize that our supposed hour-long conversation has run for over two hours, and we hastily collect our things. Dropping Zahra back off at home, I hug her and thank her for a wonderful time. She says, "No, thank you for the hot chocolate and for listening!"

Retellings
"My friends are different now" (Zahra, Winter 2016)

My attention turns to when Zahra said, "The reason I made new friends is because you guys didn't treat me like a friend." Zahra has shared many stories of experiences with friends she says have taught her about trust. As Zahra enjoyed hot chocolate and I had coffee, Zahra discussed how she negotiated a recent learning experience about a friend she grew up with who had been talking about her to other friends. She said that she had not been aware that the friend was upset with her, and she described how she negotiated the unexpected conflict. Giving a sense of her belief in talking openly and honestly, Zahra explained, "I went to her and said, 'If I did something wrong, just tell me to my face ... and I'll do the same for you.'" Zahra said that after trying multiple times to talk openly with her long-time friends, she learned to avoid the back and forth gossip that might arise: "Other girls come and tell me things and I'm like, 'It's okay girls, just leave it' because then they're going to go behind my back and tell her. They've done it before, so I don't say anything."

Several months later, as we enjoyed breakfast at one of our favourite restaurants in the winter of 2016, Zahra said that her long-time friends "are different now": "Before, they were nice and actual friends ... I was like, 'Oh, they're my best friends,' and we were always together. And it's like now they sometimes don't even want to hang out with me. I was really upset at first.... in the beginning of the year, I was so sad.... Girls are so mean to each other nowadays.... And it's not visible; it's with the things they say or the way they look at you." Zahra said she negotiated the pain of feeling rejected by becoming closer to "friends who I can trust" and sharing these experiences with Ayesha: "I would always tell her and feel better about it after."

"I could imagine myself with her" (Zahra, Fall 2015)

Over the last two years, I have witnessed and experienced how for Zahra, love and care for others are rooted in her appreciation for the complexity of their experiences and perspectives and in her ability and willingness to travel to their worlds (Lugones). Thinking back to when Zahra said, "My mom is going through a hard time" and "I could imagine myself with her," I am once again awed by her ability to travel to her mother's worlds.

As Ayesha and I enjoyed lunch in the spring of 2016, we discussed Zahra's ability to travel to her mom's worlds with loving perception:

> Me: Zahra told me something that I just had to share. She said that she loves when you go to lectures because it makes you happy, and when you're happy, that makes her happy.

> Ayesha: Yeah. She told me that too, and I was so happy when she said that ... sometimes she just [tilts head] and looks at me, and I ask, "Why are you looking at me?" and she says, "I just like looking at you" and it just makes me laugh and laugh [laughing].

> Me: She said you like attending things where you'll learn and grow.

> Ayesha: And she always asks me when we leave those kinds of places, "Are you happy? Did you like it?" And I just feel sometimes for her age to be like this is just amazing.

Rooting (Hard) Stories Alongside Ayesha—Winter 2015

Glancing at the digital clock on my car's dashboard, I resist the urge to speed up. I am running ten minutes late for my dinner date with Ayesha. She sent me an unexpected WhatsApp message a few hours ago asking me if I had plans tonight, and I answered, "Nope, what do you have in mind my friend?" After Ayesha and I agreed to meet at one of my favourite restaurants for a late supper, I hurriedly finished making dinner and waited for Wissam to come home from work so that I could head out. He, of course, could not leave work on time, so I sent Ayesha a message to let her know I might be ten to fifteen minutes late. She replied, "That's okay luv, take your time. I will get us a table."

Making duaa as I walk into the restaurant, I spot Ayesha seated at a booth close to the entrance. We hug as I laughingly thank her for getting me out of the house. She laughs and thanks me for meeting her on short notice. She explains that she has been preparing all week for a large dinner party with family friends tomorrow and needed to get out of the house, too. We excitedly look over the menu as we wait to order. After we order way too much food ("We can take our leftovers for lunch!" I reason as Ayesha laughs), Ayesha tells me more about the new job she started about three months ago. Ayesha explains that especially in comparison to her old job where she "never felt appreciated," she loves working at this new position: "I am enjoying it and the people are amazing … I've never worked with people like this; they are so nice."

Ayesha says that she is feeling more confident as a result of feeling respected and appreciated at work. She shares how after a recent argument with someone she loves, she reacted in an uncharacteristic way:

> Ayesha: And the funny thing is that instead of having a panic attack like I usually do, I was like, "Go ahead. I don't care" [in relation to an ultimatum that was given to her]. I don't know if it was my job, getting so much respect and attention…. I mean, it was surreal to me to have the kind of treatment that they gave me. I don't know why they treated me like I am a very high person, just so good, I was never treated like that.

> Me: You deserve to be treated like that.

> Ayesha: I don't know. I just felt like … not arrogant, but like I'm worth it.

After comforting one another as we share stories of familial conflict, our conversation turns to the recent terror attacks in Paris. Ayesha says that she has not felt a shift in attitudes or perceptions at work after the tragedy: "Nobody talked to me about it … but whoever I'm talking to, I talk mostly about my private life a lot—what I'm doing with my daughters and things like that—so they know that this is a person like me, and they have a family like I do."

She laughingly continues, "And those people in reception, they are the key people. They have been there a long time, and if they know you, then everybody will know you." I laugh and say, "That's like administrative assistants in schools." And Ayesha responds:

> Yeah, and I can't defend any of those things. It's not my responsibility to defend it ... and I can't. I just don't understand why people do such bad things. But we can't live in fear; we need to try to be positive. Fear feeds on fear, so it just builds paranoia. One of my friends, she's so sweet, but she gets so anxious ... and I told her that we have to make sure these things don't disrupt our inner peace.

Over dessert, our conversation shifts to Ayesha worrying that Zahra is experiencing pain because of her friends. However, she says that she knows that Zahra will be okay because "she's so mature for her age. Subhan Allah, I told her that I couldn't have come up with this duaa for myself that Allah gave you to me in this form. And she was like [sweetly], 'Oh Mom.'" Ayesha says that she shared with Zahra her own experiences with feeling left out:

> Ayesha: I told her I grew up being so unpopular all the time.
>
> Me: You? I'm shocked.
>
> Ayesha: Yeah, no, I was so passive ... I don't want my children to be like that but Alhamdulillah they're not. So I tell Zahra all the time, "When I was your age, I would *love* to be friends with you. I was never like you!" And she's like, "Oh Mom. I feel bad for you!" [laughs] ... Alhamdulillah.

I express how I am really beginning to appreciate the many ways that Zahra can show love and care for Ayesha and her sisters. Ayesha says the following:

> Yeah, when she feels I am upset, Zahra will tell her sisters, "Just let Mom be relaxed for a while." She does that all the time and sometimes I get mad at her like, "Zahra, I can take care of it!" But she says, "Mom, I just want to help," and I feel so bad. I don't want her to feel the responsibility to keep the house going, you know? She's not responsible for that. I don't want her to feel responsible; otherwise, she will be abused.

I wonder yet again at Zahra's ability to travel to her mom's worlds as Ayesha speaks further:

> Like even this week, I was so stressed out ... sometimes when their rooms are messy, it doesn't bother me, but sometimes I go into their rooms, and it's messy and I get mad. We get mad at our children, and it has nothing to do with them ... like you'll come home and the shoes will be all over the place and you'll say [in a singing voice], "Oh they're home!" but another day you'll see the shoes and you'll say [in an angry voice] "Put your shoes away!" It's *us*, and I hate that. What happens to us?

Feeling a heady sense of resonance with her words, I stammer, "Subhan Allah ... I do that all the time." Ayesha sighs and says, "Subhan Allah."

Almost three hours after our conversation begins, we reluctantly get up and prepare to leave. Outside, I hug Ayesha tightly, and we agree to meet with our children during the winter break in a few weeks. Her vulnerability and her words live in me as I drive home, and I make duaa that Allah (SWT) showers us, our families, and loved ones with countless blessings as we grow into the New Year.

Retellings
"I sometimes don't know how to help her"
(Ayesha, Fall 2015)

Ayesha's question—"What happens to us?"—still lives in me as I write this, over a year after she posed it. Ayesha has questioned, or expressed uncertainty about, her parenting practices many times during the course of our inquiry. I am drawn to a conversation we had in the fall of 2015. Ayesha sent me a WhatsApp message that Zahra was "thinking of taking her hijab off" because "her new friends don't wear hijab and she says she fears being left out by them too." I replied, "I'm so surprised and sorry that Zahra has been feeling left out." Ayesha's next message left me tearing up: "I sometimes don't know how to help her when she feels so empty." Reflecting upon Ayesha saying "I don't want her to feel the responsibility to keep the house going," I was awakened to the realization that Ayesha is repeatedly travelling to Zahra's worlds, even as Zahra travels to hers. After several minutes of struggling to form a response, I typed the following: "I'm so sorry. Can we talk in person or over the phone soon? I wanted to share a story that this reminds me of, but it will be hard to text it." Over the phone, we talked about how hard it can be to make and/or maintain friendships, and I share some of my experiences with feeling excluded in junior high school. I said that I do not have answers for what they are experiencing, but that it always helped me to know that I had a loving family supporting me. And I asserted, "I know that Zahra has that too."

"We can't live in fear" (Ayesha, Winter 2015)

As Zahra, Ayesha, and I composed our inquiry, we talked about terrorism and politics during times of disturbing rhetoric and/or terror attacks. Our discussions make me think about how terror attacks, and the narratives that stem from them, can reverberate across the globe and how they can shape our lives and the ways we story ourselves and others. In the summer of 2015, as we were fasting during the month of Ramadan, Ayesha mentioned the upcoming Federal elections and we discussed some of the troubling things that were being said and done by the former Conservative government, including the passing of Bill C-51[23] and C-24.[24]. Surprising me with her words, Zahra said, "We can't be afraid. We need to be honest and keep speaking up."

Later, as we engaged in a breakfast conversation in Zahra and Ayesha's home in the fall of 2015, Ayesha and I were talking about voting in the next day's Federal elections, and Zahra shared a story of being made to feel uncomfortable in her grade seven social studies class. She said that candidates from numerous political parties in her school riding had visited her class to introduce themselves and their platforms. She talked about how the Progressive Conservative Party candidate said, "I don't support the wearing of the niqab during

23 Bill C-51, the "anti-terrorism" legislation championed by the former Conservative government, has been criticized for being too vague and lacking in adequate oversight (Watters).

24 Bill C-24, also known as the Citizenship Act, was controversial because it allowed dual citizens convicted of terrorism to have their Canadian citizenship revoked. This was regarded by many as creating two-tiered citizenship (Globe and Mail, "Globe").

citizenship ceremonies." Zahra, who believes in the need to be "honest and keep speaking up," said that she felt upset and was just about to challenge his words when the Green Party candidate's response helped put her at ease: "He said, 'We don't ask you to take your turban off. Shame on you!'"

Months later, a few days after a terror attack in which a Muslim American man and his wife killed fourteen people and injured twenty-two others at an office party in San Bernardino, California, on 2 December 2015, Ayesha sent me a YouTube video about the need to remember ourselves and our faith as attackers hijack our religion to sow fear and division. On WhatsApp, Ayesha wrote, "I am so tired of this. With Paris and now this, it is too much!" She continued, "I try not to think about it, but it is hard." Her words reminded me of how during a breakfast conversation a few weeks before Ayesha sent me the video, Zahra said, "What happened in Paris made me so upset and scared. I still think about it ... I'm traumatized by it." The pain Zahra and Ayesha expressed pulled at the deeply rooted sorrow I have felt mourning innocent lives in incomprehensible terror attacks alongside the sharp pain of feeling shamed and blamed by those who commit horrific acts in the name of my faith and those who generalize these horrific acts to Islam and all Muslims.

Several months later, in the spring of 2016, Ayesha sent me a few WhatsApp messages of her worries after a Muslim man killed fifty people and injured fifty-three others in a gay nightclub in Orlando, Florida. She wrote that "Orlando is being used by Donald Trump so badly against Islam" and that "The crime has really affected Zahra." During a conversation I had with Zahra in the summer of 2016, she shared a class discussion her teacher had initiated the day after the shootings:

> She was like, "Okay, so there's something we need to discuss as a class, have you guys heard about the Orlando shootings?" and some people didn't know about it, and she explained it to them. And then she was like, "So what do you guys think?" and everyone was saying that just because you don't agree with people about something doesn't mean you need to ruin everything ... you have *no* right to tell people what to do.

Ayesha had earlier, in the winter of 2015, expressed appreciation for the way Zahra's teacher encourages these types of class discussions: "Her teacher makes people aware about the things that happen and talks about how we should react, which is so good, right?"

In the late fall of 2015, Zahra discussed her pain and confusion following several terror attacks. As a Muslim woman who deeply believes in the interconnectedness of peace and justice, her words strummed resonant chords within me. Zahra, who has talked about experiencing nightmares and feeling "traumatized" as a result of terror attacks, felt outrage, confusion, and pain at the attackers' unfeeling brutality: "When I think about it, I get so sad. And I wonder about them [attackers], like, 'Do you not feel bad about doing that? Do you not feel *anything*?' I could never ever hold that much guilt. I promised myself since I was a kid that I would never hurt or wound anybody because if I were to have that much guilt in my heart it would just kill me."

Deepening Our Inquiry—Winter 2015

I am in the kitchen getting ready for Ayesha and Zahra's visit, and I hear a soft knock at my door. I open it and invite Zahra and Ayesha in. They both look so lovely in their elegantly draped hijabs and outfits. It is close to noon as Zahra, Ayesha, Noor, Yehia, Hannah, and I enjoy pancakes and traditional breakfast food, and we talk about how nice winter break has been, especially being able to sleep in.

Our conversation turns to Noor recently purchasing a cell phone. Zahra has had a cell phone for a few months already, and she and Noor have a good time making fun of familial cell phone rules: "No phones at the table." "No phones before bed." "No phones if you don't do your chores." "No phones when ..." They laugh openly, and Ayesha and I (unsuccessfully) try not to smile as we look at each other. I say, "Hmm ... no phones in general might be a good idea," and Noor groans, "Mommm." I think of The Parent Contract as Zahra and Noor look at each other knowingly. After everyone helps to clear and wipe the table, I ask Noor and Yehia if they can look after Hannah in the next room while Zahra, Ayesha, and I talk.

Zahra begins by telling me she brought some of their favourite photographs to show me. I had asked Ayesha and Zahra to bring familial artifacts and was excited to see what they wanted to share. Zahra passes me the first photograph, and I see two young girls about four or five years old grinning at the camera. One of the girls was dangling from a couch with the other behind her:

> Zahra: I was four or five, and my mom was taking a picture of me and Sarah, and she's like, "Cheese!" and I'm like, "Wait let me hang off of this first" [laughing].

> Ayesha: Making a duck face [laughing].

> Me: And you're wearing a bracelet too. You *still* look fashionable! [laughing].

> Ayesha: She was always wearing accessories, ever since that time she is like that.

The photograph prompts Ayesha and Zahra to reminisce about the townhouse that it was taken in. Zahra recalls loving the house because it had a basement that she and Sarah thought of as their very own playground. We talk about Ayesha and Zahra's many moves over the years (seven times in total) as well as the homes they lived in before they moved into the one I originally visited them in. They lived in the home from the photograph for the longest stretch of time, six years, before moving into their current home.

We discuss which home was closest to Zahra's former elementary school. Ayesha says that some of their homes were farther away from the school than she would have liked to drive but that she loved that the school offered Arabic and Islamic classes alongside the Alberta Program of Studies. She also loved the familial atmosphere of the school: "I was so involved and volunteered all the time. It was so nice; it felt like a family there." I ask Zahra if she felt this way about her former school, and she says, "Yeah, I guess." I ask her if she feels as comfortable in her current school:

> Zahra: Well, at first, it took me a while to understand because I missed the orientation where they show you where your locker is, where classes are, and everything because I was in B.C. with

my mom. So I was looking for my homeroom, and I couldn't find it, and then the bell rang, and I still couldn't find the class. So they looked in the office to get my timetable, and then I went to my class.

Me: And this was the first day of school?

Zahra: Yeah, and I wasn't sure what to do with my school supplies, and then my homeroom teacher said, "When they call for the lost children, just go with them," and I was like, "Okay" [laughing]. She's a funny teacher.

Me: Okay, so it was a joke.

Zahra: Yeah it was a joke ... and then some school people came and asked, "Who doesn't have a locker?" and me and my friend went with them, and then they showed us where our lockers were. I shoved everything into my locker and just grabbed a pencil and went to my classes. I lost my timetable again the next day and found it a week later [laughing].

Me: It sounds like it was a confusing first week.

Zahra: Yeah, it took me about a week to be fully adjusted.

Zahra then shares a story about almost getting in trouble in class:

Zahra: One time, I was on my phone in class, and the teacher was like, "Why are you on your calculator?" and I was like, "*Oh,* you're right, my bad." And she was like, "You're smarter than that" ... and I was like, "Thank God I didn't get in trouble for that!"

Me: That's interesting because you once said that your friend is the one who gets in trouble for talking even if it's you.

Ayesha: [Laughing] I taught her how to win their trust at first. Tell Muna about that.

Zahra: She was like, "You have to be really good at the beginning. Do everything they want, be quiet, study, get your homework done, and all that." So I did all that and then they never had any problems with me.

Ayesha: I said just do that, and then all year long, you won't have problems; they will just love you [laughing].

Zahra: Yeah, I owe it all to my mom [laughing].

The next photograph Zahra hands me features Ayesha behind a stroller with a rosy-cheeked baby inside. There is snow all around, and both are bundled up from the weather. Zahra explains that "I was thinking about one with both of us, and I remembered my mom and me and the snow and this snowsuit and I was like, 'Oh yeah, we have to show Muna this one.'" Reminiscing about when Zahra was a baby, Ayesha shares, "She was such a playful baby, always happy, always talking. I mean she would just always play and talk with anybody." We laugh as I say, "I feel like you're still like that Zahra!" Ayesha laughingly responds, "Yeah ... if she saw someone, she would just say, 'Hi! Hi! Hi!' She pretended, 'Oh I'm speaking English,' and she would just say something ... but she only spoke Farsi with us at home."

The third photograph Zahra shows me is of Zainab being potty-trained by Sarah, and she talks about her relationship with her sisters. Our conversation then shifts to Zahra talking about feeling excluded by her friends. She says, "I'm not surprised, though. I knew that would happen." I ask, "That they would change?" She answers, "Yeah. And they did." I am confused at first, but then Zahra explains some of the history of their relationship:

Zahra: Well, I was a bit of a bully when I was younger. I was so bossy, and then, in grade four, my entire class just got so fed up that they didn't want to play with me. I was so upset, but then the teacher had a class meeting, and they were all like, "You're so bossy!" And I said I'm sorry and then I tried not to be bossy and to be nicer, but they didn't want to be nice back, and I found out it was all because of one girl. She ruined my life.

Me: How?

Zahra: Because she told everyone so many bad things about me and told the teachers so many lies that I even had to go to the principal's office because of her.

Me: Oh wow.

Zahra: And I hated myself for the longest time because I thought it was my fault, that I did it, but I didn't, and I don't know why I believed that for the longest time.

Me: You thought that you deserved it.

Zahra: Yeah, and everyone hated me, and then she left, and it got so much better. My friends told me the stuff she would say and that they didn't really like her or believe her.

Ayesha: And they never said anything until she left. They were so afraid.

Zahra: But I didn't have any friends for the longest time, and now they're back to that.

I express my sadness that Zahra is feeling excluded by the same group of girls who had mistreated her in elementary school. Ayesha says, "I think we sometimes take it for granted that the people closest to us will be the ones who can be the most hurt from us." Zahra looks at her mom and says, "But you guys were there for me. You've always been there."

Retellings
"I wouldn't do it again, I'll tell you that" (Zahra, Summer 2016)

Zahra shared many stories of her grade seven experiences over time. In the winter of 2015, she talked about being surprised by some of her experiences in the first few months of junior high:

Zahra: In grade six, we were all excited because it will be different, but then after a few days, life carries on. I had an idea, based on a few books I've read, of what junior high would be like, but it's totally different.

Me: Really?

Zahra: Yeah. I thought that there would be this really popular mean girl and stuff like that but there's no such thing.

Me: Well that's good [laughing]. So what else surprised you?

Zahra: Well, we aren't allowed to go to our lockers between classes and stuff like that, but I guess I adjusted-ish.

Although she shared many painful stories of feeling excluded by her friends as they transitioned from elementary to junior high school, Zahra talked about feeling supported in different ways in her transition from a faith-based elementary school program to a public junior high school. She said that "there are lots of Muslim kids in [her] school" and that she was happy that there was a designated space for prayers at lunchtime: "Even the students who aren't Muslim know a lot about Islam, like they'll ask, 'Do you go to the mosque? Oh, that's cool' and stuff like that." She also talked about enjoying school because of a few teachers she likes: "My L.A. [Language Arts] and Social teacher, she's easy to talk to and is really nice; she is not the type to just talk about school, like she'll turn talking about a book into something personal somehow. And my gym teacher is also my homeroom teacher, and she's really nice, like our entire school loves her. She's that type of teacher who makes everything fun."

In the summer of 2016, as Zahra and I talked at our favourite breakfast restaurant, I asked Zahra how she experienced the last few months of her grade seven year. She responded, "It was stressful." After I asked why it was stressful, Zahra said, "Finals. Studying and studying and paying attention in class. It was Ramadan, too, so I'd go home and sleep late and then I'd get up late and go to school late. I was so tired." However, Zahra said that being able to "leave [school] after exams" and "sleep lots after school" helped to lessen her fatigue.

Although both Ayesha and Zahra said things had gotten better for Zahra in the second half of grade seven, she told me the following in the summertime: "I hated this year; it just really sucked." She explained, "It was the first year, a lot of change, you know, people changed, and you change too ... it was hard and it was fun and it was bumpy." After Zahra paused, I responded, "So there were good moments, but ..." and Zahra completed my sentence by saying, "I wouldn't do it again, I'll tell you that."

"I learned that I have to stand up for myself" (Zahra, Fall 2016)

Our many conversations about bullying make me wonder about how these experiences, once planted, continue to live in us. Although Zahra said she knows the hurtful things said about her in elementary school are not true, she often described her younger self as a bully—a label Ayesha rejects. During a dinner conversation alongside Ayesha and Zahra in the fall of 2016, Zahra talked about learning from her experiences with friends: "If I'm nice to someone who's mean to me, it just gets worse. You have to show them, whoever it is, that it's not okay, and that worked for me. Because I used to try to be nice to some of the people who were mean to me, and it wasn't good, so now I can be mean right back. I learned that I have to stand up for myself." I asked Zahra when she started to realize that she needed to stand up for herself:

Zahra: After a really long time. Like, I had one friend who wasn't nice to me, and so I started saying, "No, I'm not doing this anymore."

Me: But I wonder if you're being *mean* when you do that. You're standing up for yourself, which is very different from being mean.

Zahra: Yeah, I guess, just showing that this is the kind of quality that I want in my friendships and if you give me less, then I don't want that friendship anymore.

Ayesha: But maybe you were like this even when you were younger?

Zahra: No.

Ayesha: But your friends used to say that you're bossy.

Zahra: Because I was bossy. I was so mean. I was really a bully at that age.

Ayesha: I don't think that you were.

Me: You sharing that story of learning to stand up for yourself, that's so important. Because even me sometimes, even though I know that it's not okay, too often we teach girls to just be nice, not stand up for their rights ... just don't make a big deal about stuff.

Ayesha: Yeah, and something we don't do as much in [is] teaching them to set boundaries. Especially as women, we just give and give and give, and I guess not really demand anything in return or just the minimum. That's how our value is sometimes forgotten.

Ayesha was trying to remind Zahra that her assertiveness in speaking up is likely what contributed to the perception that Zahra was bossy in elementary school. She was trying to remind Zahra that the stories others told about her in elementary school were not true. In questioning whether Zahra standing up for herself was being mean, I was also thinking that Zahra once shared the following: "I promised myself since I was a kid that I would never hurt or wound anybody because if I were to have that much guilt in my heart it would just kill me." Zahra's earlier experiences with being storied as a bully, however, continue to live in her. These stories are deeply rooted and continue to reverberate in the stories she composes alongside others. As will be revisited in future tellings and retellings, Zahra has learned that speaking up and sharing her opinions can sometimes be perceived by others in unintended ways.

Continuing to Grow Alongside Zahra—Winter 2016

Driving to our favourite breakfast restaurant, Zahra tells a story about the time her dad's car got stuck in the mud when they visited the Dinosaur Provincial Park a few years ago. We are still laughing as we are seated at a small table at the back of the restaurant. Ordering our usual— blueberry pancakes—Zahra surprises me by talking about the possibility of attending a different school for her grade eight year:

Zahra: My mom wants me to switch schools ... they [possible new school] have this program called pre-AP. They teach the way I'll really be able to learn. Instead of just doing paper and pencil stuff, they teach with projects. It's the same curriculum, but they teach you differently.

Me: Are you still thinking about moving schools or you've already decided to?

Zahra: I'm thinking about it, but my mom's already made up her mind I think.

Me: How did you hear about this school?

Zahra: My friend goes to that school, and she told me about this program and so then I told my mom about it. I kind of don't like my school but I do sometimes ... I'm confused [laughing]. So I told my mom, "Let's go check it out." But I told her that I'm scared that I'll be the new girl and not know anyone.

As we eat our pancakes, our conversation turns to Zahra talking about how her friends have changed this year, and I ask if she thinks she has changed too:

Maybe? I don't know ... I do feel like since all my friends aren't with me anymore I'm more confused. My self-esteem kind of dropped a little. I felt bad about myself and didn't want to go out as much anymore. I kept telling myself, "No, no, you should be proud of yourself and not feeling bad about who you are." So I started pulling myself up like, "You know what? You need to stop."

After we share stories about negotiating friendships, Zahra talks about how she really enjoys her social studies class this year. I ask her if she remembers a time when she did not enjoy a class for any reason:

Zahra: That's never happened in this school, but in elementary school, there was a teacher who if you spoke up, you were considered disrespectful because he was a Sheikh. Everyone respected him so much, it was insane. I mean, yes, he taught us Qu'ran, but he also said a lot of things that weren't fair, like he said, "Oh girls, you're not supposed to do this or that," and we'd be like, "Why?" He always said things I disagree with.

Me: And how would you feel when you heard "You shouldn't do this or that?"

Zahra: Annoyed. Don't tell me what to do or what not to wear.

We end our conversation earlier than usual because I promised Ayesha that I would drop Zahra off to their volunteer commitment at a Helping Hampers organization. On my drive home, I sit with Zahra's stories, and I make duaa that Allah [SWT] guides and protects her.

Retellings
"You're better than this" (Zahra, Winter 2016)

As we engaged in discussion that day, I gained a strong sense of Zahra's self-awareness. After she described telling herself, "No, no, you should be proud of yourself and not feeling bad about who you are," Zahra expressed disappointment in herself for behaving in uncharacteristic ways alongside friends: "Sometimes my friends say really inappropriate things, and I just laugh because I want to be their friend. Then I think about it and say, 'What is wrong with me?' and I really feel bad about it. I say, 'Why? Why are you doing this to yourself? You're better than this." In the summer of 2016, Zahra talked about reminding herself of who she is (and who she wants to be) when she realized that a girl who had once mocked her was her classmate: "When I saw her on the first day of school, I was like [to herself], 'Ew, go away,' and later on, I was feeling jealous of her because she had things I didn't have, so then I said to myself, 'Zahra, you're not that kind of person. Don't do that to yourself.' And the funny thing is that we are now close friends."

During our breakfast conversation in the winter of 2016, Zahra talked about imagining her experiences as a YouTube video and encouraging herself when she is feeling down:

> I just talk to myself like, "It's okay," you know? And in grades five and six, I used to watch a lot of "Draw My Life" videos, and when something big happens, I'm imagining how I could draw it out in a YouTube video. So in every video, it goes, "I went through this," about the hard times, and so I always think, "Well everyone goes through this. It's just a rough patch, it'll be over— just try not to make yourself feel bad."

"You shouldn't force someone to do something" (Zahra, Summer 2016)

Zahra has repeatedly expressed her belief that people should not be forced to behave or dress in certain ways. Like Ayesha, she believes in the profound right to choose. In the summer of 2016, Zahra shared a story about a recent experience that reminded me of how she spoke of her Qu'ran teacher telling girls how they should behave: "This older guy we know walks into the party, and he's kind of weird. I mean he stares at women, and it's creepy. And then he comes up to me and was like, 'Oh, you're not wearing your hijab?' and I was like, 'Who are you to ask me that?' A lot of people have so much respect for him but he doesn't deserve that respect." Later in our conversation, Zahra expressed indignation that a classmate "got dress-coded:"

> In my school, you can wear anything, but if your stomach shows or if you have tiny straps, they dress-code you. My friend got dress-coded once for wearing a short shirt, and you could kind of see her stomach. One of the teachers called her over and took her outside and talked to her. I was like, "How embarrassing!" I don't get it, out of school everyone can dress the way they want, but in school they can't? It doesn't make sense.... It's their decision, you shouldn't force someone to do something or wear something because they'll start to hate it.

Growing Stories to Mother By Alongside Ayesha— Spring 2016

I take a deep breath outside the restaurant doors. I am late for my lunch date with Ayesha because I was trying to make sure everything and everybody was settled at home before I left. It is spring break and the kids are home, but when Ayesha asked me if I wanted to have lunch a few hours ago, I replied "Yes!" almost immediately. A few days ago, she had shared, through a WhatsApp conversation, that her mom had a stroke last week and Ayesha has been spending all her free time by her side. Ayesha said she would be heading back to the hospital right after we have lunch. I pause to make duaa and try to feel a little more grounded as I walk into the restaurant.

I walk up to the front and tell the hostess that I am here to meet a friend who has already been seated. Without asking me for my friend's name, the hostess immediately leads me to Ayesha. Admittedly mischievous, I ask her, "How did you know she was the person I was looking for?" She shifts uncomfortably and I laughingly say, "I'm just kidding." Ayesha laughs heartedly as we hug. She looks beautiful, although I know she has not slept well in days. Before I can ask her the same question, Ayesha asks, "How are you doing?" with concern in her eyes and I try to fight back tears. Ayesha knows that the last few weeks have been very hard for me. Along with worrying about Hannah's upcoming appointment at the autism clinic, I have been grieving for an incredibly gifted, kind, brave, and loving friend, Dr. Julie Long (may she rest in peace). I have also been deeply worried about, and making duaa for, my cousin Billal (Allah yirhamu), who was recently diagnosed with a rare and aggressive form of cancer. I wipe my tears as I say, "I'm doing okay Alhamdulillah … I'm sorry, I don't mean to cry." Ayesha then makes me laugh:

Ayesha: No it's okay. Just let it go. You don't have to say sorry.

Me: I think it's the Canadian in me. I always feel like I have to say sorry [laughing].

Ayesha: [laughing] That reminds me of some comedy thing I watched … "No I'm sorry!" or even, "Oh, thank you and sorry for opening the door!" [laughing].

Wiping my tears as we laugh, I ask Ayesha how her mom is doing: "Alhamdullilah, she's a lot better. She's a person who really takes a lot of stress in. She always thinks about everyone and is always thinking about everything, and she worries so much. I told her, 'Mom, you need to forget about us and just live your life, maybe go to English classes or computer classes … keep your mind off your kids!'"

Later, as we enjoy our appetizers, Ayesha tells me about how Zahra recently asked her for permission to attend a school dance: "I said, 'A year ago, you wouldn't even think of this, and now you think it's okay. How much have you changed?' The next day, I texted Zahra. "Thank you so much for not going. I'm so proud of you." And she texted me back and said 'Mom, I'm so sorry. I was going to go but I just saw your message.'" Ayesha said that Zahra's friends had been pressuring her to go to the dance: "Her friends were telling her 'Why aren't you coming?' and I told her, 'You have to say, "Why are *you* going?"'" I say that I cannot imagine Zahra saying something like that to her friends, but Ayesha says, "She used to do it, but she stopped ... kids would call her grandma because she would be like, 'Oh, you have to put this away,' and then her friends called her bossy. I would explain, well this is probably happening because of this or that, and she would learn. Some people don't learn no matter what you say, but she learns."

I ask Ayesha how Zahra was feeling when she got home that day: "She was a little edgy and uncomfortable, but I didn't have time to spend with her. I wanted to take her for coffee or something, but that was the day I had to take my mom to the hospital." Ayesha says she is so proud of Zahra and how she is negotiating all the challenges she is facing: "I can understand how she must be feeling because at that age that's all you want, right? You don't see the bigger picture." She explains that she and Zahra talked about the school dance at length during one of their nightly bedtime conversations: "I try not to make her feel bad if she does or doesn't do something. We talk about it." I am amazed that Ayesha continues to have nightly bedtime conversations with each of her girls, but she says, "I'm not able to talk to them for as long because it's been so busy. But they like it so much; it's their special time."

As we eat, I ask Ayesha about the possibility of Zahra attending a new school: "We were thinking about it, but we will probably not move her; she's doing so well this year. Zahra's getting straight A's, and she's now established herself. I don't think her circle of friends is that good, but if she goes to a new school, maybe worse people will be there. Who knows? Changing schools doesn't solve the problem, right?" Ayesha says that Zahra seems to be doing better at school, so she is not as worried about her. I ask Ayesha how she has sustained herself during the challenges of the last year: "From different things ... I go to lectures or listen to them. I read, or watch videos ... if you only look at all the things that are wrong, you're stuck in one spot, and your heart is just so hard. I just try to distance myself from that. I don't need that in my life."

Retellings
"She has an old soul" (Ayesha, Fall 2015)

While talking about how classmates likened Zahra to a "grandma," I was reminded of Ayesha telling me in the fall of 2015 that she sometimes feels guilty for speaking so openly with Zahra about topics that might be too mature for her: "But she's so easy to talk to and really understands ... she has an old soul." Later, as we enjoyed dinner in the winter of 2015, Ayesha said, "She's so mature for her age. That's what her teacher told me too. She said that she's one of those students who actually thinks about what I [the teacher] say and then asks thoughtful questions."

However, after being storied as bossy and a bully, Ayesha said that Zahra learned not to share her thoughts or opinions with friends. I got a strong sense of Zahra's reluctance to express her opinions about others' choices when we had breakfast in the summer of 2016:

> I have this friend who I really like to talk to, and we laugh a lot, but when she's with our other friends, she's so different and will do and say things that are really inappropriate. And I won't say anything because I don't want to be the one who's acting like the mom. They told me they hate it, and I realize that it's true, I do act like that sometimes ... So when people do something I don't like or wouldn't do, I just sit there and laugh ... I can't tell them what I really think because they'll just get mad.

She said she has learned to share her thoughts only when asked: "If they ask me for advice, then I *would* talk about what I think with them."

"I understand why my mom doesn't think it's a good idea" (Zahra, Summer 2016)

During a breakfast together in the summer of 2016, Zahra shared her perspective about not going to the school dance: "I wanted to go with my friends and my mom was like, 'No, you're not allowed to go.' I was about to go anyways behind her back, and then she texted me, 'I'm so proud of you for not going.' And I was like, 'Oh great, why mom, why?' and so all my friends went, and I had to be like, 'I can't go.'" Zahra discussed the dance during a bedtime conversation with Ayesha, explaining that her mom reminded her that dancing in a mixed-gender setting is not advisable as a Muslim girl. Zahra continued, "I was mad at first, but I understand why my mom didn't think it was a good idea." In the fall of 2015, in relation to this familial bedtime routine, Zahra said: "Every night before bed, she comes in and says goodnight and talks with us in our rooms for a little while, each one of us. Sometimes I say, 'Mom, if you're tired, you don't have to,' and she's like, 'No, I love doing this with you guys,' so I don't tell her not to because she really likes it." Both Ayesha and Zahra spoke about how much the other person enjoys their bedtime conversations. From what I witnessed and heard alongside them, they are both right.

Growing Forward Alongside Zahra—Summer 2016

Zahra's letter to me (shared with her permission)

I hug Zahra tightly when she opens the door to her home. It has been a few months since I have seen her and I exclaim, "I miss you!" Zahra covers her mouth as she laughingly says she misses me too. Ayesha comes to the door, and we hug before Zahra and I head to my car. As we walk away, I ask Zahra, "How do you feel about your new braces?" and she says, "Ugh. I'm not used to them." During our drive, I notice that she often covers her mouth.

After we order pancakes, Zahra asks how my writing is going. We had met alongside Ayesha a few months ago to negotiate a chapter I was writing about coming alongside one another. At that time, Zahra surprised and honoured me with a letter she had written to me as part of a class assignment.

We talk about the research writing and reminisce about our relationship:

> Me: I'm finding it hard to write because when someone trusts you with their stories and experiences, how do you write about it faithfully?
>
> Zahra: It's so hard.
>
> Me: But even though we'll be ending our research conversations soon, we'll still be seeing each other lots, insha'Allah, because you guys are like family now.
>
> Zahra: Yeah, my mom always talks about you and says, "I'm so happy we know her," and I love meeting up with you.
>
> Me: Me too wallah.

Zahra then talks about how things have gotten better with her friends since we last talked, and she discusses how the end of the school year was stressful because she was writing finals during Ramadan. After Zahra talks about why she "hated this year," I ask her what advice she would give to others transitioning into grade seven:

> Zahra: Hmmm ... I'd tell them to learn how to open a combination lock.
>
> Me: That's so funny! Another participant said the same thing [laughing].

Zahra: When I first got there, I didn't know how to do it, but one of the teachers was like, "Let me show you how to do it" [laughing]. I'd also say, "Keep yourself organized." Organization is literally one of the biggest things because if your stuff isn't organized, be prepared for a year of getting yelled at. I swear, one kid who isn't organized, a teacher yelled at him every single day and I'm like, "Why don't you organize your stuff?" and he was like, "No" [laughing].

Zahra reminds me of Ayesha's advice about "how to win [teachers'] trust," when she says, "I would also tell them to be careful not to get in the teacher's face, especially in the beginning." She then shares the story of her friend getting dress-coded and says, "You shouldn't force someone to do something or wear something because they'll start to hate it … that's what my dad did with me. He forced me to wear the hijab, and now I hate it." Although I have sensed in the many seasons we spent alongside one another that Zahra felt pressured to don the veil, I have never heard her say it in such a clear and troubling way. I reach across the table to hold her hand and say, "I'm so sorry Zahra. It's not okay that you were made to feel like that."

After thanking me for my words and thinking quietly for a few moments, Zahra continues speaking:

Zahra: And I'd say to the girls, don't let boys be annoying and mean.

Me: How can they be annoying and mean?

Zahra: They weren't mean to me, but my friend got involved with a group of friends, and there were a bunch of guys there, and you know how guys can be. So I told her, "You need to back off; these guys are crazy." But she didn't, and then they started a rumour about her that went around the entire school. I felt so bad for her.

I express my sadness for what her friend experienced, and then I say, "It's interesting that you said, 'You know how guys can be.' That reminds me of our first conversation when you said, 'Boys will be boys' about the group of boys who used to bully you in grades one and two." Zahra says, "They were more teasing, rather than bullying. I was very dramatic." I say, "Subhan Allah, you used to consider it bullying last year and now think it was just teasing ... why do you think your perspective has changed?" Zahra responds, "I think when I got older, I realized how boys are." I ask, "I wonder though ... the expression, 'Boys will be boys,' do you remember when you first heard it?" Zahra says, "I don't know. It's funny, we say it, but don't think about what it even means," which reminds me of how Ayesha said Zahra has an "old soul.'"

As we enjoy our pancakes, Zahra talks about how people have changed over the year: "I can't really explain it, but it's like they're different. Like you know this person, but kind of don't know this person anymore.... Even me, I've probably changed in the way that I've thought of other people, and the way I thought about a lot of things." She explains how she has learned not to give advice unless she is asked because she does not want to "be acting like the mom." I ask her if she remembers giving someone advice recently

> This good friend asked me, "Zahra, do you think it's bad that I changed? Some people tell me I've changed, and I don't know if it's good or bad." Because she used to be really quiet and now she is way more outgoing. I was like, "It's not a bad thing that you've changed. It's normal, and it's okay. And it's good that you are more open." I said, "You should do what makes you happy."

Pausing for a few moments, Zahra continues, "So another thing, when you were asking what advice I would give, is that you need to find a good friend who you can talk to ... a lot of things are going to change. The way you think will change, the way you see yourself will change. You're going to have other friends, but you need at least one good friend who you can *really* talk to."

As we prepare to leave the restaurant, Zahra says she looks forward to being taught by her favourite teacher next year: "She was about to leave the school, and we were all so sad, but then she told us she was staying and that she will teach us in grade eight.... We were all so happy; the whole room was like, 'Yeah!' because she is one of the teachers who you can never forget ... she's amazing."

Retellings
"You're a woman now. You have to do this and that"
(Zahra, Fall 2015)

Zahra has expressed her tensions with her hijab several times during our inquiry. Her relationship with her hijab reminded me of my own journey with donning the hijab and taking it off multiple times as a child and youth. However, my decision to don or remove my hijab has always been my decision. I began to get a strong sense that Zahra felt pressured to wear the hijab during my many conversations alongside Zahra and Ayesha. In the fall of 2015, Zahra shared that she felt that she had to wear it after she reached puberty and also talked about feeling increased expectations alongside this milestone: "My dad's always like, 'You're a woman now. You have to do this and that,' and I'm like 'Don't remind me ... please.'" Ayesha had earlier told me in the fall of 2015 that her husband viewed hijab as obligatory when a girl reaches puberty. She said she worried about Zahra and how Hassan would react if Zahra ever decided to remove it. Ayesha repeatedly emphasized the importance of choice during this discussion. Almost a year later, Zahra asserted, "You shouldn't force someone to do something or wear something because they'll start to hate it ... that's what my dad did with me. He forced me to wear the hijab and now I hate it."

It is very difficult to type these words. Throughout my life and scholarly work, I have challenged the single story that veiled girls and women are forced to cover. However, as Adichie reminds me, "The single story creates stereotypes. And the problem with stereotypes is not that they are untrue, but that they are incomplete. They make one story become the only story" ("Danger"). Although countless Muslim girls and women, including me and other co-inquirers, chose to don the hijab, many others have been unjustly pressured or forced to do so. As someone who, like Ayesha and Zahra, believes in the profound (human) right to choose for ourselves, hearing Zahra say, for the first time, that she hates wearing her hijab because she was forced to wear it filled me with sorrow. For this reason, when I met with Ayesha, Zahra, Sarah, and Zainab alongside my children for lunch in the late summer of 2016, I was happy to see Zahra walk in to the restaurant without her hijab. Zahra looked at me somewhat self-consciously and hugging her joyfully, I said, "As always, you look so beautiful habibty."

I did not speak with Zahra about her decision to remove her hijab until a month later in the fall of 2016. Ayesha had recently separated from her husband, and I knew that Ayesha, Zahra, Sarah, and Zainab were in the process of learning to compose their lives and relationships in different ways. I also knew that Zahra and her sisters were just beginning to renegotiate their relationships with their father after weeks of not seeing him after their parents' separation. I picked Zahra up for a dinner date at our favourite pasta restaurant, intending to simply enjoy her company that night. I did not want to pressure her into talking about anything she was not ready to talk about. As we followed the hostess to our booth, Zahra nudged me and whispered, "Did you see that?" After we were seated, I asked her, "See what? Sorry, I didn't notice anything." Zahra replied, "That guy made a face and moved away from you when you walked by." I said that I did not notice him doing that and asked Zahra if she noticed anything different in other people's behaviours towards her after removing her hijab. Zahra replied to my question with sympathy in her eyes and voice, "Yeah. I'm sorry to say this, but it's *so* different Muna. I feel like I don't have to do anything extra to show people that I'm normal."

Epilogue: Negotiating Our Narrative Account [and boundaries]—Fall 2016

Waiting for Zahra and Ayesha at our favourite pasta restaurant, I reflect upon the many seasons we have lived alongside one another. Images flash in my mind of some of the moments we have lived together. Laughing with Zahra in my car. Talking over yet another dessert and laughing over yet another coffee or tea with Ayesha. Raking the sand with my feet as Zahra and I talk on the playground swings, sharing secret stories with the same abandonment as our swinging. Hugging Ayesha tightly and telling her how brave she is and how much I admire her. Giving Zahra my Just Olive Tree[25] bracelet that I often see her wearing and telling her I hope it helps

---

25 This is a bracelet I purchased from justolivetree.com. The website says this company "is a Canadian-based Jewelry company specialising in genuine Middle Eastern Olive Wood Jewelry collections for a Just cause—the Palestine Children's Relief Fund."

ground and sustain her as it has for me. Feeling Ayesha's hand on my shoulder as she says, "It will be okay, Muna. Allah will guide and protect her."

I smile when I see Ayesha and Zahra approaching, and we exchange hugs and Salams. As we get settled into our booth, I ask Zahra how grade eight is going so far. They moved again in August following Ayesha's separation from her husband, and Zahra and Sarah are now attending the junior high school in their new neighbourhood. She responds, "It's okay. I like the teachers a lot, and it's a good school. And I like walking to school with Sarah. I poke her when I see her in the hallway [laughing]." Zahra talks about making a lot of friends at her new school, but as "the new girl," it is hard to become close with someone.

After we order, we talk about the writing of our narrative account. In specific, I ask about the inclusion of a few (difficult) stories—stories that continue to shape their life-making:

Zahra: I think it's okay if you say, "Later on I found out that" but not the details.

Me: Okay. And what about you Ayesha?

Ayesha: I think I want to share the details actually.

Me: The thing is that your stories are going to be like this [making an interconnected steeple with my fingers], so if Zahra doesn't want it in the writing, it can't go in.

Ayesha: What I want is for women who read ... this is something that could help someone. I've already had women telling me that my story helped them.

Zahra: I'm just scared that someone will read it and know it's me, especially specific people. I have a lot of people in mind who have said mean things about me in the past.

Ayesha: But those people will never read this right?

Zahra: You never know.

Me: That's right. I can't guarantee they won't.

Ayesha: But the thing is they will never find out it's us because our identities will be hidden. Even if you read it, you might not realize it's yours and be surprised it is you.

Me: I honestly can't guarantee that, but you know what? Just think about it and let me know later. You don't have to decide tonight. I don't want you to feel pressured or to put something in that will make you feel bad. Ever.

I later ask Ayesha, knowing what she knows now, what she would share with other moms whose daughters are transitioning into adolescence: "My advice would be to communicate with your child as much as possible, to empathize with them. That's the hardest part sometimes, but find out what it is that they're thinking and feeling, and encourage them to grow." Ayesha talks about how her faith has been her sustaining story alongside practicality:

Ayesha: My faith did give me so much hope—hope that the problem will go away, that it's not going to be there forever … but to also be really practical, like how am I actually going to work this out. Faith is good for guidance, but you still actually have to find a way to make that happen.

Me: That's so important to think about because sometimes when things are really hard, people will tell you "Just make duaa."

Ayesha: Or that "you have to trust Allah."

Me: And it's true. We do have to have faith and trust Allah, but …

Ayesha: But you also need to do something, you need the tools to actually do it … I would ask questions from my friends and even from you, mash'Allah, and people in my circle, some of the girls who went to school here, like how do I do something about this?

Ayesha emphasizes the importance of choice and talks about the challenges as they continue to learn to live in new ways alongside one another:

Ayesha: As moms, we have to give our kids power to make decisions. I've been trying to form the structure of that. What things should they decide for themselves? What things should I decide? What things we'll decide together? We didn't grow up with that, and our parents didn't really teach us that way. And for the longest time I haven't really disciplined the kids because there was so much happening.

Zahra: I was wondering about that [everyone laughing]. I was like, "So wait, I can do anything, and she won't take my phone? Ohhhh …" [laughing].

Ayesha: Yeah and I did that intentionally because they were going through so much, and I didn't want to or even couldn't do it. But now I feel like we are in a place where we should set the rules, we should set those boundaries.

Driving home that night, I continue to reflect on composing this inquiry alongside Ayesha and Zahra. I think about how strangers can become friends and friends can become family. Feeling profoundly grateful, I think about growing our relationships over time, and I wonder what future seasons will bring …

Maya's beautiful artwork is displayed with her permission throughout the following chater.

Chapter 5

A Narrative Account of Living and Growing Alongside Maya and Layla

> Like the seeds dreaming beneath the snow,
> your heart dreams of spring.
> —Khalil Gibran, *The Prophet*

Layla and Maya's Family

Layla—Mom
Mahmoud—Dad

Children by Birth Order

Ahmed
Maya
Adam
Rema
Jamal

Maya's Aunt/Layla's Sister

(who joined many of our conversations)

Sara

Growing Forward ... Alhamdulillah

Watching her gracefully whirl and spin and move her body, I feel a surge of love, pride, and admiration. As someone who trips over my own feet, I am fascinated at the way Maya can smile as she maintains her balance in the midst of improbable positions on the ice. I look over at Layla and smile at the way she is lovingly watching her daughter with riveted attention, knowing she is feeling an even headier overlapping of emotions than I am right now.

I think of how different this skating exhibition feels from the one I attended last year. I remember how nervous I had been for Maya at that time. She had experienced a heartbreaking moment at a skating competition a few months before last year's exhibition. Still reeling from her Tata's sudden death (Allah yirhama), Maya had been unable to complete her routine, leaving the ice in tears. However, I remember how she had bravely laced her skates up once more a few months later and skated as gracefully at last year's exhibition as she is now.

Maya waves at the crowd of loved ones who have come to support her, and we all wave enthusiastically back. She blows a kiss at Layla who blows several back to her, and I am surprised by the sudden tears welling in my eyes at their display of love. I know that Layla and Maya have weathered many changes in the seasons we have lived and inquired alongside one another, but their loving exchange reminds me that they have weathered these changes together.

I close my eyes for a brief moment to make duaa that their relationship continues to grow and flourish, and to sit with the immense gratitude I am feeling at having been blessed with the opportunity of living and inquiring alongside Maya and Layla over the last several seasons, Alhamdulillah.

How Do Friends Become Co-inquirers?—Summer 2015

After parking my car on the side of the familiar street, I think of how strange it feels to be walking up to this home—one that has been one of my home places for almost fifteen years—with information sheets and notebook in hand. I have lived many stories alongside one of my closest friends, Sara, in her familial home. This home is also where I had the privilege to become friends with many of Sara's family members over the years, including her younger sister Layla. In February 2015, as Sara and I discussed my research, she asked me, "Why don't you invite Layla and Maya? I'm sure they would love to participate." Confused, I ask, "Wasn't Layla born in Canada?" Sara responded, "Yeah, but her husband Mahmoud was born in Lebanon."

While I thought it would be fascinating to inquire alongside a mother and daughter who were both second-generation Canadian Muslims, I was unsure about inviting Layla and Maya to participate in this inquiry for several reasons. I was concerned that Layla would feel pressured to accept my invitation because of our long-term friendship. I was also hesitant because Layla and Maya live in a small town that is an over two-hour drive from the City, and I was unsure about how often we would be able to engage in discussions. Because of these considerations, I waited several months before inviting Layla and Maya to participate in this research. I eventually decided to discuss the possibility of participation with them after seeing Layla at a community function. After we exchanged hugs and Salams, Layla excitedly asked, "So when are we going to start the research?" Amused but not surprised that Sara had already mentioned the research to Layla, I laughingly replied that I would call her soon.

Layla's enthusiastic, unprompted question during that community event helped ease my concern that she would feel pressured to participate in this study. Later, I discussed with my supervisor, Dr. D. Jean Clandinin, the possibility of inviting a third set of co-inquirers, and we both agreed that engaging in inquiry alongside Layla and Maya would allow us to inquire into, and learn about, their experiences composing their lives in a rural Albertan context—a place that is different from the large, urban setting where other co-inquirers and I live.

During a telephone call with Layla a few weeks later, we agreed to meet at Layla's parents' home, close to where I live, because they would be in the City that weekend. Layla said that she drives to the City almost every weekend to visit with family, and she suggested we meet to talk on the weekends when possible. As we spoke, I (silently) exhaled a sigh of relief. I realized that I had been thinking about the reasons why inquiring alongside Layla and Maya may not be advisable rather than focusing on the unique experiences and knowledge they embody and can share as Canadian, Muslim, and Lebanese females making a life in small-town Alberta.

I walk up to their parents' house, amid the sights and sounds of Sara and Layla's children playing outside, and I see that the garage door is open and that Sara and her mom are sitting at a picnic table loaded with fruits and snacks. I smile at them and this familiar sight. It is one that greets me almost every time I visit their home during the summer season. As we exchange Salams and hugs, Layla joins us in the garage. After we catch up for a few minutes, Layla's mom says that she will be going inside to change for her errands run. Layla asks her mom to tell Maya to join us in the garage, and within moments, Maya approaches me and says, "Hi A3mto Muna!" We hug, and I marvel at how much she has grown since I last saw her. With her jet-black long hair and sun-kissed skin, she is as beautiful as ever. I ask Maya how she is enjoying the summer so far. She tells me about some of her adventures since school ended a few weeks ago and asks me about Noor: "Did you bring her with you?" I reply, "Not today, because I wanted to talk to you a little more privately about the research I'm doing for school." Sara excuses herself and starts to head inside as Layla asks, "Sara can't be here when we talk about this?" Smiling, I reply that Layla and Maya are more than welcome to ask anyone they wish to be alongside us in our conversations. Layla laughingly calls out to Sara, "Sara! Get back here."

As we fill our plates with snacks, I tell them about the study and how it has been unfolding thus far alongside four mother and daughter co-inquirers. Maya asks thoughtful questions as we talk, "A3mto Muna, I'm not always the best at telling stories; my mind goes too fast sometimes, but I'm good at writing and drawing?" In response, I bring out the bag of research-related supplies I prepared and explain that I have given the same supplies to other girl co-inquirers. I place a large sketchbook, pack of gel pens, journal, and disposable camera in front of me and tell Maya that she can take the supplies and use them in whatever way she likes: "You don't have to use any of these supplies for the research, but I would love to include whatever you decide to use." Maya excitedly asks, "Can I start right now?" Smiling at her, I say that she can take whatever she wants, even if she doesn't think she wants to participate. Layla laughingly says, "Muna, I think we have both already decided we want to be part of this." I bring out the information sheets and ask if we could please read them together first, just to make sure they are fully aware of what the research will entail. Layla jokingly rolls her eyes and says, "Okay, go for it." As I read, I notice that Maya is doodling in the sketchbook, and I smile because I too like to doodle when I am listening to something or someone.

Later, I realize that I have already been there for almost two hours, and I ask Layla and Maya if they have any questions before I leave.

They both respond that they do not, so as I pack my things up, I leave two consent forms on the table and ask them to please consider participating over the next few days. I say that I love them and will understand if this commitment does not work for whatever reason for them. Layla laughs and signs her consent form in response. Maya does the same. Waving away my protests, Layla hugs me and says she really looks forward to being a part of this research and that she is so proud of me. With my heart feeling full, I turn to hug Maya before I leave, and she thanks me for the research supplies and promises to write as much as she can over the summer. I say that I would love to see anything she chooses to share with me. Still smiling as I drive home, I reflect on my relationships with Maya and Layla, and I wonder how our long time knowing of one another will shape our inquiry ...

Retellings
"We Trust You" —
(Layla and Maya, Multiple Conversations)

I smile often listening to the audio recording of our research conversations over many seasons. The sounds of doors opening and closing, phones ringing and pinging, and children laughing take me back to many different places as a co-inquirer alongside Layla and Maya. These sounds, overlapping with our meandering discussions, are similar to the sounds accompanying countless get-togethers over many years of friendship, and I continue to wonder about how our long-term friendship, our knowing of one another, has shaped our research inquiry and our relationship.

Since Sara introduced us over thirteen years ago, Layla and I have built a friendship of mutual love and appreciation. We have visited and celebrated with each other, laughed often with and at each other, and supported one another during pregnancies, illnesses, ambitions, and disappointments. My children call Layla "A3mto" (Auntie), and her children do the same with me, for they have grown up alongside us and each other. Our love for, and comfort with, each other was always present during our conversations, and in the early winter of 2016, Layla articulated what I was feeling after several seasons of inquiring alongside each other: "You know, it's hard to remember what we're talking about sometimes because we're friends and we just talk anyways. I love talking to you, because there's a friendship behind it too, but I learned to love you even more than I already did, Alhamdulillah."

As we engaged in multiple conversations for the purposes of this inquiry, I was both heartened and fearful of the level of comfort we had with one another. I was heartened by it because I know that Maya and Layla trust me to take care of the stories they shared and lived with me. However, this trust is also what I fear. When Maya and Layla repeatedly say, "We trust you," I feel their trust as a blessing and as an *"Amanah,"* which is an Arabic word meaning "a trust." In Islam, the concept of *Amanah* signifies a faith-based, moral obligation to uphold and carry out a sacred obligation. Making duaa as I type this, I pray that I am able to fulfill this *Amanah* to the best of my abilities. Insha'Allah.

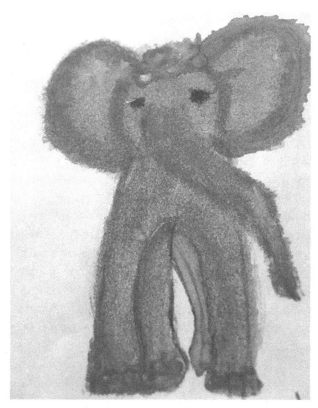

Maya's artwork depicting one of her favourite animals.

Rooting a Research Relationship—Summer 2015

Standing in front of what Sara's children have called the Toys R Us Room, I marvel at the number of toys on display, and at their organization. Sara is showing me around Layla and Maya's home as we wait for Layla to join us. We arrived in Tree Town (pseudonym for their town) about ten minutes ago with five children clamouring to get out of their seats after a more than two-hour drive. Noor, Yehia, and Hannah, along with Sara's children, Mariam and Omar, were greeted by Layla's children as soon as we parked the car. Noor and Maya immediately disappeared to Maya's room while the older boys stayed outside to either play basketball with Layla's eldest son Ahmed and two of his friends, or ball hockey with Layla's third child, Adam. As Layla's youngest children, Rema and Jamal, guide our younger children to the Toys R Us Room inside, Layla calls and says to please make ourselves at home while she runs a few errands and that she will be returning home soon.

I stand in front of the toy room, after Hannah impatiently wiggled her way out of my arms to go explore the forest of toys, and I say "mash'Allah." There are rows upon rows of shelves with bins upon bins, all labelled, of toys. Sara laughs at my expression and explains that since Layla has five children, she has been collecting their toys— many of which were gifts from friends and extended family—over the last thirteen years. I can see that the kids are enjoying playing in this room immensely, and I now understand why Layla urged me to bring Noor, Yehia, and Hannah with me today: "Believe me Muna, they won't be bored at our house."

Sara then gives me a tour of her sister's home. It is beautiful, spacious, and incredibly clean and organized. She tells me that it was built a short while after Layla and Mahmoud first moved to Tree Town. Shouting out greetings, Layla joins us as we finish touring her home, and with whirlwind expertise, she carries several bags into the kitchen. Sara and I follow her to offer assistance when Layla stops, looks around, and asks, "Where's Maya? I thought you would be talking to her by now?" I say that we have just finished touring her home and that Maya and Noor are catching up with each other in Maya's room. Layla calls out "Maya! You need to come to the kitchen so A3mto Muna can talk to us!" I laughingly say that we do not have to rush our talk, as Maya and Noor walk into the kitchen. Layla asks, "Okay, so how are we going to do this?" Feeling multiple eyes on me, I stammer, "Um ... I know that a private conversation isn't going to be possible right now, so how about we just talk and see how it goes?" Maya asks if Noor can stay in the kitchen with us, and I respond, "Of course she can, if that's what you want." My original plan for this first research conversation was to sneak away to a quiet place to begin composing annals alongside Layla and Maya while Sara and Noor help to look after the younger children, but I now know that this will be challenging considering how the children have been walking in and out of the kitchen from the toy room and from outside. Unsure of how an unexpected group conversation will proceed, I prop my cellphone on the kitchen table and ask if I can begin recording? Layla says, "Of course," and I press record on the audio recorder.

I ask Maya how school is going, and she responds that the first few weeks of her grade six year have already been really boring, but "recess is fun though." I notice that Maya is turning the journal I had given her a few months ago over in her hands: "I didn't take pictures or anything, but I've written this." Maya hands me her journal, and I leaf through several pages, exclaiming, "Habibty, you wrote so much!" To which Maya replies, "Yeah, I tried." Layla says, "Maya is a good writer ... her teacher says she loves to read her stories." I turn to the front page of the journal to a page titled "Things I Love" and ask, "Can I read this out loud?" Maya says, "Yeah," and I begin reading, "Figure skating, piano, swimming, baseball, drawing, unicorns, my friends." After reading the long list of things Maya loves, I exclaim, "I love how you drew little symbols next to each item, so creative!"

Later in our conversation, Layla shares that her children were born in Tree Town, except for Ahmed and Maya. They moved to Tree Town when Maya was about six months old, and "most people in town know each other or at least recognize them." She says that there are three elementary schools, and "next year, all the kids will be together in the only junior high, so it'll be a culture shock for a lot of these kids." I ask, "Why will it be a culture shock?" Layla responds, "My kids go to the school where there are a lot of low-income families, and there is a school that is more middle [income] and one with wealthy people." She continues, "The kids' school is next to our restaurant, so they can walk there after school, and Mahmoud can pick them up if something happens. Plus, not everyone's born rich, and we don't want to make our kids *shayfeen hallun* [the Arabic word for "arrogant"] and cocky, you know? This is what we can afford, and we treat everyone equal no matter what." Layla explains that Tree Town "depends on oil" but that the downturn in oil has "hit a lot of people really hard":

Layla: Work is slow now because so many people who used to work in oil lost their jobs because there's no work anymore. People got laid off because there's no work for them.

Maya: But in the elections, Elizabeth May [leader of the Green Party of Canada] was saying how we need to get rid of oil.

Layla: Yeah, but if it wasn't for oil, Tree Town wouldn't exist Maya, and Baba's [The Arabic word for "dad"] business wouldn't exist either.

Me: You know, we hear the arguments about the need to get rid of dependency on oil, but the discussions don't always keep in mind the communities that depend on it.

Layla: Especially here in Alberta, the rest of the world doesn't really live off it, but Alberta really does.

As we enjoy pizza, fruits, and veggies after filling plates for the younger children, we talk about Maya's love of figure skating, and Layla says, "Maya, tell A3mto Muna about the exhibition. [Turning to me] I'm going to get you guys tickets!" Maya says, "Yeah, our exhibition is in February. Rema and Jamal will be in it too. [Turning to Noor] I want you to come." Noor and I say that we would love to watch Maya's exhibition, and I thank them for inviting us. Maya talks about how a lot of her friends attend figure skating lessons with her, and Layla says, "That's the thing about this town, when you're in activities you meet other people. So when they go to junior high, it's not so hard. Like Ahmed [her eldest son] is in hockey, so when he went to junior high, he knew a lot of the kids. For those kids that are from out of town or that don't do much outside of school, it's so hard."

As Sara and I prepare to leave, I tell Layla how amazed I am that over thirteen children have been coming and going in her home, but they all seem to be having a wonderful time either outside or in the Toys R Us Room. Layla reflects, "You know, I used to play with a girl next door because she had the nicest baby stroller, and I never really had much toys." Sara says, "Our parents weren't used to having toys as kids. That's the thing, our kids are used to having lots of toys, but we didn't have that growing up." Layla responds, "I don't know what it was. My neighbour had tons of toys ... our toy room? She had that."

Hannah toddles in to the kitchen for a third time alongside Layla's youngest child, four-year-old Jamal. He proudly announces that he helped Hannah find the kitchen. Smiling widely, I thank him and tell Layla that he has grown so much already: "I remember how small he was when he was born!" Layla responds, "And I remember how I made you take me to my doctor's appointments when I was pregnant with him." I laugh and say, "You never made me Layla. I wanted to." I had been so scared for Layla at the time. She had been living in the City for the duration of her high-risk pregnancy with Jamal so that she could be closer to her in-laws and extended family. Layla continues, "No, I remember how much you were there for me, and I appreciate it." Shaking my head, I say, "And I appreciate how you and Sara were there for me when Yehia was in the hospital."

Driving home after our three-hour afternoon visit to Layla and Maya's house, Sara and I laugh at some of the events of the day. Later, I sit in silence while most of our children sleep, and I silently say "Alhamdulillah" for this opportunity to inquire alongside wonderful friends.

Retellings
"We have so much stuff going on" (Layla, Winter 2016)

Listening to the recording and reading my field notes and transcript of our first research conversation, I once again get a strong sense of the bustling, busy lives that Layla and Maya live. Neighbours and friends joined Layla's children in play throughout the afternoon that we spent there, and later, in the course of the many seasons we engaged in inquiry alongside one another, I was introduced to several of Maya's and her siblings' closest friends and neighbours, who Layla said "are part of the family" (Fall, 2015).

Layla's comment that "when you're in activities you meet other people" gives a sense of the importance she places upon extracurricular activities for her children. For example, figure skating is only one of the many activities that Maya enjoys. She has also learned to play the piano and is an avid swimmer. During a conversation in the winter of 2016, Layla proudly shared that "Maya could be a lifeguard with the level of swimming she's completed." Maya's siblings are all registered in multiple activities too, including hockey, figure skating, archery, wrestling, and gymnastics. Alongside almost weekly travels to visit with family members in the City, helping with schoolwork, and driving her five children to their many activities and visits with friends, Layla is also a weekly volunteer in her children's elementary school; she works with and helps translate for newly arrived Syrian families, and she sometimes helps her husband with the restaurant he owns in Tree Town.

Although Layla believes it is important for her children to be engaged in extracurricular activities, she knows that the demanding schedule of their activities has contributed to her neglecting her own needs. In the winter of 2016, during a telephone conversation, Layla said that although she loves that her children can pursue their passions, she feels fatigued: "We have so much stuff going on. I honestly don't have time to take care of myself, too. By the time we wake up and I clean up, make food, drop them off at school, pick them up, and all their activities, have supper and clean up again, my whole day is gone. And going to the City every weekend and all the work that comes with it? My body is tired." When I asked Layla if she has considered limiting her children's extracurricular activities to one activity for each child, she responded, "I would feel bad if I did that though; they love their activities." I laughingly countered, "Layla, only Noor and Yehia are in activities right now, and I told them that they can only be part of one activity per season in order for me to stay semi-sane." Laughing, Layla said, "I think that I just have to get better at asking for help when I need it."

"I wish for our daughters something different" (Layla, Fall 2016)

Layla's musings about her childhood neighbour's toy room is a persistent thread running throughout our conversations. In many different ways, Layla has expressed her desire—and I have witnessed her actions—to ensure that her children enjoy experiences she wishes she would have had the opportunity to enjoy. The first time I gained a strong sense of this was in late fall of 2015 when Layla discussed her dream of Maya attending a post-secondary institution: "I want Maya to have the full university experience because when I got married, I used to see Sara come and go with her friends and with you, and she really got to experience that time of her life and I didn't have that. I enjoyed it for Sara and so I want that for my kids. I don't regret getting married and having kids, but I'd like those experiences for Maya." Layla, who is younger than me by a year, married Mahmoud when she was nineteen years old. Wissam and I married when I was twenty years old in the summer before my last year of undergraduate studies. Reflecting on getting married so young, Layla said, "I wish for our daughters something different Muna. I wish for them to finish school and take their time and enjoy it."

(in the midst of) Tending to Life and Relationships— Fall 2015

The familiar smells of *qahwa* (coffee) and *shai* (tea) being prepared, as well as the sights and sounds of children and visitors coming and going amid multiple overlapping conversations, make me smile. If I closed my eyes, I would think I was in my parents' home right now. I inwardly chuckle at how Layla texted me earlier in the day to ask if we could meet talk at her in-laws' house, since the house would be empty. I happily agreed, as I thought it would probably be quieter there than my home, and I wanted to begin composing annals alongside Maya and Layla in a quiet setting. I walk into the home I have visited numerous times over the years, and hug Layla, Maya, and Sara at the door and we head to the kitchen table, which is, of course, already bearing several plates of snacks. Just as we begin to talk, Maya's paternal grandmother (Allah yirhama) walks into the room, wearing her seemingly perpetual smile. I rise from my seat to greet her the way I was taught to greet elders with kisses on alternating cheeks and "Assalamu Alaikum Hajji!" ("Hajji" is an Arabic word used to address a woman who has completed the Hajj pilgrimage. I was taught to address female elders as "Hajji" and male elders as "Hajj" as a sign of respect.) I ask Layla and Maya if we should postpone our conversation because I know that Maya's grandmother (Allah yirhama) is feeling anxious about her surgery tomorrow, but Sara says that she will gladly spend time with her so that we can talk. I am happy to hear them laughing a few minutes later.

As we enjoy huge slices of carrot cake (with Layla pressuring me to eat) and as more people begin streaming into the house, Layla says, "I'm sorry. This house is always like this, but I really thought it would be quieter tonight." I laughingly reply, "My parents' house is the same way, but I don't want to be making you feel like we have to continue this conversation right now. We have lots of time insha'Allah." Layla replies, "No wallah, it's fine, we love you and want to do this." Maya and Layla then talk about having fun at a trampoline park earlier in the day. I ask Maya about how school has been going in the last two months:

Maya: It's kind of boring.

Layla: Why is it boring?

Maya: Well, it's fun when we do social and science.

Layla: Tell A3mto Muna why you like social and science.

Maya: I have an awesome teacher. She taught me last year, and she's teaching grade five and six in the same class this year. But I like social and science because we get to go to the grade six class where all my friends are.

I ask Maya who her closest friends in school are, and she names a few girls: "But Yasmeen is my best friend. We've always been best friends, ever since we were babies."

Later, Maya talks about an upcoming skating event she is looking forward to, and Layla interjects, "Her first skating competition; it's at a place that's an hour and a half drive from Tree Town." Maya exclaims, "I will be doing my first solo routine, but I'm not sure about two of the jumps in my routine." Layla smiles at Maya, "You'll get it insha'Allah." With pride, Layla tells me, "Her skating teacher is so impressed with her, and I am, too." Maya excitedly talks about how she also practices multiple routines for the Tree Town Skating Exhibition in February. Layla says that she volunteers as one of the organizers of the exhibition and that her basement is currently "full of boxes." Perhaps recognizing my look of confusion, Layla explains further:

Layla: I'm in charge of ordering all the younger kids' costumes, but this year we have to sew our own for Maya because the costumes are too short.

Me: Oh okay.

Layla: She wears thick tights anyway, so it's okay [laughing]. But some of them are *really* short; it's okay though. I always order the same material for her dresses.

Maya: I don't like it when they're so short like that.

Layla: But do you have a hard time because your costume is different?

Maya: Kind of, but I don't really care because I always have nice dresses. I mean everyone has long sleeves though.

Layla: They all have long sleeves, but they're usually very short. Like last year, I just added an extra piece of material at the bottom, so it didn't really make much of a difference. It just looked more flowy.

Layla's question to Maya about feeling different prompts me to ask if there are many people of Muslim background in Tree Town. Layla answers that there are a few dozen families, "but only three hijabis," who make a life in Tree Town. I ask if they are ever made to feel different because they are Muslim:

Maya: What I see on social media and stuff, I don't see any of that at school. There's one kid, he's from ... I'm not sure where, but he was in my class because he was kept back a grade, so I see grade fivers saying mean things to him like, "Go back to your country!" and I'm like, "This *is* his country."

Layla: Good for you.

Me: So when you defend him, do they say or do anything to you?

Maya: No, nothing. They don't say anything.

Layla: Good for you for speaking up though.

Later, as we begin to compose annals alongside one another, Maya and Layla share stories of their earliest memories. As a self-described "small-town girl," Layla says, "I was born in the City but I only remember living in First Town." Maya interjects, "Same. I was born in the City and only remember Tree Town." Layla describes her many moves after marrying Mahmoud: "We got married and moved around a lot—in First Town for a year, in Second Town for a few months, in the City for less than a year—and then we finally moved to Tree Town. and we've stayed there since." Layla explains that she and Mahmoud finally settled in Tree Town after taking advantage of an opportunity to buy the restaurant that they still own. I ask Layla why they only stayed in Second Town for a few months: "We moved to Second Town because Mahmoud found work there, but we just hated it. It was so different there, like even though there were lots of Muslims, just because I'm a hijabi, they would call me Hajji, and I was only twenty years old!"

Later in our conversation, Layla asks me, "Did you see on Instagram and Facebook how I got surprised with flowers?" I shake my head and say that I'm not on social media, but I heard about how, after the Paris attacks a few weeks ago, Layla received a gift delivery of flowers and a supportive note from an anonymous friend:

Layla: And do you know what? I never found out who they were from, but I posted that I really appreciated it because I did. The thought was so nice, especially when so much is going on with the politics and all the talk about Muslims and whatever.

Me: Do you guys feel a difference since the attacks at all?

Layla: [To Maya] Do you feel like anyone says anything because you're Muslim?

Maya: No. Everyone likes me.

Layla: But it's tied to popularity at this age I think, so because she's popular, it's fine, you know?

Maya: Well, in school we talk about that, like my teacher is against people doing and saying mean things to other people because of things like culture.

Layla: That's so good. And you know, I don't really feel racism in town. I really don't. *But* we have an opinion page in Tree Town, and I see a lot in there. I don't see it when I'm out and about or at the arena or anything. At the arena, we're like a family. All the people who have their kids in hockey and skating, we all kind of know each other. And you know how I am. I'm pretty bubbly and will talk with them so they have almost no choice but to talk to me [laughing]. I'm not doing it for any specific reason wallah; it's just me. It's who I am, and they might be like, "Well how can I be rude to her and she said, 'Hi, how are you?'" and maybe they think about it and things change. And yes, I might get a few stares here and there, but I don't think about it.

Me: That opinion page you were talking about, that was in the paper?

Layla: No it was online. There's lots of racism in there actually, like one guy was responding to a lady who was like [in relation to recent terror attacks], "They're not real Muslims," and he was like, "No, they're all like that." I don't really respond on there, but I did report his comment because you can report stuff like that.

Troubled, I ask Layla if she knows the person who posted that comment:

No, because he commented anonymously. But there's this one dad from Ahmed's hockey team that wrote something in the opinion page. He said, "*They* need to do something; their people need to stop them," and wrote, "Don't say I'm racist because my buddy is Muslim." It's true, because he talks to Mahmoud and kicks jokes with him. So I said to Mahmoud, "It's funny that he thinks we can do something, like I forgot I have ISIS on my callers list [sarcastic tone]." I mean we don't know who these people are and we can't stop them, but others think we can. I wish we could, but we can't. I told Mahmoud that if I ever see him at the arena, I'm going to say, "So you think I have these people on my speed dial or something?" but I didn't see him yet.

In response to Layla, Maya says, "I don't think Muslims can do that kind of stuff. They're not Muslim. And there are no terrorists in Canada! But, yeah, they think we're terrorists, but just because one person does it, doesn't mean everyone will." I ask Maya why she said that "they all think we're terrorists," and with tears in her eyes, she says, "Well I listen and I know about it. Because you know in the Paris attacks, one of the guy's brothers didn't know that he was doing that and everyone just assumes that the whole family is like that." Layla listens to Maya with concern in her eyes and says, "Yimkin flitna bi'l hakee shway [an Arabic phrase for "Maybe we let our conversation get out of hand"], but they have to know about it too. I always tell them don't ever be ashamed of who you are."

Retellings
"Don't judge a book by its cover" (Maya, Summer 2015)

Maya's response that it can be "kind of" hard to be different than her skating peers because of the alterations Layla makes to her costumes is a recurring thread running throughout our conversations. Earlier, in the summer of 2015, I read the following excerpt from Maya's journal aloud: "At school when it's hot out and all of the girls are wearing shorts and tank tops, and I can't wear that stuff it's kind of hard. And when I swim, all the girls wear bikinis, and I have to wear shorts and a swim shirt, but clothing has nothing to do with my personality in other words—don't judge a book by its cover." After I finished reading that excerpt, I looked at Maya and said, "I totally understand. It's so hard when it's hot outside and you're so covered." Maya sighed, "It sucks. My friend Yasmeen is Muslim and can wear shorts, tank tops, and even bikinis." Layla interjected: "It's hard because I know that clothes are a really big deal for her. I try to tell her that not all Muslims practice the same and that we don't have to do what everyone else is doing."

Expectations related to how Maya should dress can be hard for Layla to negotiate too. During a telephone conversation with Layla in the early winter of 2016, she felt frustrated after a female family member expressed displeasure after seeing a picture of Maya in one of her skating costumes:

Layla: You know how they have a professional photographer who takes pictures that you can pay for. Well, there was one of Maya jumping and it's one where her legs show, and the skirt looks really short, and she [the family member] was like, "Hmm ... no comment."

Me: Yeah, but I saw her skating that day, and she was wearing really thick tights too.

Layla: Yeah, and Maya wanted it because it shows her jumping really high, but I was so surprised at Mahmoud. When he heard that Maya might not skate next year, he was like, "Why?" and I was telling him she might want to try something else and it's okay because I know he doesn't like the outfits they wear sometimes, and he was like, "The ones she's been wearing are fine, I want her to skate if that's what she wants to do." He doesn't want to take that from her, you know? I was so happy he said that.

Me: Okay. Did you tell him about the comment you got about her skirt being too short?

Layla: Yeah, and he said to just ignore it, but it did bug me. I get it, you know, someone seeing a picture, it can come across like, "*Shoo labsee?*" [an Arabic phrase for "what is she wearing?"], but at the same time, that's the problem with our kids, they can't participate in anything because of stuff like that, you know? It's not fair to our kids to say no to participating in sports and activities because of things like that, and Maya doesn't seem to care that I alter her costumes; she just loves skating. I asked her if she minded, and she said no, and you *know* that she'd tell me if she didn't like it [laughing].

Later, during that same telephone conversation, Layla talked about being surprised at the reason Maya was unsure about participating in a swimming field trip:

For Muslim girls it's hard sometimes ... the other day, Maya was saying how, for their gym options class, they're going swimming for the day and she said, "I want to go, and I don't want to go." And I was like, "Why? Because you have to wear shorts and your rash guard and everyone else will be wearing swimming suits?" And she was like, "Kind of," and then I said, "So you're not going to have fun with your friends because of what you're wearing? I don't think they care what you're wearing." And then she was like, "Yeah, you're right, I'm going."

I contemplate Layla's words, and I wonder when Maya started to notice that she was expected to dress differently than her friends. I think about how, for me and Noor, difficulties with expectations related to dressing are perhaps not as pronounced because the majority of Noor's friends attend Islamic school with her. They know that, upon reaching puberty, choosing to observe hijab may, depending upon the interpretations of Islamic texts they follow, include covering their hair and other parts of their bodies. The stories Layla and Maya shared, however, make me contemplate how expectations related to dress and other cultural and faith-based/religious beliefs and practices can, in myriad ways, be extremely challenging for Muslim girls and their mothers to negotiate.

"Good for you for speaking up" (Layla, Fall 2015)

Intricately connected to Maya's belief that it's misguided to "judge a book by its cover" is the way that she actively defends those she believes have been arrogantly perceived. Maya's story of coming to the defence of a boy in her class who was told to "go back to [his] country" is only one of many stories she or Layla have shared of Maya speaking up in defence others. In the summer of 2016, as we enjoyed Ramadan *iftar*[26] in Sara's home, Maya talked about becoming friends with a girl whose poetry she admired:

Maya: She's so nice, and she's always been taller than everybody. The other kids don't really make fun of her, but they don't really talk to her either. And this is the first year I actually started talking to her because she's in my class this year and she's so nice, and funny too, so I told her I have her back [laughing].

26 This is an Arabic word for the meal that breaks a fast. We were fasting during the long, hot summer days of Ramadan at the time.

Me: It was nice of you to notice that, people don't often notice when others are ignored.

Maya: Yeah I notice everything, like for example there's this new kid in school, and he's kind of chubbier, and some of the other people have first assumptions, but I talked to him, and he's nice. And when some of my friends said mean things about him, I was like, "Well, I like him; he's nice." And there's this other guy in my class, he came to the school in grade three, and he was taller and bigger than everyone. So everybody made fun of him when he ran in gym, but he's so nice and so funny too, and I would tell them to stop. And then in grade four, everyone started noticing how funny and smart he is.

Several months later, as we enjoyed another dinner in Sara's home in the winter of 2016, Maya shared a story of a younger girl trying to "add [her] on Instagram." Maya explained why she declined the girl's request: "I told her, 'Nope. You're mean to my [younger] brother.'" She continued, "I feel like I'm even more friendly this year, but I can be tough. If someone isn't nice to my family or friends, I can be tough."

In the winter of 2017, as Maya, Sara, Layla, and I talked into the night, Maya shared a story of speaking up for a friend who had been the subject of many rumours:

Maya: I was mad at my friend because she called one of my other friends a "Ho."

Me: What? Who?

Maya: [Name of friend] called another one of my friends a "Ho and an alcoholic."

Layla: And Maya was like, "You don't even know her. Why would you say that about her?" So Maya got mad, and then [the friend's] mom noticed they weren't acting the way they usually do, so she called me and asked what's going on, and I told her what her daughter said. And she [friend's mom] was so mad because she said, "I never want my daughter to say that about anyone." I'm so happy Maya told her it's not okay.

Maya: [Tearfully] I feel so bad for her because so many people think that about her and they keep spreading that rumour. They talk about her because she's so pretty and ...

Me: So others just assume these things because she's pretty?

Maya: Yeah, but we've been friends for a long time, even before we went to school together, and she's not like that.

As I think about this troubling story, and many others that Maya shared, I think about how brave Maya is to speak up in defence of others, especially when she's defending others to her friends. I wonder if Maya's experiential knowledge of being a Muslim girl expected to dress in different ways, as well as of being the daughter of one of a few veiled women in Tree Town, helps her to travel to the worlds of others who are judged and/or ridiculed for being different. I think of Maya saying, "I told her I have her back" and of how often Layla has said "Good for you" or has otherwise encouraged Maya to speak up. I wonder if Maya draws some of her strength and courage from the knowledge that Layla will have *her* back.

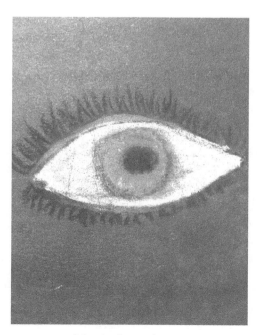

Maya's charcoal art.

Facing (internal and external) Arrogant Perception(s) Alongside Maya and Layla

Inquiring alongside Layla and Maya for many seasons, I have often wondered about arrogant perceptions, including my own. As I prepared for our inquiry, I expected to hear stories of discrimination because, I am ashamed to admit, the single story I held of small-town Alberta was one of discomfort with, or even intolerance of, difference. However, in coming alongside Maya and Layla and their stories of making a life in Tree Town, I quickly learned that my arrogant perception of rural Albertan communities was constructed without wakefulness to my lack of experiential knowledge of small-town life. In the fall of 2016, Layla and Maya spoke of building a sense of community in Tree Town:

> Layla: I'm finding that Maya doesn't want to come to the city as often on the weekends anymore; she wants to stay in Tree Town.
>
> Maya: Because I get to hang out with my friends.
>
> Layla: And in a small place like Tree Town you have to *make* a community. Our friends are like our family.
>
> Maya: Because they're good to us and we're good to them.
>
> Layla: Like ladies from the school will come over for coffee or if we have a skating meeting, I'm always the first to offer my house, and they always laugh and tell me, "Oh, you're such a good hostess."
>
> Me: And has it been like that since you've moved there?
>
> Layla: It happened more when the kids started school and their activities. But have I ever felt that anyone was mean to me? No. In the beginning it might have been a bit weird like, "Oh, she's Muslim" or whatever, but now it's, "Oh, that's just Layla," which is nice. I find that in the City, there seem to be more looks and racism to be honest.

Although in my everyday life and scholarly work, I warn about single stories and arrogant perceptions in relation to Muslim people and communities, Maya and Layla helped me to realize that I too can engage in arrogant perception of people and places I have limited knowledge of. .

My conversations alongside Layla and Maya have repeatedly reminded me about my ability to be an arrogant perceiver, including the ways I might judge others' parenting practices. Layla's experience with a female family member who was unimpressed with Maya's skating costume makes me think about how mothers can be subjected to the arrogant perceptions of others and how we can also be perpetrators of arrogant perceptions. In the winter of 2016, Layla shared how a friend questioned her parenting after she learned that Maya and her siblings are permitted to participate in sleepovers outside the home. Laughingly, Layla shared how this same friend then allowed her daughter to participate in an overnight camping field trip. In response, I said, "Moms can be so judgmental of other moms." Layla said, "Yeah, I can be judgmental too though." I replied, "Me too."

Layla and I also discussed the arrogant perceptions others may hold of us as Muslim women and mothers. In response to a story I shared of an experience with feeling arrogantly perceived as a veiled mother to a child with ASD, Layla said, "It's so sad because people see us and make assumptions about our kids or the way we are as parents. It even happens with people from poor communities or with moms who smoke or with people who are a different race. The stereotypes are so strong sometimes." Layla's words make me wonder about deeply rooted single stories that shape so many lives. I think of Maya's tearful words "They think we're terrorists" and of Layla's sentiment "I always tell them don't ever be ashamed of who you are," and I wonder about the myriad ways single stories and arrogant perceptions—whether they stem from family, friends, classmates, and/or strangers—shape the experiences of Muslim children growing into adolescence and adulthood. How do single stories and arrogant perceptions shape their knowing of themselves and of their families and communities? However, Maya's tearful comments during our conversation makes me wonder yet again about how parents and other educators can discuss stereotypes and assumptions others may hold of Muslims, particularly with children and youth, in ways that encourage awareness while rejecting fear and cynicism.

STORIES WE LIVE AND GROW BY

Growing Forward Alongside Layla and Maya in the Shadows of Loss—Winter 2016

Breathing deeply as I set the table, I make duaa that our conversation will be calming after what I know will be an emotional afternoon for Maya and Layla. Along with Maya's younger siblings, and Sara and her children, Layla and Maya will be coming over for a late lunch conversation. Layla just texted to let me know that they are running late after deciding to visit her mother-in-law's grave (Allah yirhama). A few months ago, Sara tearfully informed me that Maya's grandmother (Allah yirhama) passed away because of unexpected complications related to her day surgery. Shocked, I tearfully recited the words my mom taught me to recite upon hearing news of death: "*Inna li'Allah wa Inna Ilayhi Raji'oon*" ["We belong to Allah and to Him we are destined to return"]. As I arrange the table, I think of Layla and Maya's visible heartbreak when I saw them at Maya's grandmother's funeral.

Maya's grandmother's funeral (in accordance with Islamic custom that burial of the deceased should take place as soon as possible) was held the afternoon of her passing (Allah yirhama). With a heavy heart, I walked into the Masjid and through the doors to where I knew Layla and Maya would be sitting along with the rest of their family to accept condolences. Remembering Jidee's and Yehia's (Allah yirhamun) funerals, I made duaa that Allah (SWT) pours sabr into the hearts of all who mourn this incredibly kind woman (Allah yirhama). Walking into the room, I began offering my condolences to the first row of women, all of whom I know, saying "Allah yirhama" repeatedly. By the time I reached Layla and Maya, I am crying silently, and I wordlessly embraced them each tightly. I held them longer than is customary in offering condolences, for there were others who were waiting to offer condolences, but I did not want to end our embrace while they held me as if they too were reluctant to let go. In my ear, Layla whispered, "Subhan Allah, we were just together in her home, Allah yirhama."

After the Janaza prayer (Salat Al-Janazah, the Muslim funeral prayer, is offered in congregation), I made my way outside to where I knew Maya and Layla would be standing to say their goodbye's before Maya's grandmother (Allah yirhama) is driven to her final resting place. I noticed Sara, Layla, and Maya standing to the side and walked over to them to hold Maya tightly as the hearse carrying her grandmother (Allah yirhama) drove away. We stood like that for a very long time before someone called out to Layla that they needed to leave. Hugging Layla and Maya one more time, I left the Masjid, but my heart remained with them.

The knocking on the door interrupts my thoughts, and I usher Layla, Maya, Sara, Jamal, Adam, Rema, Jamal, Mariam, and Omar inside with hugs. As we fill the younger children's plates with food, I ask Layla and Maya how they have been doing:

Layla: It's been a bit tough Alhamdulillah, but Maya has been doing a good job of taking care of her Jiddo, she's so *hannunee* [the Arabic word for tender hearted]. I don't know; it's been hard. But next week, you guys have to come to Tree Town for the skating exhibition.

Maya: Yeah!

Me: I'd love to wallah.

Layla: Bring all the kids too.

As we settle down in our seats with our plates in front of us, Layla remarks, "Subhan Allah how the last time we talked was right before she passed Allah yirhama. How have things changed for you since then Maya?":

Maya: Bad. Bad changes.

Sara: What? Why?

Maya: [Tearfully] I don't know ... everything sucks.

Me: I'm so sorry habibty. The last couple of months have been so hard.

Maya: Yeah.

Heart aching, I try to give Maya space by asking Layla if the boxes of skating costumes are still in her basement. Her eyes brimming with unshed tears in response to Maya's words, Layla laughingly replies, "Yeah, it's like Party City [supply store] ... the other moms were saying, 'Oh, the costumes are so ... *warm* this year.'" We laugh as Layla says, "How can you expect little kids to skate in those tiny costumes on the ice? It's so cold!" Maya says, "I love skating, but I hate the competitions. I failed horribly." Layla explains further:

Layla: Remember her grandma passed and then the week after was her competition? So I asked her if she still wanted to go, and she did. But this rink was different because in Tree Town, we have lines on the ice and this one didn't.

Maya: And I just froze.

Layla: Yeah.

Maya: And then I got scared, and I started crying, and then I left.

Layla: But Mama [my child], there were lots of emotions going on, and that's just normal.

Later in our conversation, Layla talks about visiting Maya's grandmother's (Allah yirhama) grave in a way that surprises me:

Layla: You know, I had never been to a graveyard before, and so my kids learned it [the protocol for visiting graves] earlier than I did ... they've learned that it's *wajib* [the Arabic word for "duty" or "responsibility"] to go visit their grandma and anyone that has passed. And if they go with us, that's what they'll know, right? And the sad thing is that sometimes it takes a sibling or a mom or a dad or grandparent to make you go.

Me: Jiddee and Yehia (Allah yirhamun) are buried there, but I've never visited their graves.

Layla: Oh really? I'm surprised Muna.

Me: My whole body tenses at the thought of going.

Layla: I thought it would be hard too, but honestly it's relaxing. Isn't it relaxing when you go see Tata [an Arabic term of endearment for grandmother], Maya?

Maya: No not really.

Layla: Well for me, it's relaxing. I cry when I'm there, but I don't feel bad.

Maya: They brought a bench to Tata's grave.

Layla: So we can sit and read Qu'ran to her ... wallah, you'd get a sense of relief if you went to visit them Muna. It will be hard, and you'll cry, but it'll be a good cry and Subhan Allah it's so peaceful, and it feels so good to just talk to her alone.

As they prepare to leave, Maya talks about being disappointed in herself for not doing as well as she expected in her recent report card:

Layla: But you did so good.

Maya: I got four excellent's ... But I didn't get any medals.

Layla: [To me] You need to get an excellent in everything to get a medal, and so she beats herself up if she doesn't get a medal. She has such high expectations for herself, and it's good to have high expectations, but you don't have to push yourself so hard Maya. I'm so proud of you for doing so good and for trying.

Maya: [Sighing] But it sucks.

Later, I wave goodbye and promise to see them in Tree Town for Maya's skating exhibition next week. I close the door with a heavy heart and make duaa for Allah (SWT) to guide and bless them and for Maya's skating exhibition to be a joyful time for all.

Retellings
"We learned to appreciate life and our family a little bit more" (Layla, Summer 2016)

Living alongside Maya and Layla as they mourned the death of Maya's Tata (Allah yirhama), as well as transcribing and listening to our conversations during their process of learning to live in different ways in the wake of her loss, has been an incredibly emotional experience for me. Maya's special relationship with her Tata reminds me of my relationship with Sittee (Allah yirhama), and my heart aches at the profound pain Maya feels. Throughout our conversations, I would revisit my memories alongside Maya's Tata (Allah yirhama)—the most recent being when Maya, Layla, and I talked on the eve of her surgery and listening to the part where I exclaim "Assalamu Alaikum Hajji!" and her quiet response. During their process of mourning and learning to live in new ways with their stories of Maya's Tata, I would also revisit my stories of Jiddee and Yehia (Allah yirhamun) often.

Maya's tearful comment that "everything sucks" in the months following her Tata's death (Allah yirhama) prompted me to be cautious about asking about her Tata. I wanted to be respectful of Maya's mourning process. However, I later discovered that in the spring of 2016, Maya wrote the following passage in her journal: "I'm back ... It's been a long time since I wrote in this journal. I stopped writing because my Tata left us last year. It really hurt, and I really miss her a lot but I'm staying strong."

Later, in the fall of 2016, a few weeks into Maya's grade seven year, Maya opened up about her deep pain over her Tata's (Allah yirhama) passing. In my home, I had asked Maya and Layla to construct annals of their experiences in a form similar to cardiographs so that the emotional highs and lows of their lives could be visually represented. I was surprised to see that much of their annals looked almost like continuous highs, with the exception of a deep dip in both their annals:

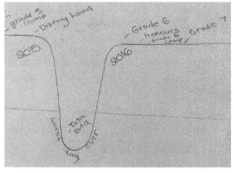

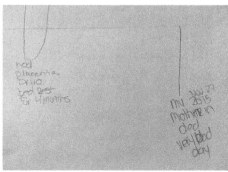

Top: Part of Maya's Annal   Bottom: Part of Layla's Annal

Me: Wow, you both have a lot of highs Alhamdulillah.

Maya: Yeah, all of these are highs, until Tata passed away.

Layla: Alhamdulillah, there was good and bad in that though.

Maya: There was no good in it.

Layla: No, there was good and bad that came from it Maya. She's at rest and isn't suffering anymore, and we became closer with you guys because of it, right?

Maya: Yeah.

Layla: We learned to appreciate life and our family a little bit more. So Subhan Allah, there was good and bad that came from it.

Reading their words, I am awed by Maya's and Layla's strength and vulnerability in sharing their profound pain in the midst of mourning. I think of how Layla encouraged me to visit the graves of my loved ones as a way to encourage a sense of peace and of how she framed these visits as *wajib* in honouring loved ones who have passed. In the winter of 2017, I visited Jidee's and Yehia's (Allah yirhamun) graves for the first time and stood for a long time talking to them. Layla and Maya taught me that although it is painful to remember our loved ones who have passed, it is important for me to still be in conversation with them and to fulfill my *wajib* to them.

Rooting Beginning (and Growing) Stories Alongside Layla and Maya – Summer 2016

Tired but excited, I sip my much-needed cup of coffee as I wait for Maya and Layla to join me. Seated at a booth far away from the entrance of the restaurant, I text Layla that I am here for our lunch date but to please take her time and drive safely. I cradle the cup of surprisingly good coffee as I think about the morning I have had. Encouraging Hannah, Yehia, and Noor to have breakfast and then help clean the house is always challenging, but doing so after Hannah's continuous night waking was especially difficult today. Wissam had returned from a month of visiting with his family in Lebanon a few weeks ago, and his departure and arrival have meant that Hannah's routine—a routine that she particularly needs as a child with ASD—has been severely disrupted. We are in the process of trying to return to a regularish routine, but it seems that routines are easier to break than they are to recreate. Wissam felt guilty that his trip contributed to our collective sleep deprivation, but I reminded him that he did not have much of a choice. If my dad were sick and oceans away, I, too, would be on the next flight to see him.

I notice Layla and Maya smilingly approaching me. Although we have enjoyed Maya's skating exhibition, a water park play date, and a Ramadan meal and sleepover since our last shared conversation, I hug Maya and Layla and exclaim, "I miss you guys! It feels like forever ago that we had our last conversation together!" Layla laughs and says, "I know, Alhamdulillah we are all so busy, but I'm so happy to be here now!" I laughingly reply, "Me too." As we choose our appetizers, Maya shares her excitement about meeting new friends at "grade six camp" in June: "Four people from every school are in each group," but Layla interjects, "And they invited the three elementary schools." Maya continues, "Yeah, before grade seven, so we can all meet each other and hang out." Layla explains that in Tree Town, there are annual camps in grade five and six for students from the three elementary schools in town to become acquainted with one another before they all attend the same junior high school. Grade five camp is an overnight camping experience, and grade six camp is a day camp. Layla says, "My mom never let us sleep outside the house, but I wanted Maya to experience grade five camp."

I ask Layla why she thinks her mom did not want them to sleep outside the house:

Layla: I think she was super protective, but my mom doesn't really talk about why, like if you ask a question, she will answer, but we don't have any stories from my mom. You know? My dad is the talker, so the stories we know are from my dad.

Me: I wonder why that is. Have you ever tried to ask her?

Layla: No, we never really had that friendship with her in the beginning. We were never friends, but we are different as moms. We tell our kids we love them, sit and talk, like "How was your day?" We never had any of that. My dad was more like that for us.

Me: Where do you think that came from then, that desire to be like that with your kids?

Layla: Maybe from growing up here, I don't know. But not everyone is like that even in Lebanon. I just think my mom grew up like that. Her dad died young, and her mom had to be a young single mom. I think my mom was about seventeen when her dad died.

Me: My mom was around thirteen when her dad died, and it's hard for her to talk about her earlier years too.

Layla: Maybe they're not used to it because their moms just didn't have much time to sit and talk with them, especially as single moms. They were too busy trying to figure things out, getting their kids to school and work and trying to raise their kids, you know?

Pausing for a moment, Layla says, "And it was just so busy in our house; we had all of my dad's family living with us after they came from Lebanon and, we had The Ma7hal [an Arabic way of saying "the shop"] too." I smile, thinking Layla could be describing my childhood, and say, "Subhan Allah. We had that life, too." Layla says, "It was work, work, work ... we grew up in The Ma7hal and worked there when we got older." I laughingly respond, "Yup, us too." Maya makes us laugh when she says, "I remember growing up in my dad's ma7hal too, but I don't think my dad wants his kids to work there."

As we enjoy the unhealthiest dishes we could order, Layla talks about her uncertainty concerning a recent decision she made for her youngest daughter, Rema:

Layla: I'm feeling guilty about agreeing to repeat Rema's grade one year.

Me: But didn't you repeat grade one too, Layla?

Layla: Yeah, because I didn't speak English that well. I talked A3raby [the Arabic word for the Arabic language] all the time ... and now my kids can barely talk A3raby.

Me: It was the same for me in school too. I only spoke A3raby before kindergarten.

Layla: It's the worst, and our parents don't make it any better; they talk to them in English all the time, and I'll be like, "Talk to them in A3raby! What are you doing?"

Me: My parents are the same way [laughing]. But was it hard to make the decision to repeat Rema's grade one year because of your own experiences repeating grade one?

Layla: Well, they say you won't remember, and I do remember it. I remember the older kids saying, "Weren't you in class or in playschool with me?" People still remember and I didn't want that for Rema.

Over dessert, I share my discomfort at a new rule in Noor's Islamic school: girls in junior high must wear the hijab as part of their school uniform. "I teach Noor wearing hijab is a choice she can make out of deep faith, but what do they do? They force it." Layla responds:

Layla: My parents didn't even discuss the hijab when we were growing up. My mom didn't wear it until she was forty-five. When I wore it, my dad was so proud. I think he's proud that we did it without them ever saying anything about it. This generation and our parents' generation is so different though. I think my mom wore it out of a sense of "Ok, I'm now forty-five years old and maybe it's time." It's more of a cultural thing, whereas lots of these girls are doing it for the faith part, not the cultural part of it.

Maya: I'm going to do it before graduation.

Layla: Insha'Allah, you never know Maya. And it's funny that you say that now because remember not too long ago, you said you never want to wear it [laughing].

Maya: [Laughing] First of all, I was a brat back then. But I'm going to wear it one day anyways so maybe I should just start early.

Layla: But don't make your decision based on what you think you'll feel; it's day by day. Because it's a hard decision to put it on too, right? And thinking "I might as well just do it" might not be the best way to make a big decision [laughing].

Maya: [Laughing] But you know that hijabi figure skater Zahra Lari? She's my hero. I even wrote about her for school.

Layla: That's amazing. What made you write about her?

Maya: Because she's a hijabi sister who skates [everyone laughing]. And I love how she doesn't care what people think about her.

Retellings
"It was work, work, work" (Layla, Summer 2016)

Many of the stories Layla shared of her childhood experiences resonate with me. I think of how Layla said, "It was work, work, work ... we grew up in *The Ma7hal*." And remember how, during our first conversation in Tree Town, Layla said that her earliest memories were of being in *The Ma7hal* her parents still own: "We were there all the time, and I remember even when we weren't there because we used to live right behind *The Ma7hal*. My mom would use the back alley and bring us food back and forth, and we used to sneak away too, back and forth." I said, "I know what you mean; [for] us too, my dad's *ma7hal* is still a huge part of our lives." Layla replied, "And now our *ma7hal* in Tree Town is a big part of our lives, Subhan Allah." Maya echoed our experiences as *ma7hal* kids: "Yeah, I grew up in our *ma7hal*."

Another resonant moment for me was when in the fall of 2016, Layla explained some of the memories and events she had represented in her newly constructed annal:

Layla: One of my earliest memories is when my dad's family came [from Lebanon] to live with us in First Town. I was five, maybe.

Sara: I was in grade seven, so you were closer to seven, I think.

Me: Yeah, I was around ten years old when my dad's family came to live with us.

211

I felt another heady sense of resonance with Layla when she later explained how becoming a mother helped her to lovingly travel to her mom's worlds (Lugones):

> I feel like my mom was so busy with everyone all the time and that our relationships with her suffered because of it. We're close now, but she didn't have the time to be that close with us back then. She was so busy taking care of everyone else. It took us as adults, becoming moms, to realize that that's why my mom wasn't able to develop the kind of relationships we saw other moms and daughters developing. She really just didn't have the time for it! She was taking care of too many people, just think about it, nine people from my dad's side coming and living with us. And I think about what she went through, and I don't think I could've done it.

My mom and I became closer after I became a mom, and I think about how arrogantly I had perceived my mom's worlds growing up. I told Layla "my mom juggled our *ma7hal*, and so many people in our house when we were growing up; I don't know how she does everything she still does mash'Allah."

I think about learning to travel to my mom's worlds and about Layla describing gaining a more loving perception of her mom's worlds. Motherhood stories are rooted so deeply in us. Alongside our mothers' love and care for us, Layla and I have also learned about maternal selflessness and self-sacrifice, plotlines that are all too present in dominant stories of (good) motherhood. I think of Layla saying, "We have so much stuff going on, I honestly don't have time to take care of myself too," and of how I have been trying to negotiate parenting, school, and household responsibilities in the midst of sleepless nights. I think of our wonderment at how our mothers contended with so many responsibilities alongside raising us ... and I wonder if Layla and I have more in common with our moms than we realize.

"I'm worried that her generation is going to lose their A3raby" (Layla, Fall 2015)

I think back to when Layla, drawing upon her experiences of repeating her grade one year, felt guilty for allowing Rema to repeat grade one. Although Layla said that she agreed to repeat Rema's grade one year because she believed it would "give her more time" to grow socially and academically, Layla repeatedly expressed her discomfort at the thought of Rema experiencing the embarrassment Layla felt as a result of repeating grade one. In the fall of 2016, as we discussed the annals Maya and Layla had just composed, Layla described repeating grade one as "a bad time in [her] life":

> Layla: A bad time in my life was getting put back in grade one. I think I didn't feel bad at the time, but then when I was older, thinking "I went to school with these kids and now I'm with these younger kids, how embarrassing." I was always the oldest in class.

> Maya: But Rema's age is really close to the rest of the grade one's.

> Layla: I know it wasn't that big of a deal, but it's just me, some self-esteem stuff, right?

Earlier, in the fall of 2015, Layla explained that she repeated her grade one year because she only spoke A3raby at home before going to school:

> Layla: I got put back in grade 1 because I only talked A3raby before I got to school. And I remember getting special help, like going to another class; we used to always go with a teacher to another room and read and stuff like that.

> Me: I remember getting pulled out of class in grade one, too.

> Layla: I got pulled out of class all the time and I remember getting embarrassed, just hating it so much … it was just so embarrassing.

> Me: I know. You didn't have problems with English at school, did you Maya?

Maya: No, because I barely spoke A3raby.

Layla: I feel bad because I feel my kids don't speak A3raby as well as they should.

Layla elaborated on these feelings in a telephone conversation with me in the winter of 2016. Discussing her work alongside Syrian newcomer families in Tree Town, Layla said the following: "I'm worried that Maya's generation is going to lose their A3raby. I tell her, 'see how we talk to our grandparents and can help translate? Or when I went to the school and translated for [girl in school]? Or when I went to help Syrian families who came to Tree Town?' I want her to be able to do things like that when she's older." Later in our conversation, I began to get the sense that Layla's fears of her children losing A3raby are intricately connected to her memories of repeating grade one— memories Layla repeatedly described as "embarrassing." Although Layla attributes repeating grade one to her lack of proficiency in English, she worries that her children will experience a reverse hardship—experiencing embarrassment because of their lack of proficiency in A3raby:

Layla: Alhamdulillah, we have to be so grateful for our kids, like my biggest worry right now, Alhamdulillah, is just the A3raby, especially Maya. If she thinks it's not coming out of her mouth properly, she doesn't want to say it; she doesn't want to even try it because she's a perfectionist right? And unfortunately, when we're together, ninety percent of our talk is in English, right?

Me: Yeah, us too.

Layla: I don't want her to ever feel put down because I hear things like, "Oh, why don't they know how to speak A3raby?" It's not the end of the world or anything, but at the same time I just want her to have that card in her hand so that nobody ever puts her down and says, "Oh my God, you don't know A3raby?"

Layla discussed her efforts to help her children learn A3raby, including computer software, private lessons, and planning an upcoming trip to visit with relatives in Lebanon. I was reminded of how Layla encourages her children to pursue multiple activities and passions and also of the Toys R Us Room that she lovingly maintains for her children. I think about how I ensured that Noor and Yehia are well versed in swimming and skiing—activities I wish I could have participated in as a child. I think of Layla saying, "I wish for our daughters something different," and I wonder how often we try to mother in ways that shield our children from the challenges, disappointments, and/or embarrassments we experienced growing up.

"I just love my hijabi sisters!" (Maya, Summer 2016)

I think about how Layla cautioned Maya against donning the veil without thoughtful consideration: "Don't make your decision based on what you think you'll feel; it's day by day. Because it's a hard decision to put it on too, right?" Layla's comment takes me back to when in the fall of 2016, Layla said that shortly after giving birth to Maya, she decided to don the veil following a conversation she had with a close friend:

> She was just diagnosed with cancer. and I was like, "How are you laughing when you have cancer and you have two kids?" And she was like, "*Battikkul a3la Allah* [the Arabic phrase for "I put my faith and trust in Allah"] and wearing hijab is a part of it." And I'd go home and cry and think about it, and she was alive when I wore hijab, and it was because of her, how brave and amazing she was. But I'm glad I did it when I was young and innocent because I think that the older you get, the harder it is to put on.

Layla spoke about experiencing hardship in relation to her hijab soon after she donned it. Before she and Mahmoud eventually decided to move to Tree Town, Layla talked about living in Second Town, another small town in Alberta, for only three months: "We moved to Second Town and that was absolutely terrible. We lived there for only a few months; everyone called me Khalto and Sittoo and Hajji because I'm hijabi." I remember being surprised at Layla's words: "But I remember seeing lots of hijabis in Second Town when I went there a few years ago?" Layla responded, "Then maybe things have changed because when I was there, other people, *Muslims*, made fun of me for wearing it so young." Shaking my head, I said, "Subhan Allah. I can almost understand when people who don't know much about Islam give you a hard time about it, but it it's even more disturbing when other Muslims do it." Layla responded, "But Muna, that's the thing. A lot of people in Second Town didn't know much about Islam."

Layla's gentle rejoinder reminded me of how during our lunch conversation, Layla said, "This generation and our parents' generation is so different ... lots of these girls are [donning hijab] for the faith part, not the cultural part of it." Layla's words resonate with me because I remember how when I tried to wear the hijab in grade six and then again in grade eight, many relatives chided me for acting like a "*Khityara*" [an Arabic word for "old lady"]. For many of my relatives at that time, observing hijab was considered a cultural rather than faith-based practice that was reserved for elders in our communities. For my family and for Layla's family, however, inter- and cross-generational culture-based perceptions of hijab and other Islamic practices have shifted alongside advancements in literacy, increased availability of Islamic centres in Canada and around the globe, the advent of the Internet, and the unprecedented access to Islamic texts in many different languages.

Discussing the Summer Olympics of 2016, Maya, Layla, and I marvelled at young female athletes in hijabs representing multiple countries in multiple fields:

Me: Subhan Allah, our children are seeing women in hijabs doing amazing things like that, Alhamdulillah.

Layla: All over the world. And that it doesn't stop them from doing what they want to do. Maya knows it won't stop her from doing what she wants to do if she chooses to wear it.

Maya: I just love my hijabi sisters [everyone laughing].

I think of Maya choosing to write about Zahra Lari, a veiled Muslim figure skater, as her (s)hero for a school assignment, and I wonder if Maya sees a version of herself growing in the light that Zahra Lari casts for other Muslim girls and women?

Maya's charcoal art

Rooting Stories of Being and Becoming Alongside Maya and Layla—Fall 2016

"Alhamdulillah for Sara," I think as Maya, Layla, Noor, and I settle into our seats at my kitchen table. Yehia and Sara and Layla's younger children have already filled their plates with the snack foods spread across the table and just as we are about to follow suit, Hannah pulls my hand to indicate that she wants to go outside. Sara offers to sit outside with Hannah so that Layla, Maya, and I can talk. Listening to the sounds of Hannah playing outside, I say Alhamdulillah once again for Sara's friendship.

Layla and I talk about how busy things have been since Eid Al-Adha[27], and we then laugh at how Rema and Jamal convince Maya to spray the whipped topping intended for the strawberries straight into

27 These two Muslim festivals are celebrated to commemorate important events in the Islamic lunar calendar: Eid Al-Fitr is celebrated after the completion of the holy month of Ramadan, and, a few months later, Eid Al-Adha is celebrated after the completion of the annual Hajj pilgrimage during the holy month of Dhul Hijjah.

their mouths. Layla exclaims, "Oh my God, they're so embarrassing; that's the only way they like to eat it!" Still laughing, I ask Maya how the first few weeks of her grade seven year have been:

Maya: It's been pretty good, but I was not really excited the first day.

Layla: She was nervous.

Maya: Yeah, I was really nervous the first day.

Layla: And now?

Maya: I'm excited to go to school and don't like the long weekend.

Layla: And how about your old friends?

Maya: My old friends just went away from me, and I was like whatever.

Me: Really?

Maya: Yeah.

Layla: Because she was excited to see her other friends.

Maya: Yeah, they stopped talking to me. I say "Hi" to them, and they don't say "Hi" back.

Surprised, I ask Maya, "They weren't impressed that you were making new friends?" She replies, "I don't know. I don't know why. They don't tell me. They don't even text me anymore or anything. They just stopped talking to me." Layla interjects, "Maya made a lot of new friends from grade five and six camps and from skating; they [her old friends] kind of stuck together, but she made new friends." Maya exclaims, "Because I'm nice to everyone!"

Maya talks about how much she enjoys junior high school so far: "Learning to open my lock was crazy but fun [laughing]." She continues, "And there's a lot of different teachers, and I like that because if I don't like a teacher, I still have a lot more teachers. But I like all my teachers so far." Laughing, Maya continues, "On the first day [of school], I screamed at Ahmed [her older brother] "Hey twin!"

so loudly at the assembly, and he was like [unimpressed face]." Layla laughingly says, "He was like, 'Who are you? I don't know you [sarcastic tone].'" Maya continues talking about some of her junior high experiences:

> Maya: And all the girls from Ahmed's grade come and talk to me and I'm like, "I don't know you, but okay."
>
> Layla: They're maybe just trying to be nice.
>
> Maya: Like one time I was in class, and this girl in his grade walked by and was like, "I like that girl Maya," and I was thinking, "I don't even know who you are," but I was like [giving exaggerated thumbs up sign].
>
> Layla: [Laughing] It can be like that when you have an older brother that girls like. And Ahmed keeps an eye out for her too, like when this one kid wanted to hug her.
>
> Maya: Yeah, this boy from my class literally said, "Let me hug you so your brother can get mad," but I wouldn't let him hug me.
>
> Layla: And when Maya told Ahmed about it at home, Ahmed texted that kid and said, "Don't you ever do that again."
>
> Maya: And the next day, that boy was like, "I hate your brother; he's such an asshole."

Sara and Hannah join us at the table as I ask Maya and Layla to construct annals of their experiences as emotional highs and lows, as discussed earlier. As they compose their annals, Layla and Sara reminisce about their childhood:

> Layla: I have a lot of highs; wallah, we had a lot of good times.
>
> Sara: I remember thinking that we were so happy growing up.
>
> Layla: Yeah and I always tell my husband that I want my kids to feel the way that I felt growing up, like Rema tells everyone that her dad's the president.
>
> Me: The what [laughing]?

Layla: She tells everyone that her dad's the president [laughing]. I don't know of what, and I think, Subhan Allah, the way that kids see their dads and how important it is for them to be able to love and respect them.

Sharing parts of her annal later in our conversation, Maya says, "Some of the best times in my life were at my dad's *ma7hal*.... And I remember how me and Yasmeen [her childhood best friend], we were always at her dad's *ma7hal* ... and then we would go to the back of my dad's *ma7hal* and play all the time, every day." Layla and Maya discuss the deep valleys in both their annals after Maya's Tata's passing (Allah yirhama), and then Layla says, "We learned to appreciate life and our family a little bit more. So Subhan Allah, there was good and bad that came from it. Mahmoud changed because of it, with me; he's more appreciative because he sees how his dad is so sad over his mom Allah yirhama."

After two hours of conversation, Layla announces that they have to leave to visit with friends and family for Eid. Wishing each other "Eid Mubarak" (May you have a blessed Eid) again, Layla, Maya, Sara, and I hug and promise to see each other soon. I close the door, and my heart is singing Alhamdulillah for many blessings and for the love and joy that seem to blossom in Maya and Layla's presence.

Retellings
"I'm nice to everyone" (Maya, Multiple Conversations)

Although Maya said "I was like 'whatever'" in response to her being ignored by her childhood friends in the first few weeks of her grade seven year, she later said, in the winter of 2017, that she was hurt and confused by their treatment: "This year has been kind of hard because I would smile at my elementary friends in the hallways, and they wouldn't say anything. We used to be really close, and they would tell me their secrets, and I would tell them mine and now we barely even talk."

During a dinner conversation alongside Maya, Layla, and Sara in the fall of 2016, Layla shared stories of her changing friendships and of being considered part of "the popular group":

Maya: I guess I'm part of [using air quotes] "the popular group" this year.

Sara: What does it mean to be popular?

Maya: [Theatrical whisper] I don't know. Everyone says that I'm part of [using air quotes] "the popular group," but I'm like, "What? I don't get it" My elementary friends have all stayed friends, and I've moved on, but I'm still very nice to them.

Layla: But are they mad at you do you think?

Maya: Kind of.

Sara: And how does that make you feel?

Maya: [Shrugging] I'm just like, okay if they're mad at me just because I made new friends, whatever, that's okay.

Me: So you wanted a change and to hang out with different people at that point?

Maya: Yeah, Yasmeen was kind of changing, but two of them are way different than they used to be. Me and Jessica are still best friends because we're neighbours and both of us are figure skaters, and Yasmeen and me are best friends because we grew up together, and our families are really close, but these two other girls, they just want to party and hang out with boys and stuff. And this year they didn't make any new friends, but they tell me, "You're friends with everyone," and I'm like, "Because I'm nice to everyone."

Later, in the winter of 2017, Maya expressed her frustration at the term "the popular group" being replaced by the label "the it group" and "the plastics" to describe her group of friends. (This is a reference to the 2004 movie *Mean Girls*. In the movie, the "mean girls" were a group of pretty, popular girls labelled "the plastics.")

Maya: I'm friends with almost everyone at school and they know I joke in a funny way, and they know I'm not a mean girl and they don't take my jokes personally. I don't take it too far. But everyone calls me, and my friends "the it group" and ...

Layla: See, I don't like the label they gave you guys. Who came up with that name?

Maya: [She names a student in her school.]

Layla: But did your friends like that name? Were they happy with it? Or did somebody tell them that that's who they are?

Maya: No, they don't think of themselves as "the it girls" or anything. Other kids started calling us "the it group" and "the plastics" because all the girls I'm friends with are pretty and popular ... and everyone is like, "Oh, they're so mean," and I'm like, "No they're not, you don't even know them!" It's not fair.

In the winter of 2016, Maya shared the following wisdom after I asked her what advice she would give to other girls transitioning to grade seven: "Don't listen to other people's opinions about others. Like one of my friends, people would talk about how snobby she is, but she's so nice because I got to know her before I judged her. So get to know someone before you judge them."

As I (re)consider Maya's words, I wonder at the way she used air quotes at the labels "the popular group" and "the it group" to describe her new friends. I think of how often Maya has stressed that she's "nice to everyone" and cautioned against judging others before getting to know them. I think of how difficult negotiating her grade seven year must be for Maya, not only because of the way her long-time friends reacted after she made new friends, but also because of the way she and her new friends have been arrogantly perceived and labelled.

"We look like twins!" (Maya, Summer 2016)

I think about Maya's story of the boy in class wanting to hug her to annoy her older brother Ahmed and about how Maya confided in Ahmed about being made to feel uncomfortable. I know that Maya and Ahmed have a close relationship. Although Layla's comment during our conversation that "Ahmed keeps an eye out for her," might give the impression Ahmed monitors Maya at school, Layla later shares how she appreciates the ways Maya "helps to watch out for Ahmed too." In response, Maya spoke about how she makes sure that Ahmed gets to school and his classes on time.

Maya repeatedly laughed at her stories of/with Ahmed, including her theory, shared in winter 2016, that Ahmed got on the honour roll "because of his looks!" Layla replied, "I've got teachers telling me how good looking he is, and I'm like, 'Umm, he's thirteen,' and next year, they'll be in school together, so we'll see how that goes." Several months later, as we enjoyed iftar at Sara's home in the summer of 2016, Maya talked about looking forward to her grade seven year alongside her "twin":

> Maya: I think it'll be okay. Well, it's just that lots of people know me from skating and stuff and my brother, and the girls are so weird [laughing]. They literally try to follow me on Instagram and try to be my friend and I'm like "I don't know you."
>
> Me: He's adorable though; you can't blame them [laughing].
>
> Maya: We look like twins [laughing].

A few weeks later, as Maya, Layla, and I were preparing to wrap up our lunch conversations late in the summer of 2016, Layla encouraged Maya to share a recent experience that troubled her:

> Layla: Don't shut off the recorder yet Muna. Let Maya tell you about how she was upset because she felt like some girls were being her friend because of her older brother.
>
> Maya: Yeah, because everyone has a crush on Ahmed, like everyone! And now one girl is trying to talk to me. We were really good friends in grade three because people would bully her, and I would stick up for her and then in grade four she went to another school, and then in grade six she wanted to start talking again. And then I saw her on Ahmed's Instagram, and she would always write thing like "Hot." I was like, "What?"
>
> Layla: I told her that it will probably work both ways, where people will maybe talk to Ahmed to get closer to you and vice versa. Because lots of these girls are crushing on Ahmed and when they find out she's his sister, they'll try to get close to her. And I told her to be careful, like not to think everyone is using her, but to be careful.

In the fall of 2016, a few months into Maya's grade seven year, I asked Maya if she still feels like girls sometimes try to get close to her to try to get closer to Ahmed:

That was in the beginning of the year because there were a couple of girls who would just go after my brother right away. So after that, I felt like my friends sometimes talk to me just to go after Ahmed. But the girls I'm friends with now, they stay loyal to their girlfriends and aren't that obsessed about boys, and that's nice. And I know that a lot of people like me because of me, because I'm pretty chill [laughing]. I'm not stuck up and annoying. I just go with the flow, and I'm funny.

Although Maya loves Ahmed, she often worried that people would try to befriend her to get closer to her handsome older brother. However, the last time Maya spoke of her friends, she was confident she could make friends who liked her for her.

"Subhan Allah the way that kids see their Dads" (Layla, Summer 2016)

The adorable way that Rema tells other children that her dad is "the president" brings to mind the multiple times that Layla and Maya have shared their stories of Maya's dad, Mahmoud. During our conversation in the summer of 2016, Layla said that Mahmoud changed since Maya's Tata died: "With me, he's more appreciative because he sees how his dad is so sad over his mom Allah Yirhama." I am reminded how Mahmoud advised Layla to "just ignore" the judgments and comments from family members who were unimpressed with Maya's skating costumes and how Layla felt surprised, but supported, by his encouragement.

As we spoke on the phone in the winter of 2016, Layla shared stories of Mahmoud negotiating parenting a girl who is in the process of becoming a woman:

He made me laugh the other day. He was looking at the Visa bill and asked me, "What is all this stuff from Le Vie En Rose and Pink?" [Two retail stores that sell undergarments and lingerie]. And I was like, "It was stuff for Maya," and she was standing right there, and he was like, "Oh okay, yeah, get whatever you want Baba" [this an Arabic way of saying "my child"]. He doesn't want to hurt her; he's tougher on the boys, but with Maya he wants her to enjoy herself, you know? And she told him the other day, "Oh Baba, I got 91 percent on my test the other day," and he'll say, "Oh mash'Allah, I'm proud of you." She likes that encouragement from him and tries to make him proud.

A few weeks later, during a dinner conversation in Sara's home, Maya said, "I tell my dad about my marks, and he's always like 'Keep it up.' He knows I'm smart [laughing]."

In the winter of 2017, during a late-night conversation in Sara's home, Layla and Maya laughed at how Mahmoud jokingly intimidates boys who might be interested in his daughters:

Layla: Maya was sitting at a restaurant with a whole group of kids, girls and boys, and her dad didn't say anything. I was surprised actually because Mahmoud is the kind of guy who, if a kid goes to the ma7hal, will ask him, "Hey, do you know my daughter Maya?" and if he says yes, Mahmoud will say, "Okay, well don't talk to her" [laughing].

Maya: Yeah, every boy in my class, I tell him, "If you go to my dad's shop, don't tell him you know me" [laughing].

Layla: Yeah it's a joke now because even when they're really young, like for Rema, when a kid goes to his shop, he'll ask, "Do you know Rema? Don't talk to her." And the moms and dads will laugh and say, "Oh my God, your husband is so funny" [laughing].

After many seasons of inquiring alongside Layla and Maya, I think that Layla's belief that the father-daughter relationship is important stems from Layla's own love and respect for her dad. In the fall of 2015, Layla described her dad as "more understanding" and "modern" than many of her extended family members: "He wanted us get our driver's licenses and to finish school and get jobs; he got us cars as soon as we could drive." Later, in the summer of 2016, Layla shared that in her family, her dad was "the person who would sit with us and talk to us" and how Mahmoud, whose father was "tough," learned to appreciate her dad's style of parenting: "The way I grew up was so different than the way Mahmoud was raised; it was more of a learning approach rather than a tough one, and I feel like Mahmoud understands that, and he sees how we all respect my dad, and he tries to be like that too."

Although our inquiry centred around the experiences of Muslim mothers and daughters during this time of significant life transition, the stories Maya and Layla shared of their dads and the stories other co-inquirers shared of their (grand)fathers, brothers, husbands, and uncles make me wonder about the ways that male family members shape the lives and experiences of girls and women.

Rooting Transition Stories Alongside Maya and Layla— Fall 2016

I smile at Sara, Layla, and Maya as I open Layla's car door. Sliding into the back seat beside Maya, I laughingly say "Hurry Layla, let's go before they call me back!" Laughing, Layla drives away from my house and towards my favourite restaurant. When Layla, Sara, and Maya invited me out for lunch a few days ago, I had originally said, "Maybe we can have lunch at my house instead. Sunday afternoons are hard for me because Wissam usually gets home from work at around six in the evening." Noor heard me on the phone and offered, "Mama, you can go out with your friends. I'll look after Hannah." Tears welling my eyes at her thoughtfulness, I ask, "Are you sure Noor? Maya will be coming too, and I know you like hanging out with her." Noor relied, "It's okay. I can hang out with her another time insha'Allah." I admire her maturity and kindness as I hug Noor and say, "Thank you so much habibty."

As we look over the familiar menu, Maya reaches into her bag, hands me her journal and sketchbook, and says, "I wrote a few more things in my journal and made some charcoal and watercolour art." Sara, Layla, and I appreciate Maya's artwork:

Layla: She's very good at drawing and painting.

Sara: So talented ...

Me: It's beautiful Maya. What were you thinking about when you made this? [It is watercolour of a tree. This artistic work is displayed on the first page of this account.]

Maya: I just love trees and drawing them and the whole design and look of circles.

Layla: So you can maybe use it as a cover of your book. I feel bad that we're so busy, and Maya doesn't really have the time to make more of her art.

Maya: And I love this one [it is a watercolour of an elephant with a flower crown displayed earlier in this chapter] because I love elephants. And me and [neighbour and best friend] Jessica did this one together [it is watercolour of half a tree displayed on the last page of this chapter]. We each painted half of the same tree.

Me: I love them all Maya. They will look beautiful in our chapter insha'Allah.

Maya offers to read the last entry of her journal, and we listen as she reads with quiet confidence: "I'm in the second month of grade seven and I really like it. I've been doing pretty good from the last time I wrote. I don't think I've changed much, but I did get taller I guess. This year I was so happy for fall but it snowed early, but that's Canada for you." Smiling at Maya's words, I say, "I wonder if we can revisit that first entry you wrote—the one of your favourite things" We laugh as Maya edits the over-a-year-old list of her favourite things: "Oh my God, unicorns, rainbows, and bows? Nah [scratches them out], and I'm going to take out baseball and write basketball instead." She explains that she's now on her school's basketball team and is thinking of joining other school teams; she adds rugby and hockey to her list.

Maya's revised list of her favourite things

We discuss other changes Maya has experienced in her transition from elementary to junior high school, and she surprises me with a forward-looking story of being an orthodontist:

Me: So Maya, you said you don't think you've changed that much in the past year.

Layla: But you have. I feel like she's all about her friends, yes, but school is still very important to her. She's a go-getter. She's more mature and knows what she wants.

Maya: School is the most important thing, and that comes with being a braces person.

Me: A braces person?

Maya: Yeah, an orthodontist.

Layla: [Laughing] She watches these videos on root canals and how to do braces.

Maya: And wisdom teeth.

Layla: She's preparing herself for her future. The other day she was like, "Mama, look how they did this root canal!"

Maya: No, wisdom teeth. With a root canal, they drill the teeth. I love it. Anytime I see anyone with braces I'm like, "Let me see your teeth?" [laughing].

Later, after Maya shares how her relationships with her elementary school friends have changed, Layla mentions how it is sometimes hard to negotiate relationships with other moms. She shares a story of a relative being annoyed that her daughters' friends seem to really like hanging out with Maya:

Layla: That's not fair, like Maya wouldn't care if [the woman's daughter] hit it off with her friends. Sometimes family can be hard to deal with too.

Me: And I was just reading an article, Subhan Allah, about how important it is to teach our kids to be wary of emotional manipulators—people that don't want you to be friends with others and try to control you.

Layla: Yeah and there's a lot of that in our families.

Me: We were taught to be trusting and that it's okay if someone mistreats you when it's people in our families who aren't being kind; they love you, so it's okay.

Layla: Just suck it up.

Sara: Because you have to be respectful.

Me: It's not our place to not like it.

Layla: Yeah, exactly.

As we enjoy our meals, Layla and Maya share a story of a family friend who storied Maya's love of attending school sports games in an unsettling way:

Layla: So Maya and some girls went to watch the game, and Yasmeen's mom goes there and texts me, "Your daughter is not in the gym." So I texted Maya, "Where are you?"

Maya: I was at a friend's locker.

Layla: Because A3mto said she'd seen you with boys.

Maya: I'm with my friend at her locker, and these boys were following us and even asked us to sit with them, and I was like "No."

Layla: But Yasmeen's mom took it that these guys are hanging out with them, so she called me after the game, and I told her that Maya said that these boys were following her and she was like, "I was going to tell you but I wanted to see if she would tell you first."

Maya: I got really mad.

Layla: She was like, "Don't get mad at me, but your daughter doesn't really watch the game."

Maya: No duh. It's boring. We suck [laughing].

Layla: And I don't like that about A3rabs, like when they see a girl talking to boys, they think that there's something going on, and I don't like that. I used to talk to boys all the time, and they were just friends. My teacher's son used to drive me to work experience every day because I was like, "Hell no, I'm not walking all that way alone." And it's funny because my dad knew, but my uncles didn't know because they wouldn't like it.

I shake my head at Layla's words, and say, "So true, it's not fair." Layla continues:

You know, if someone doesn't accept her for who she is and she has to hide things, then they can just get lost. You know I have a friend that to this day, over ten years after she got married, still lies to her husband about being allowed to go to grad with one of the boys in her class. Why? This is me. You want me for who I am? Great. You don't? Hit the road Jack. This is how we live. I'm not going to hide or put on a lie for you.

Retellings
"Don't say or do this or that" (Maya, Summer 2016)

I re-read our words that day and think about the story Layla and Maya shared of the family friend who felt the need to make Layla aware of Maya's whereabouts during the game. I am still troubled by the way Yasmeen's mom arrogantly perceived (Lugones) Maya's actions, and I think of the many stories Maya and Layla shared of being judged by others—often by those who are closest to them. In saying, "Don't get mad at me, but your daughter doesn't really watch the game," Yasmeen's mom, who Layla considers one of her closest friends, knew that she was insinuating much more than Maya's lack of interest in watching a sports game. For Layla, her words "were a slap in the face" because she was insinuating that Maya was more interested in hanging out with boys than watching the game. As a Muslim and Arab woman who knows the cultural and religious implications of insinuating that a girl of Muslim and Arab heritage is not being truthful about her relationship with boys, Yasmeen's mom knew that her words would be hurtful, but she nonetheless expressed her disapproval. Later, in the winter of 2017, Maya tearfully shared her pain at Yasmeen's mom's arrogant perception of her actions: "She said that I always hang out with boys, but my own brother who goes to school with me said that's not true!"

In the summer of 2015, during our first conversation in Tree Town, Maya and Layla shared another story of feeling judged. As we conversed, I laughed as Maya and Noor posed for a selfie. Layla incredulously asked, "Are you guys taking a selfie while we're talking?" Noor nonchalantly responded, "Yeah, I'm posting it on Snapchat." Maya added, "Mama, I just downloaded Snapchat." Layla replied, "Remember what A3mo did when you got Vine?" Maya responded, "Yeah, he's so annoying." Layla and Maya explained:

Maya: So I posted a video of Jamal saying, "Heyy Girlll!" on my Vine [laughing].

Layla: And her uncle must've seen it and he called Mahmoud, and was like, "Mahmoud, did you see what your daughter is doing?"

Me: For God's sake, our girls are so policed.

Layla: I know.

Because of their experiences with Maya's Vine being policed by her uncle, Layla felt it was important to remind Maya to be careful with her activities on social media.

As we engaged in inquiry, I started to get a heady sense that Maya was not the only one who felt policed by others' arrogant perceptions (Lugones)—Layla often felt the same way. Layla and Maya shared the following story in the summer of 2016:

Layla: I just told [a female relative] "I'm going to come get her from your house, because we have an appointment to do Maya's eyebrows," and she was like, "Why are you taking her to do them? She's still so young!" ... like *calm down*, it's not a big deal.

Maya: She [the relative] is so "Don't say or do this or that." It's so annoying.

231

The stories Layla and Maya shared of feeling policed by others' judgments resonate profoundly with my experiences of feeling judged as a girl, woman, and mother. I think of the countless times I have been told by those closest to me why something I do or say or that my children do or say is not appropriate. I think of how Layla and I discussed being raised to be quietly respectful and tolerant of loved ones who try to 'advise' us, even if their 'lessons' are unfair and hurtful. Although we were both annoyed with these early stories, they are deeply rooted in us. Contemplating the many arrogant perceptions Maya, Layla, my children, and I have experienced, and will likely continue to experience, I think about how we can continue to disrupt these stories in ways that affirm our right to speak, act, and live in ways *we* deem appropriate, even if – maybe especially when – these hurtful judgments come from loved ones.

"I can do anything" (Maya, Winter 2016)

I smile as I think of Maya updating her list of favourite things in her journal and of confidently expressing her dreams of becoming an orthodontist. Throughout our inquiry, I have admired Maya's quiet confidence, her passionate defence of the people she loves, and her ability to speak her mind. Maya has often shared her love of reading, writing, drawing, painting, skating, school, and sports, and I have admired how she expresses her belief that she is good at the activities she loves. I think I admire Maya's confidence most because as a middle-aged woman and mother, I still find it difficult to have confidence in myself and my abilities.

In the winter of 2016, Layla expressed her admiration of Maya's love of learning, and Maya responded with her unique way of speaking with confidence, humour, and thoughtfulness:

Layla: She does so good in school, and I like that she cares and that she loves learning.

Maya: At recess, I act funny because I'm obviously a funny person [laughing], and when I make a joke, everybody laughs and it's nice because I don't want to be that serious person who's annoying and controlling. But in class when I need to listen, I listen.

During our conversation, I was reminded of Maya becoming more confident that her friends "like [her] because of [her]" after she initially feared that some girls try to get close to her brother Ahmed by befriending her. I asked Maya what advice she would give other girls transitioning into adolescence: "Don't try to be someone else. I know this one girl who tries to be like other people, and lots of people call her fake. Like you might think this girl is so great and try to be like her, but she's actually not who you think she was, and less people will want to talk to you and you won't have many friends. You just have to be yourself basically."

Later, as we enjoyed dinner in Sara's home, Maya talked about feeling more confident than ever: "I can do anything. I can clean for myself. I can get a job for myself. I'm independent." I think of Maya resisting the single story of being part of "the it group" by repeatedly emphasizing, "I'm nice to everyone," and I am reminded of the conversation Layla and I shared over the phone in the winter of 2016. Layla expresses her love and pride in Maya, and then shares the changes she has noticed in Maya during her transition into adolescence: "I feel like she's gotten more kind and more understanding of where I'm coming from; she's also helping me out more, and she's just even a better person. I'm so proud of her. She knows what she wants, and she's a good student and a good person mash'Allah."

I marvel at Maya's ability to maintain her confidence and humour amid the ongoing arrogant perceptions of others, and I remember the wisdom that Layla shared during that conversation: "I want my kids to *feel* my love and support. They already have enough to deal with without me adding more. They need to see their mom supporting them and telling them that they're awesome and that they can do it. So that's what I try to do for them." I think of how Maya and Layla taught me how important it is for me to regularly express my belief in, love and support for, my children because one of my duaas as a mother is for Noor, Yehia, and Hannah to confidently believe in themselves and say, "I can do anything."

"This is how we live. I'm not going to hide or put on a lie for you" (Layla, Fall 2016)

As I continue to admire Maya's confidence and Layla's loving support of Maya, I am reminded of Layla's assertion: "This is how we live. I'm not going to hide or put on a lie for you." Layla's belief that it is important to live unabashedly was elucidated during a conversation we had in the winter of 2016. She discussed her fears of her children being judged because of their lack of proficiency in the Arabic language and/ or Islamic scholarship:

> But then I think about it like, okay yeah we don't have the A3raby and all the knowledge when it comes to Islam, but I feel like we're *living* our faith. I live in a way that shows that I'm not ashamed of being Muslim, especially here where I was the first woman to wear hijab. And even with helping Syrian families in town, I try to help in whatever way I can. Allah gave me that chance, Alhamdulillah.

Layla's words bring to mind the countless times I have been alongside her as she *lives* her beliefs. During a 2016 lunch conversation, Layla interrupted Maya's story when she felt that Maya was being judgmental of another girl: "Maya, it's not nice to talk about other people like that. There's going to be a day when people talk about you, and you don't want that."

I smile and think of Layla living her beliefs, even when she would rather not. In the winter of 2016, Layla spoke of her recent experiences with her swimming instructor, laughingly saying, "She pushes me too hard." Likely noticing my surprised look, Layla explained that a summertime scare motivated her to register in private swimming lessons:

> Layla: We were on our boat, and I really wanted to try to go on the tube, and Mahmoud was like, "Just put a lifejacket on and go. What's the worst that can happen?" And so I went on, but nobody told me not to put too much weight in the front and I did, so I started to panic and got scared and flipped into the water. And everybody started screaming! But then I calmed down and said, "Okay, this life jacket is going to work." And so I kept telling myself to stay calm, and Mahmoud was yelling out,

"Layla, you're going to be fine! You just have to relax!" But I think it didn't take me long to calm down.

Maya: At first when you fell, you were scared, but Baba was coming and you were like [making calm face], and Rema was screaming!

Layla: Subhan Allah, when you hear your kid screaming, you calm down. She was so scared. When I fell, I couldn't figure out what to do, so I just told myself, "Don't move because the lifejacket will make me float." So anyway, when I went back to the beach, I was soaking wet and still shaking, and Rema was still so scared and was like, "Oh my God, are you okay Mama?" And I was trying to sound calm, and was like, "Rema, look at me, I'm fine!" And inside I was like, "Alhamdulillah, Alhamdulillah, Alhamdulillah!"

Maya: Mama, see what happens is, if something scares you once, it takes you a while to calm down, like if a big dog is chasing you, you will still be scared even after it's gone.

Layla: Yeah, and you know, everything happens for a reason and maybe I needed to do something about my fear of being in the water.

Although Layla could have chosen to stay away from large bodies of water, she instead decided that she needed to "do something" about her fears because "everything happens for a reason" and registered in private swimming lessons. Smiling as I type this, I marvel at Layla's courage and at the rich curriculum she is composing alongside Maya, Ahmed, Adam, Rema, and Jamal as she lives her beliefs and faces her fears.

Epilogue: Nurturing Stories of Growth Alongside Layla and Maya—Winter 2017

Carrying a tray of Tim Horton's coffee drinks, I walk into Sara's house and laughingly say, "I'm so happy to be here right now." I had just put Hannah down for bed when I received a text from Sara on our shared WhatsApp group with Layla: "Hey, we're going to be hanging out at my house tonight if you can come over." I replied, "I'd love to. I'll pick the Tims' [coffee] up." About a half hour later, at close to 10 p.m., Maya and Layla rush through the door, with Layla exclaiming, "Sorry we're late! It took us forever to get away!"

As we settle into the living room couches with plates of snacks, Layla and Maya make me laugh as I try to talk about our research journey:

> Me: I was thinking about how this is one of our last research conversations.
>
> Layla: I was thinking the other day about how bad I feel that you have to go back and listen to these conversations again [laughing]. Maya, can you get closer to A3mto Muna's phone so she can hear you later?
>
> Maya: Want to listen to me chew A3mto Muna? [laughing as she chews near the phone].
>
> Layla: [Laughing] This girl is so not me. She's social, but she's so sarcastic too.

Still laughing, I try again:

> Me: [Laughing] Maya, remind me of the advice you gave to girls transitioning into grade seven from the last time we talked.
>
> Maya: I think I said, "Be yourself" ... and something like, "Don't let other people choose your friends."
>
> Me: I think you said, "Get to know someone before you judge them."
>
> Maya: Yeah, because "the it girls" are all my friends, and they're really nice. And I think I'd tell them that I was really nervous and worried for nothing, like you expect things to be like the movies, and it's not like that. You have more freedom, and you can talk to more people and make new friends, like if someone isn't working out for you as a friend, then you can get closer to someone else.

Layla compliments Maya on her advice to other girls and then offers advice to other mothers during their daughters' transitions into adolescence:

I would tell mothers that their daughters should have more freedom but that you still have to guide them. Their bodies are changing; their thoughts are changing. You don't always want to be saying "No, no, no, and *haram* [the Arabic word for "forbidden"], *haram*, *haram*." Let them live and have fun too. I really try to be fair with Maya; she's so good, and she cares about school. So why would I say "No" to everything that she wants? Why would I tell her "stay at home" while I'm dropping her brothers off to have fun with their friends? It doesn't make sense. It's not fair to let Ahmed do what he wants, so I expect the same things from them both. And that's where we sometimes go wrong in our community. We say that boys will be okay no matter what and [that] girls need to be protected. And that's not fair. So I would tell moms to be fair and expect the same things from their children.

With Layla's powerful words still echoing in the spaces around us, I check the time and am surprised to discover that it's past midnight. Promising to see each other soon, we leave Sara's house with hugs and more laughter. Getting into my car, I say "Alhamdulillah" once again for my relationships with Maya, Layla, and Sara. Driving back home along the familiar snowy roads, my heart dreams of spring.

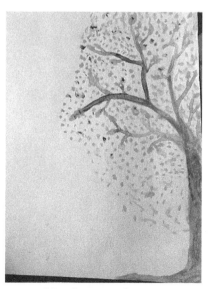

Maya's watercolour art

Growing Forward ... and Rooting Resonant Threads

I sit in quiet contemplation as I stare at the empty screen; my fingers hovering above the keyboard. I find it hard yet sustaining to transition from the intimacy of inquiring alongside Rayyan, Safaa, Zahra, Ayesha, Maya, and Layla, to co-composing and negotiating research texts alongside them—work rooted in relationality. I feel a profound sense of responsibility preparing to write about what I see as some of the resonant threads flowing through our narrative accounts. How do I stay in relation with co-inquirers as I try to give a sense of the resonances between and among our diverse experiences? How do I honour and thoughtfully engage with the stories we live by, with, and in (Clandinin, "Engaging") in ways that make our unique and interconnected lives visible but do not somehow reinforce single stories of our experiences as Canadian Muslim females?

Looking across the narrative accounts that I composed alongside co-inquirers, several resonant threads "that echoed and reverberated across" (Clandinin et al., *Reverberations* 14) the stories we live *by*, *with*, and *in* were made visible. In the following chapters, I explore three threads echoing across the stories we lived, shared, and inquired into alongside each other: composing our lives in the midst of arrogant perceptions; planting, living, and growing stories of relational resistance; and imaginatively composing our lives *in relation*. It is important to note that this research should not be used to make generalizations about the experiences of all Canadian Muslim girls and women, daughters, and mothers in the midst of life transitions. Rather, to understand our multilayered experiences, Safaa, Rayyan, Ayesha, Zahra, Layla, Maya, and I invite you to come alongside us and metaphorically lay the multiplicity of stories you live *by*, *with*, and *in* alongside the multiplicity of ours.

Chapter 6

Composing Our Lives in the Midst of Arrogant Perceptions

Once, a man was travelling with his son, and they had a donkey with them. The man decides to let his son ride the donkey and walk beside them. A bunch of people saw them, and said, "Oh look at the foolish man! He's walking instead of riding the donkey." So he decided to ask his son to get off the donkey, and now the son was walking as the man rode the donkey. And then a bunch of people saw them and said, "Oh look at that cruel man! He's sitting on the donkey as that boy walks!" So now the man is confused, and he got off and walked beside his son. So a bunch of people saw them and said, "Look at that stupid man! He's walking beside a useless donkey!" So then they both sat on the donkey and a bunch of people said, "Oh what a cruel man! That poor donkey is carrying too much weight." And then he decided to carry the donkey, and people were just hysterical about that! He was trying to please the people. But that's the point—no matter what you do, people will find something to talk about.

—Ayesha, Winter 2017

Reflecting upon coming alongside Safaa, Rayyan, Ayesha, Rayyan, Layla, and Maya over the last two years, I think about my assumption—born of experiential, embodied knowledge (Johnson)—that they would likely share stories of being made to feel judged and/or discriminated against as Muslim girls and women. And I did hear these stories. My heart hurt as Rayyan and Safaa shared the story of a woman approaching Rayyan to say "Don't worry, when you're eighteen, you won't have to wear that [hijab] anymore." I experienced pain upon hearing that Rayyan's eldest sister was told to "go home" by a belligerent man on a bus as she was returning home from school. I was disturbed by Safaa's story of her daughter Sadia being made to feel uncomfortable in class by her teacher's words about Muslim perpetrators of terror attacks. I shook my head in troubled indignation as Layla shared the story of an acquaintance's online opinion post, "*They* need to do something; their people [other Muslims] need to stop them [ISIS/terrorists]." I felt waves of sorrow when Ayesha and Zahra expressed how, in different ways and at different times, they had been made to feel the need to prove that they are "normal". Alongside mother co-inquirers, I puzzled about how to talk with our children during times of increased vitriol and rhetoric, particularly in the wake of several terror attacks[28] committed by those who identify as Muslim and during the 2015 and 2016 Canadian and American federal election cycles.

However, although I was expecting to hear stories of discrimination, I was surprised by their stories of feeling arrogantly perceived (Lugones) in many other ways, sometimes by those closest to them. I was surprised by my surprise, for I too have experienced multiple forms of arrogant perception. As a Muslim woman, mother, teacher, student, and scholar in a hijab, I, too, have experienced arrogant gazes perceiving me as not Canadian, Muslim, critical, scholarly, or "good" enough from within and across Muslim and other communities in Canada.

Although co-inquirers and I have all, in different ways, expressed our frustration with contending with multiple forms of arrogant perception, I was not wakeful to this deeply reverberating thread at first. Rather, it was a slow dawning of awareness following many months of inquiry alongside co-inquirers. The first time I puzzled with

---

28 However, terror attacks in Africa, the Middle East, and South Asia (which often target Muslims) do not typically provoke the international news coverage and/or global indignation that attacks committed in Western nations do. Also, although terror attacks committed by those who identify as Muslim are extensively discussed and covered in the West, the majority of attacks in the West are overwhelmingly committed by those who do not identify as Muslim (Global Research, "Muslims").

the idea of multiple forms of arrogant perception was in the winter of 2015. Deeply troubled by the story Rayyan and Safaa shared of a group of girls in Rayyan's Islamic school calling her younger sister, Marwa, "dark chocolate" in a derogatory way—and of her teacher's attempt to smooth over the racist intent behind their words—I wrote the following:

> Sitting with the stories Rayyan and Safaa shared today, I'm so troubled and disgusted at how lip service is paid to Muslims being one Ummah while racism and discrimination within Muslim communities is an often unacknowledged, silenced story. Friends and former students have shared countless stories of feeling discriminated against by other Muslims because of their race or cultural heritage or how "pious" (or not) others deem them to be, and in so many other ways.

As our inquiries alongside one another deepened over the seasons, mother and daughter co-inquirers repeatedly called my attention to the array of arrogant perceptions they face from other Muslims. I think of Layla's stories of being made to feel uncomfortable in Second Town because, as a woman in hijab, she was mockingly called Sittoo, Hajji, and Khalto by other Muslims. Rayyan, Zahra, and Maya also shared stories of contending with judgments or bullying by other Muslims girls and women. Rayyan's stories of experiences with racism, bullying, and discrimination included a deeply rooted story of being made to feel excluded by girls in her Islamic school kindergarten because her classmates did not approve of the traditional Somali lunches she brought from home. Later, in grade seven, Rayyan experienced verbal assault and physical intimidation from another girl at her Islamic school because of a perceived slight. At different times, Zahra shared stories of experiencing bullying, and of being storied as a bully, by long-time friends and classmates from her elementary Islamic school. For Maya, feeling judged and arrogantly perceived painfully stemmed from females within and across Muslim and other communities in Canada, including the mother of one of her best friends, a Muslim woman she has grown up referring to as A3mto.

Stories of "Good" Girls and Mothers

> We teach girls to be likeable, to be nice ... Many girls remain
> silent when abused because they want to be nice. Many girls spend
> too much time trying to be "nice" to people who do them harm ...
> This is the catastrophic consequence of likeability. We have a
> world full of women who are unable to exhale fully because they
> have for so long been conditioned to fold themselves into shapes to
> make themselves likeable.
>
> (Adichie, *Dear* 37)

A I reflect upon the stories of arrogant perceptions that co-inquirer
mothers, daughters, and I lived, shared, and inquired into alongside
each other, I wonder about some of the expectations of what/who/how
we *should* know/be/behave, some of the stories of "goodness," we
negotiated as Muslim females. I consider how, while there are countless
stories—constructed and enforced by different people, families, and
communities—of who can be deemed a "good" girl and mother, each
construction involves the creation and perpetuation of a single story
(Adichie, "Danger") of "goodness." Because these single stories can be
deeply rooted, those considered to be on the margins of, or outside, the
borders of constructions of "goodness" can be arrogantly perceived as
lacking it.

The following sections make visible how co-inquirers and I
experienced single stories of "goodness" as (Muslim) girls and mothers.
I place brackets around the word 'Muslim' not to bracket out the
centrality of our faith or identities as Muslim women, but to give a
more expansive sense of the multilayered stories of "goodness" we
negotiated; for, as our narrative accounts and the next sections
elucidate, we faced multiple forms stories of "goodness" from within
and across Muslim and other communities in Canada. For us, these
included any combination of the following constructions and
expectations of who/how/what we *should* be or how we should act be/
act/dress/know as (Muslim) girls and mothers: modest, deferential,
should (or should not) wear hijab, bilingual, nice, and selfless, among
many other single stories. However, considering the diversity of stories
co-inquirers shared of their experiences in relation to single stories of
"goodness," it is important to note that these stories are neither fixed
nor frozen; for, as Goodwin and Huppatz assert, the form and

expression of constructions of "goodness" are rooted in ever-shifting personal, cultural, societal, geographic, and temporal/generational narratives, contexts, and expectations. Weaving the ideas of several theorists and the stories mothers, daughters, and I lived, shared, and inquired into alongside each other, the following sections make visible a number of single stories of "good" (Muslim) girls and mothers that we experienced from within and across Muslim and other communities in Canada.

Good (Muslim) Girl Stories

good + girl.

rope, by Nayyirah Waheed

As I reconsider some of the stories of judgments and arrogant perceptions that Maya, Zahra, and Rayyan shared, I think of Brown and Gilligan's discussion of how girls "at the edge of adolescence" (91) often experience increased expectations to be "good," and begin to un-know their knowing in their efforts to "connect to the world of adult shoulds." In their five-year study alongside one hundred participants between the ages of seven and eighteen from a private school in Cleveland, Brown and Gilligan show how adolescence marks a "crossroads in women's development: a meeting between girl and woman, an intersection between psychological health and cultural regeneration, a watershed in women's psychology which affects both women and men" ("Meeting" 1). During this time period, the authors posit that "girls learn to separate what they know from what good girls should know, what they do from what good girls should do, what they feel and think from what nice girls should feel and think" ("Meeting" 91). As I sit with their words, however, I think about how Shweder et al. caution against constructing generalized understanding of continually evolving selves—and the diversity within and across continually evolving communities and cultures. They argue that considerable diversity can be found within and across cultural communities, including within and across families and familial practices. Brown and Gilligan's study was undertaken in a very different context—in a different time and place, and alongside a different group of girls— than this narrative inquiry.[29] However, their discussion of narratives of "goodness" nonetheless resonates with the stories mothers and daughters lived and shared alongside me.

As I re-read Brown and Gilligan's words more than twenty-five years after they published their work, I am struck by the thought that girls transitioning into adolescence continue to face expectations of "goodness." I think of Maya's stories of feeling policed in her use of social media by her uncle, policed in her skating costumes by a female relative, and policed in her interactions with boys by her best friend's mother. I recall how, in relation to the latter story, Layla said the following: "I don't like that about A3rabs, like when they see a girl talking to boys, they think that there's something going on. I used to talk to boys all the time, and they were just friends. My teacher's son used to drive me to work experience every day. And it's funny because my dad knew but my uncles didn't know because they wouldn't like it." Like Maya, Layla felt policed as a youth by the judgments and arrogant perceptions of *some* of her family members, for not all of the adults in Layla and Maya's lives held/hold the same single stories about what a "good" (Muslim) girl should know/be/do/say/feel/think.

For Zahra, expectations to be a "good" (Muslim) girl include her dad's "adult world of shoulds" in the form of his single stories of the ways Muslim girls and women should dress/act/think/be. As I think of Zahra's father telling her, "You're a woman now; you have to do this and that," in relation to his expectations that she don the hijab upon reaching puberty, I am reminded of Ali's discussion of how, in some families and communities, Muslim youth who become *baligh* "are

29 Responding to criticisms that participants of their research were socially advantaged because they all attended a private school, Brown and Gilligan ("Feminism") acknowledge the "privileges which American society offers to those born in favorable conditions" (12). However, they argue:

Although most of the girls attending Laurel School live in middle-class or upper middle-class families and the majority are white Americans of European descent, it is important to emphasize here that 20 percent of the girls in this study are from working-class families and are attending the school on scholarship, and 14 percent of the girls in the study are of color and are of African and Asian descent. In this group of girls, then, color is not necessarily associated with low social class, and neither color nor low social class is associated with educational advantage. (12)

responsible and held accountable for observing religious practices" (8). I also think of Bateson's words, "In many cultures, menarche is the time when girls … must become docile and demure … when they are lectured about necessary sacrifices" ("Full" 54).

Zahra's stories of feeling policed by the judgments and arrogant perceptions of her childhood Islamic school friends draw attention to how adults are not the only source of a "world of shoulds." Whereas Brown and Gilligan argue that adults can perpetuate the (single) story "that 'nice girls' are always calm, controlled, quiet … never cause a ruckus, are never noisy, bossy or aggressive, are not anxious and do not cause trouble" (61), I think about how Zahra was storied by her elementary school friends as a bully and bossy because of her outspokenness and assertiveness. I reflect upon how Zahra said she learned to only offer her opinions when asked, and I am reminded of Brown and Gilligan's discussion of "the tyranny of nice and kind" (88) as girls in the midst of transitioning into adolescence may learn to silence themselves and their knowing to maintain unhealthy relationships. I am using the word "unhealthy" in a Lugonian sense because thinking with the experiences Zahra shared of being single-storied by her childhood friends, Lugones' powerful words take on new meaning for me: "I am not a healthy being in the 'worlds' that construct me unplayful" (14). Sitting with these thoughts, I wonder when Zahra's elementary school friends began to correlate assertiveness (in girls) with bossiness and when the seeds of these stories began to take root and live in Zahra.

Thinking of Adichie's ("Danger") words about "how impressionable and vulnerable we are in the face of a story, particularly as children," my attention is drawn towards Rayyan's reticence to name herself as fun and beautiful because she did not want to seem "conceited":

Me: Okay, how would you describe yourself to someone you really trust?

Rayyan: Well …

Marwa: Maybe that you are fun, beautiful …

Rayyan: That's conceited!

Although Rayyan later described herself as "pretty," "kind," and "generous" after she was assured that her sister Marwa and I would not judge her for naming herself in complimentary ways, I continue to wonder when and how Rayyan learned to silence herself from describing the many beautiful facets of her being and becoming so as not to provoke judgments in others. However, as our narrative account made visible, Rayyan seemed to *grow* in confidence during her transition into adolescence. I wonder at her increased confidence amid multiple experiences related to bullying and judgments from female classmates, and I think of the many times that Rayyan's mother, Safaa, emphasized that "everybody is different" and reminded Rayyan of her right and responsibility to advocate for herself. Safaa's words remind me of Adichie's letter to a friend who had requested advice on raising her newborn daughter a feminist: "Teach her never to universalize her own standards and experiences. Teach her that her standards are for her alone, and not for other people. This is the only necessary form of humanity: the realization that difference is normal" (*Dear* 62). In continually asserting that "everyone is different," Safaa was teaching Rayyan that arrogant perceptions—both internal and external—are unfair because they smooth over personal, cultural, racial, generational, and other forms of difference. She was teaching Rayyan that "her standards are for her alone, and not for other people," just as Rayyan cannot use other people's standards as benchmarks with which to measure herself. Safaa's words draw my attention to how internal and external judgments of who can be deemed a "good" (Muslim) girl can obscure difference(s) and impose countless single stories of "goodness" from within and across Muslim and other communities in Canada. However, my attention is also drawn to how, with her love and gentle teaching, Safaa helped Rayyan to eschew multiple arrogant perceptions and grow her confidence.

Good (Muslim) Mother Stories

> The way to mother is not writ in the stars, the primordial soup, the
> collective unconscious, nor in our genes. Our predecessors
> followed a pattern very different from our own, and our
> descendants may hew to one that is no less different.
>
> (Thurer 334)

Although I gained a strong sense that girl co-inquirers faced single stories of "goodness" relatively early in our inquiry, my realization that Safaa, Ayesha, Layla, and I faced single stories as "good" (Muslim) mothers occurred in the latter seasons of this research, as I constructed narrative accounts alongside co-inquirers. Narratively inquiring alongside Layla into the many stories she shared of feeling arrogantly perceived as a mother by friends and extended family members created spaces whereby my resonant experiences in relation to "good" (single) stories of motherhood[30]—those of Safaa, Ayesha, and Layla—were made increasingly visible.

As I reflect upon the stories mother co-inquirers and I lived, shared, and inquired into alongside one another, I am drawn towards Austin and Carpenter's discussion of the cultural narrative of (good) mother-hood[31]:

> This narrative characterizes a mother as a person in an interdependent relationship where she is self-sacrificing, nurturing, selfless, emotional, compassionate, connected to nature, and gives efficient and effective attention to everyday tasks; she is always available to her children and assumes complete responsibility for them, she is unselfish and

---

30 My thinking and writing here draws upon the work of: Austin and Carpenter; Goodwin and Huppatz; Gore; O'Reilly; and Rich, "Of Women" (among others).

31 Austin and Carpenter explore the experiences of mothers of children diagnosed with Attention Deficit Hyperactivity Disorder (ADHD). Alongside participants, the authors trouble constructions of good mothers and argue that "the term good mother establishes the possibility of the bad mother and the detailed criteria of good mothering in themselves detail the criteria of bad mothering" (383).

supportive.... This narrative of the mother describes the taken for granted assumptions of what motherhood *is* and how it *should* be enacted. (380-381)

Sitting with Austin and Carpenter's words, I contemplate the myriad *shoulds* that co-inquirers and I experienced in relation to single stories of "good" (Muslim) mothers. I think of Layla's stories of feeling policed in her mothering by extended family and friends and how after seeing a picture of Maya in her skating costume, a female relative told Layla, "Hmm ... no comment" to convey her disapproval. Maya's best friend's mother also expressed her disapproval, and arrogant perception, of Maya's relationship with boys in a manner that, for Layla, felt like "a slap in the face." Safaa was also the recipient of unsolicited mothering advice by a female relative, who told her, "You really have to take your kids somewhere where they can learn their [Somali] culture"—an arrogant perception that Safaa rejected because, as she asserted, "Alhamdulillah, I feel like they are rich. They have enough culture. And, you know, Canadian culture has so many things that are good, like they are honest, polite and my kids have that, too."

Austin and Carpenter's inclusion of the words "selfless" and "self-sacrificing" in their discussion of the cultural narrative of (good) motherhood resonate with many of the stories mother co-inquirers and I lived, shared, and inquired into alongside one another. In our narrative account, inquiring alongside Layla into our stories of learning to re-story our relationships with our mothers, I wrote

As I think about learning to travel to my mom's worlds, and Layla describing gaining a more loving perception (Lugones) of her mom's worlds, I think about the stories of motherhood that are rooted so deeply in us. Alongside our mothers' love and care for us, we have also learned about maternal selflessness and self-sacrifice, plotlines that are all too present in dominant stories of (good) motherhood .... and I wonder if Layla and I have more in common with our moms than we realize.

Reflecting upon our stories, I think of how Lugones, drawing upon her relationship with her mother, shares the following:

There is something obviously wrong with the love that I was taught and something right with my failure to love my mother in this way.... There is something obviously wrong with my having been taught that love is consistent with abuse, consistent with arrogant perception. Notice that the love I was taught is the love that Frye (1933, 73) speaks of when she says "We can be taken in by this equation of servitude with love." (6)

Although Lugones later discusses how this view of her mother's efforts is itself a form of arrogant perception, her words make me wonder once again about plotlines of selflessness and self-sacrifice rooted in single stories of "good" motherhood. Sitting with these thoughts, I consider the busy-ness of mother co-inquirers and me— and other stories we lived and shared alongside one another that give a sense of these plotlines—as we composed our selves and lives over the past two years. I think of Safaa working as a medical practitioner and a multicultural consultant alongside raising six children, and of Ayesha learning to negotiate the intense demands of a new job while taking care of her daughters, parents, and siblings. I think of Layla saying, "We have so much stuff going on; I honestly don't have time to take care of myself too," and of how I repeatedly engaged in conversations alongside co-inquirers after sleepless nights with Hannah. Echoing Lugones, Adichie writes, "We teach girls that a large component of their ability to love is their ability to sacrifice their selves" (*Dear* 56), and I wonder about stories of good motherhood planted (and rooted) in Safaa, Ayesha, Layla, and me, and the stories we are planting alongside our children.

Although "what are regarded as good mothers change with time, fashion and context" (Goodwin and Huppatz 2), mothers have always been subject to close scrutiny by others. Goodwin and Huppatz emphasize, "The good mother appears differently in different settings – she is a nuanced and multiple form" (1) and that, "Above all, mother has been established as a normative construct, a mechanism through which women do what they 'should'" (4). Thinking about the innumerable *shoulds* we have faced as girls, women, daughters, and mothers, I also wonder about how we all have expressed annoyance at being arrogantly perceived—sadly, often by other women. However, recalling a conversation alongside Layla in which we admitted that we can also be arrogant perceivers, I am reminded of Lugones' words: "So, women who are perceived arrogantly can perceive other women arrogantly in their turn" (5).

I think about how we can also arrogantly perceive *ourselves* and our mothering practices. I am reminded of Goodwin and Huppatz' assertion that "the good mother is known as that formidable social construct placing pressure on women to conform to particular standards and ideals, against which they are judged and judge themselves" (1). And I think about Ayesha's frustration with herself because she felt inconsistent in her responses as a mother: "It's *us* and I hate that. What happens to us?" Ayesha also expressed, "I sometimes don't know how to help her" as she struggled to support Zahra in negotiating unhealthy relationships with friends. For Layla, her uncertainty and guilt about agreeing to repeat her youngest daughter Rema's grade one year are rooted in her fears that Rema may experience the embarrassment she experienced as a child who repeated the first grade. Layla's also worries that her children will experience embarrassment because of their lack of proficiency as Arabic language speakers: "I don't want her [Maya] to ever feel put down ... because I hear things like, 'Oh, why don't they know how to speak A3raby?' ... I just want her to have that card in her hand, so that nobody ever puts her down." Layla and Ayesha's stories remind me of Rich's[32] words about becoming a mother: "Soon I would begin to understand the full weight and burden of maternal guilt, that daily, nightly, hourly, *Am I doing what is right? Am I doing enough? Am I doing too much?*" (*Of Woman* 223). Like Ayesha and Layla, I often worry about my expectations for Noor and for myself and about how arrogant perceptions of who can be deemed a "good" (Muslim) girl and mother can stem from single stories within and across Muslim and other communities in Canada—stories planted and rooted deep within.

Continuing to reflect upon deeply rooted single stories of "good" (Muslim) mothers, I think of Safaa's repeated reassurances when I voiced my many uncertainties and worries. I recall when, expressing embarrassment at my lack of foresight in not advising Noor to practice opening her combination lock before the start of the school year, Safaa exclaimed, "Because she's your oldest ... I have experience!" With

---

32 Rich discusses her experiences with considering herself, at turns, a good or bad mother. Critiquing the countless, often paradoxical, expectations inherent in narratives of mothers and motherhood, Rich writes, "I can imagine the guilt of Everymother, because I have known it in myself" ("*Of Woman*" 223).

quiet confidence born of experiential, embodied knowing[33] as a Somalian Canadian Muslim woman who grew up in a large extended family in Kenya, Safaa repeatedly reminded me that "everybody is different" and how parents "like everything to be perfect [but] it's not." Reconsidering Safaa's words and how often mother co-inquirers and I spoke of high expectations for ourselves, Safaa, alongside Layla and Ayesha, help me to appreciate that motherhood—as a creative and continual work in progress—cannot be reduced to single stories of *shoulds* ... and I think about how "even when we cannot quiet outside detractors, we have to resist the urge to join them" (Gore 760).

33 Mickelson highlights the experiential knowledge mothers embody is often overlooked in discussions of "expert knowledge." She asserts that "Mothers' knowledge ... is heard 'en passant,' often listened to through a filter of pre-judgments by half-blocked ears" (135).

Chapter 7

Planting, Living, and Growing Stories of Relational Resistance

Through travelling to other people's "worlds"
we discover that there are "worlds"
in which those who are the
victims of arrogant perception are really
subjects, lively beings,
resistors, constructors of visions.

(Lugones 18)

If I didn't define myself for myself,
I would be crunched into other people's
fantasies for me and eaten alive.

(Lorde 137)

Although the previous chapter foregrounds some of the ways co-inquirers and I live in relation to multiple arrogant perceptions and single stories, we all, in many different ways, also live *in resistance* to countless single stories of what we should know/say, how we should act/think, and who we *should* be. The word "resist" stems from the Latin word *"resistere"* — "make a stand against, oppose" (Online Etymology Dictionary). Together, over time and within co-composed conversational spaces, co-inquirers and I shared and lived stories that troubled, challenged, and made "a stand against" a plethora of single stories. For, as Clandinin et al. assert,

Conversational spaces are not spaces to exchange and confirm already familiar understandings, but, rather, are characterized by emergent occasions for exploring other possible stories. They are relational spaces characterized by mutuality and possibility, where embodied, lived tensions become resources or triggers for telling and retelling stories. ("Reverberations" 18)

In a paper (wonderfully) titled 'Resistance and Insubordination,' Hilde Lindemann Nelson describes a process in which groups of people come together to resist dominant narratives. She explains that we all are part of many "found" communities—that is, communities of places within which we find ourselves. Examples of "found" communities can include families, neighbourhoods, places of employment, schools, and nations. However, drawing upon the work of Marilyn Friedman, Nelson discusses the transformative possibilities of communities of *choice*:

Rather than accept as binding the moral claims of the communities in which they find themselves, Friedman points out, on reaching adulthood women can form *radically different communities based on voluntary association*. She invokes both friendship and urban relationships as models for this sort of chosen community. Because such communities can focus "on people who are distributed throughout social and ethnic groupings and who do not themselves constitute a traditional community of place" (Friedman 290) and because women are a prime example of such a distributed group, chosen communities are particularly important for women. (my emphasis, Nelson 23)

Nelson's work invites me to (re)consider how, over the course of many seasons, Safaa, Rayyan, Ayesha, Zahra, Layla, and Maya and I inquired into many taken-for-granted single stories of "goodness" from within and across Muslim and other communities in Canada. I have become increasingly wakeful to how, through our resistance alongside one another, we encouraged and inspired one another to (re)live and (re)tell "morally self-defining narratives" (Nelson 24) within our (chosen) narrative inquiry communities. The following sections highlight the many ways we co-composed and lived stories of what I now appreciate as our *relational resistance*—that is, stories of resistance to countless stories of "goodness"—alongside each other as we composed our selves and lives over many seasons of inquiry.

Relationally Resisting "Good (Muslim) Girl" Stories

"We can't be afraid. We need to be honest and keep speaking up."

(Zahra, Summer 2015)

Although Brown and Gilligan describe girls transitioning into adolescence as learning to "un-know" what they know to maintain relationships, Maya, Zahra, and Rayyan all shared stories that for me highlight the ways they have *resisted* unhealthy relationships and single stories of "goodness." As her narrative account has elucidated, for Maya, being in relationship does not entail animating arrogant constructions of what/who a "good" (Muslim) girl should be/know/say/do. Maya shared a story of refusing to befriend a girl on Instagram who was "mean" to her brother, asserting, "I feel like I'm even more friendly this year, but I can be tough. If someone isn't nice to my family or friends, I can be tough." Supported by her mother Layla, Maya often spoke out in defence of herself and others who have been arrogantly perceived. Maya's stories of resisting "the popular group" and "the it group" labels others had imposed upon her and her friends remind me of her advice to other girls transitioning into adolescence: "Don't listen to other people's opinions about others. Get to know someone before you judge them." These stories, and others Maya shared and lived alongside me, give a sense of the many times she actively resisted multiple arrogant perceptions and single stories.

Inquiring alongside girl co-inquirers made me increasingly wakeful to the ways that silence(s) can be acts of resistance. Contrary to my assumption that Rayyan did not share many stories during our first research conversation because she is shy, she *chose* what to (not) share with me because we were just beginning to build a relationship and because I had not yet shared much with her. Based on this realization, I wrote the following:

In her quiet but profound way, Rayyan drew my attention to the importance of reciprocity in every interaction, every relationship. As she spoke, I recalled our first conversation and inwardly cringed ... because, in that moment, I realized that I hadn't really shared much about myself in the beginning, and yet had asked Rayyan to share a lot about herself. I now recognize that Rayyan shared what she felt were safe stories at first because we hadn't yet built a trusting relationship. All she knew of me was that I was a former teacher to her eldest sister Leila, and that her mom felt it was important to participate in this research. Over the course of this inquiry, Rayyan has repeatedly helped me to appreciate that, while she may be quiet at times, she is not shy ... and that she will take her time deciding if/what/when she will share. She too knows the value of building relationships and communities carefully.

Rayyan's quiet but profound insistence on the importance of reciprocity in our relationship brings to mind Brown's discussion of vulnerability: "Vulnerability is based on mutuality and requires boundaries and trust. It's not oversharing, it's not purging, it's not indiscriminate disclosure ... [it's] about sharing our feelings and our experiences with people who have earned the right to hear them" (45). The stories that Rayyan and I lived, shared, and inquired into alongside each other continue to teach me of my responsibility as a co-inquirer— and as a friend—to carefully co-compose relationships with mutual vulnerability.

I think about how Rayyan's belief in the importance of mutuality in relationships is intricately connected to her belief in the importance of the Two R's of interpersonal rights and responsibilities—a deeply rooted story that Safaa plants alongside her children in their familial curriculum-making (Huber et al., *Places*). After sharing the story of her eldest sister's experience of being verbally attacked and discriminated against on a bus, Rayyan stressed, "Not every Muslim is like what you see in the news. Even if you're not Muslim, you should always stand up for people." I think of how, after being arrogantly told by a woman, "Don't worry, when you're eighteen you won't have to wear that [hijab] anymore," Rayyan responded to the woman with silence (although Safaa responded to the woman by asserting that Rayyan *chose* her hijab), but then later emphasised to me: "I will never take it off; it's important to me as a Muslim." These stories, and others that Rayyan shared and lived alongside me, reveal her confidence in resisting unhealthy relationships, arrogant perceptions, and single stories of what she should say/know/think/do, and who she should be, in her transition into adolescence.

Zahra, however, reminds me that silence can be used and perceived in different ways. For Zahra, resisting single stories and arrogant perceptions was a process of learning when to speak up and when to allow her silence to speak. Belenky et al. discuss the "roar which lies on the other side of silence"[34] (4) when women own their voice and "use it to gain control over their lives." After trying multiple times to talk openly with long-time elementary school friends about their unhealthy relationships, Zahra learned to distance herself from them and to use silence as a way to avoid having her outspokenness and assertiveness perceived in unintended ways. However, Zahra also said she has learned to "stand up for [her]self" during her transition into adolescence: "If I'm nice to someone who's mean to me, it just gets worse. You have to show them, whoever it is, that it's not okay ... and that worked for me. Because I used to try to be nice to some of the people who were mean to me, and it wasn't good, so now I can be mean right back. I learned that I have to stand up for myself." During our conversation that day, alongside her mother Ayesha, I questioned Zahra about her use of the word "mean" to describe her defence of herself:

Me: But I wonder if you're being *mean* when you do that. You're standing up for yourself, which is very different from being mean.

Zahra: Yeah, I guess, just showing that this is the kind of quality that I want in my friendships and if you give me less, then I don't want that friendship anymore.

Although the painful experiences of being storied as a bully and bossy in elementary school still live in Zahra, she has learned to live in relation to these experiences in ways that create spaces for authentic relationships built upon mutual trust, care, and respect. This embodied

---

34 Belenky et al. borrow this powerful phrase from George Eliot, who in *Middlemarch* writes: "If we had a keen vision and feeling of all ordinary human life, it would be like hearing the grass grow and the squirrel's heart beat, and we should die of that roar which lies on the other side of silence" (Eliot 183).

knowledge was elucidated in Zahra's stories of becoming close to someone she feels she "can trust," and her advice to other girls transitioning into adolescence: "You need to find a good friend who you can talk to. A lot of things are going to change, the way you think will change, the way you see yourself will change. You're going to have other friends, but you need at least one good friend who you can *really* talk to."

I sit with Zahra's words and the story she shared of reassuring a friend who was facing arrogant perceptions of what others deemed to be negative changes in her personality: "It's not a bad thing that you've changed. It's normal and it's okay. You should do what makes you happy." Zahra's words and stories bring to mind Gilligan et al.'s discussion of how adolescent participants often question whether it was "better to respond to others and abandon themselves or to respond to themselves and abandon others?" (9). The authors continue: "The hopelessness of this question marked an impasse in female development, a point where the desire for relationship was sacrificed for the sake of goodness, or for survival" (9). Similar to Brown and Gilligan, Gilligan et al. contend that girls transitioning into adolescence often face a paradoxical puzzle. Do they move away from the possibility of being authentically in relationship for the sake of maintaining inauthentic, yet familiar, relationships? Although Zahra puzzled with this conundrum many times during our inquiry, she learned to reject unhealthy relationships in her transition into adolescence and chose to move towards the possibility of being authentically in relationship. Through learning to "stand up for [her]self" in different ways, including embracing the "roar which lies at the other side of silence," Zahra resisted countless arrogant perceptions and "good" (Muslim) girl single stories.

Our narrative accounts also made visible that Rayyan, Zahra, and Maya are supported in their resistance by Safaa, Ayesha, Layla, and other family, friends, and community members. Although seemingly disconnected from their stories of resistance, the junior high school locker stories that they all shared, for me, are an educative metaphor for how Rayyan, Zahra, and Maya found and/or co-created space(s) to be and to become amid multiple arrogant perceptions and single stories of "goodness." However, I continue to wonder at the ways that family, friends, teachers, and community members from within and across

Muslim and other communities in Canada can better support girls and youth in their being and becoming or, at the very least, try not to impose single stories about what a "good" (Muslim) girl should be/know/do/say/feel/think.

Relationally Resisting "Good (Muslim) Mother" Stories

every poem. here.
is an unwrite.
of all that has been written in me without. permission.

—Nayyirah Waheed

Austin and Carpenter assert, "By speaking back, speaking out and choosing who to speak to, mothers trouble and actively challenge the notion of what it is to be a good mother" (389). As we lived stories of resistance Safaa, Ayesha, Layla, and I, alongside our daughters, also faced arrogant perceptions and single stories about who we should be and what/how we should think/know/act as "good" (Muslim) mothers. However, as our narrative accounts made visible, we also lived alongside one another in ways that "trouble and actively challenge the notion of what it is to be a good mother." My conversation alongside Layla and Maya in the fall of 2015 draws attention to the ways mother and daughter live and co-compose stories of relational resistance:

> Maya: What I see on social media and stuff [related to arrogant perceptions of Muslims], I don't see any of that at school, [but] there's one kid, he's from ... I'm not sure where, but he was in my class because he was kept back a grade, so I see grade fivers saying mean things to him like, "Go back to your country!" and I'm like, "This *is* his country."

> Layla: Good for you. Good for you for speaking up though.

As one of a few Muslim women wearing hijab in a small town, Layla teaches her children to stand up for others. She teaches them that being in relation with people with diverse backgrounds, values, practices and beliefs—including diversity within and across Muslim communities— is a part of life: "I try to tell [Maya] that not all Muslims practice the same and that we don't have to do what everyone else is doing." Giving a sense of Layla's embodied knowledge as a woman in hijab, Layla mused, "It's so sad because people see us and make assumptions about our kids or the way we are as parents; the stereotypes are so strong sometimes." However, Layla repeatedly assured Maya that although wearing the hijab is a choice that must be carefully made with awareness of multiple considerations, "it won't stop her from doing what she wants to do if she chooses to wear it."

Alongside Maya, Layla also resists single stories that some extended family members and close friends hold of "good" (Muslim) girls and mothers. When Layla felt policed in her mothering by a female relative who did not approve of Maya's skating costumes, she creatively shifted boundaries and expectations through slightly altering Maya's skating costumes and through encouraging Maya to pursue her passions. Layla's comment in the winter of 2016 gives a sense of her frustration with countless *shoulds* in relation to covering/dressing expectations for "good" (Muslim) girls: "That's the problem with our kids; they can't participate in anything because of stuff like that, you know?" Reflecting on Layla's words, I recall a conversation in the fall of 2016 alongside Layla, Maya, and Layla's sister Sara about some of our unhealthy familial relationships:

> Layla: Yeah and there's a lot of that [emotional manipulation] in our families.
>
> Me: We were taught to be trusting and that it's okay if someone mistreats you when it's people in our families who aren't being kind. They love you so it's okay.
>
> Layla: Just suck it up.
>
> Sara: Because you have to be respectful.
>
> Me: It's not our place to not like it.
>
> Layla: Yeah, exactly.

By supporting Maya to pursue her passions in the face of arrogant perceptions from some extended family members, Layla resisted single stories of "good" (Muslim) girls and mothers, and eschewed the living and telling of cover stories: (Clandinin and Connelly, "Teacher"; Clandinin and Connelly, "Teachers'"): "If someone doesn't accept her for who she is and she has to hide things, then they can just get lost. This is how we live. I'm not going to hide or put on a lie for you." I also think of Layla's passionate assertion, "We're *living* our faith. I live in a way that shows that I'm not ashamed of being Muslim, especially here where I was the first woman to wear hijab," and I am struck by Layla's strength in resisting, alongside Maya, a quagmire of arrogant perceptions and single stories of what/how/who others deem they should know/act/think/do/be.

For Safaa, resisting arrogant perceptions and single stories—including single stories of "goodness"—is intertwined with her belief in the Two R's of rights and responsibilities: "Everybody has rights and responsibilities. If we are careful with those Two R's, then you are going to survive. You have rights *and* responsibilities. I tell them, "You don't allow anybody ever to take your rights away. *Anybody*. But make sure you also fulfill your own responsibilities. If you are careful with those Two R's, then you will be okay." Alongside her children and others, Safaa lives a curriculum of the profound right and responsibility to speak up and advocate for themselves and others: "I always tell my kids, 'Nobody knows what you want, you have to ask'". I think of how Safaa encouraged Rayyan to speak out against injustice in their stories of experiences with bullying, racism, and discrimination. I am also reminded of Safaa's stories of encouraging her children to advocate for prayer spaces in school, speaking up alongside her children to resist stereotypes when a teacher painfully single-storied Muslims as perpetrators of terror attacks, and against racism at her children's Islamic elementary school. Reflecting on Safaa's resistance of a female relative's unsolicited advice about the need to take her kids somewhere they can "learn their [Somali] culture," I think of how Safaa encouraged me to draw upon my knowledge when I was given unsolicited advice about Noor: "You know your daughter and what is best for your family." I think of the many times that Safaa urged me to advocate for myself and Hannah: "You can't be shy asking for supports Muna." I marvel at how Safaa not only resisted arrogant perceptions and single stories of "good" (Muslim) girls and mothers but also encouraged and supported Rayyan and others to actively speak out and resist them as well.

I contemplate our stories of relational resistance, and think about Ayesha resisting stories that a family member was trying to impose upon her:

Ayesha: And the funny thing is that instead of having a panic attack like I usually do, I was like, "Go ahead, I don't care" [in relation to an ultimatum that was given to her]. I don't know if it was my job, getting so much respect and attention. I mean, it was surreal to me to have the kind of treatment that they gave me. I don't know why they treated me like I am a very high person, just so good. I was never treated like that.

Me: You deserve to be treated like that.

Ayesha: I don't know. I just felt like ... not arrogant, but like I'm worth it.

In affirming that Ayesha deserves to be treated with respect, I was supporting and encouraging Ayesha's resistance to unhealthy relationships. Ayesha's words also bring to mind her resistance to Zahra being storied as a bully and bossy by elementary school friends. During a conversation in the fall of 2016, Ayesha attempted to remind her daughter that these stories were likely in response to Zahra's outspokenness and assertiveness:

Ayesha: But maybe you were like this [assertive and outspoken] even when you were younger?

Zahra: No ...

Ayesha: But your friends used to say that you're bossy.

Zahra: Because I *was* bossy. I was so mean. I was really a bully at that age.

Ayesha: I don't think that you were.

Me: You sharing that story of learning to stand up for yourself, that's so important. Because even me sometimes, even though I *know* that it's not okay, too often we teach girls to just be nice, not stand up for their rights ... just don't make a big deal about stuff.

Ayesha: Yeah, and something we don't do as much in teaching them to set boundaries, especially as women. We just give and give and give, and I guess not really demand anything in return or just the minimum? That's how our value is sometimes forgotten.

Although Zahra previously shunned the labels imposed upon her in elementary school because they were "lies," she later rejected this knowing by expressing, "I was really a bully at that age." However, Ayesha attempted to remind Zahra that it was likely her assertiveness and outspokenness that contributed to the stories of Zahra being bossy and a bully. She was trying to teach Zahra that "demand[ing]" mutual care and attentiveness in relationships is important, otherwise, "that's how our value is sometimes forgotten."

Through speaking and living stories of resistance alongside Zahra, Ayesha troubled single stories of "good" (Muslim) girls and mothers. Drawing upon her experiences growing up as an Afghan refugee in Pakistan who felt the weight of additional responsibilities as the eldest sister in her family, Ayesha did not want to burden Zahra as an eldest sister: "I don't want her to feel the responsibility to keep the house going, you know? She's not responsible for that. I don't want her to feel responsible; otherwise, she will be abused." At the time of writing this chapter, Ayesha had formed a support group for Muslim women who were recently separated or divorced. I think of Ayesha's wish to include details of stories that Zahra was uncomfortable with sharing in our narrative account: "What I want is for women who read ... this is something that could help someone ... I've already had women telling me that my story helped them." I am reminded of Rich's words: "The most notable fact that culture imprints on women is the sense of our limits. The most important thing one woman can do for another is to illuminate and expand her sense of actual possibilities ... Only when we can wish imaginatively for ourselves can we wish unfetteredly for our daughters" (*Of Woman* 246). Sitting with Rich's words and the stories Ayesha, Zahra, and I lived, shared and inquired into, I am inspired by Ayesha's courage in imaginatively composing and living stories of relational resistance to "good" (Muslim) girl and mother single stories in ways that created spaces for us to "wish unfetteredly" for ourselves, our daughters, and other Muslim women.

Reflecting upon how often co-inquirers and I felt arrogantly perceived—including by other Muslim women and girls—I am reminded of Lugones' discussion of "worlds" and "world"-travelling. Lugones asserts that "knowing other women's 'worlds' is part of knowing them and knowing them is part of loving them" (17). This idea brings to mind how Layla and I discussed learning to travel to our mothers' worlds with loving perception. Recognizing that "only when we have travelled to each other's 'worlds' are we fully subjects to each other" (17), Lugones asserts that loving perception is crucial for women, who can, depending upon the situation, be arrogantly perceived and/or arrogant perceivers: "We are fully dependent on each other for the possibility of being understood and without this understanding we are not intelligible, we do not make sense, we are not solid, visible, integrated; we are lacking. So travelling to each other's 'worlds' would enable us to *be* through loving each other" (Lugones 8). Through lovingly travelling to one another's worlds and expressing "disloyalty to arrogant perceivers, including the arrogant perceiver in ourselves, and to their constructions of women" (Lugones 18), co-inquirers and I have often create(d) spaces for ourselves, each other, and other women to resist arrogant perceptions and single stories. We create(d) spaces for ourselves and others to *be* ... and to become.

Chapter 8

Imaginatively Composing Our Lives ... *in relation*

> We practice the art of living in telling stories,
> whether spoken or written or imagined in secret,
> dreamed or planned, past or future. I have come to think
> of the composition of lives as an art form, and of families
> and communities as artful tales in progress.
>
> (Bateson, "Full" 22)

Bateson's discussion of life-making as an imaginative, ongoing composition resonates with the many ways that co-inquirers and I "have worked by improvisation, discovering the shape of our creation along the way, rather than pursuing a vision already defined" ("Composing" 1). Working from within a conceptualization of life-making as an active, imaginative, experiential, embodied, storied, and ongoing construction (Clandinin, "Engaging"), the following sections highlight how mother and daughter co-inquirers and I imaginatively composed our selves and lives *in relation* (Huber) to familial and intergenerational stories, and in the midst of multiple past and ongoing transitions.

Composing Lives *in relation* ... Amid Multiple Past and Ongoing Life Transitions

> I am a woman giving birth to myself.
>
> (Rich, *Of Woman* 184)

As I reconsider some of the stories of transitions that co-inquirers and I lived, shared, and inquired into over the last two years, I think about how when I first imagined this study, I foregrounded the girl co-inquirers' transitions into adolescence as *the* primary transition for co-inquirers. However, as I think about the many changes in our selves, our relationships, and the stories we lived *by*, *with*, and *in* over time, I am now wakeful to a multiplicity of ongoing transitions that co-inquirers and I experience(d). I am wakeful to how, while transitions into adolescence were/are undoubtedly periods of significant transition, we are always in the process of imaginatively composing our selves and lives *in relation* to countless people, places, and past and ongoing stories.

Carolyn Heilbrun conceptualized transitions as

> a threshold experience … providing to the actors involved the condition of liminality. The word 'limin' means 'threshold,' and to be in a state of liminality is to be poised upon uncertain ground, to be leaving one condition or country or self and entering upon another. But the most salient sign of liminality is its lack of clarity about exactly where one belongs and what one should be doing, or wants to be doing. (3)

For Heilbrun, liminal spaces of transitions are in-between spaces of uncertainty and unsteadiness, but also of imagination and possibility. She argues, "Women have always had a particularly close relationship to changeable terrain …. [however], when recognized, liminality offers women freedom to become themselves" (1). Over the last two years, co-inquirers and I have shared and lived many experiences of life transitions alongside one another. I think of Safaa leaving the only home she had known as a young child in Somalia to live with her father in Kenya and learning to speak several new languages during her transitions into a new home, school, community, and society. I think of how, leaving Kenya to travel to Canada as a newlywed, Safaa says she "*made* a family." I think of seeing Rayyan a few months ago, after her weeks-long stay in the hospital, and how she is learning to live in different ways in relation to a life-long medical diagnosis. I think of Ayesha's stories of war and displacement in Afghanistan and Pakistan amid her transition into adolescence, and the stories she (re)told and (re)lived about learning to compose her life in different ways as a refugee in Pakistan, as a newcomer to Canada, after many moves and job changes, and in the midst of separating from her husband. I think of the stories Zahra shared of learning to stand up for herself in the midst of unhealthy relationships with elementary school friends, and the stories she shared of learning to compose her life in new ways following her parents' separation, moving to new schools, and removing her hijab. I think of the stories Layla shared of negotiating multiple moves and periods of uncertainty, and of Layla's and Maya's strength and vulnerability in the midst of profound grief at the loss of Maya's grandmother. I think of how co-inquirers supported and sustained me as I learned of Hannah's diagnosis with ASD and how, together, we navigated many transitions over the last two years.

While our narrative accounts made visible the ways that co-inquirers and I are imaginatively composing our lives in the midst of multiple ongoing transitions, they also made visible moments and/or periods of liminality we all have experienced. As I reflect on some of the stories Safaa, Rayyan, Ayesha, Zahra, Layla, Maya, and I lived and shared of facing arrogant perceptions and single stories amid experiences of loss and grief, separation and divorce, illness, terror, and trauma, I think about the ways we (re)storied many of our transitions—some of which included moments and/or periods of profound uncertainty. I am reminded of how David Carr discusses the need for narrative coherence in our storied lives: "Our lives admit of sometimes more, sometimes less coherence; they hang together reasonably well, but they occasionally tend to fall apart. Coherence seems to be a need imposed on us whether we seek it or not. Things need to make sense. We feel the lack of sense when it goes missing" (97). However, although we sometimes experienced a lack of coherence in our life-making, we continued to imaginatively compose our lives in the midst of uncertainty and possibility (Heilbrun). Our laughter and playfulness, support and encouragement of one another, and continued growing, resisting, and (re)imagining alongside one another as we composed our selves amid multiple ongoing transitions bring to mind Carr's words: "The unity of sel[ves], not as an underlying identity but as a life that hangs together, is not a pregiven condition but an [imaginative and ongoing] achievement" (97).

Composing Lives *in relation* to Familial and Intergenerational Relationships and Stories

your novels.
the classic novels of a minutia. i have no interest in.
pale. in comparison to the novels of my world.
the novel of my mother.
the novels of my grandparents.
the articulate novels of how my people walk down a street.
the novels i have been reading my whole life.

"Classic" by Nayyirah Waheed

Through our inquiry, co-inquirers and I made visible the ways we have drawn upon our experiential, embodied knowing and the stories we live *by*, *with*, and *in* in composing lives and curriculum alongside others. For me, some of the most profound stories co-inquirers and I (re)told and (re)lived involved familial and intergenerational narratives—deeply rooted narratives that are continually (re)shaped by our living. Although many of the stories in previous chapters highlighted arrogant perceptions and single stories of some of our relatives, co-inquirers and I also lived and shared many stories of learning with, and from, our families and of feeling supported and sustained by our familial relationships.

In her uniquely poetic manner of speech, Safaa often shared familial, cultural, and intergenerational wisdoms with me. I think of how Safaa said, "You know, in my [Somali] culture we have a saying, 'We learn discrimination from our mothers' wombs' ... everyone is different, Subhan Allah," and think of the parenting advice she still draws upon:

> I think I was a teenager, and I admired my aunt and said, "Oh my God, I love you so much. I wish I could be like you." She was amazing, just very kind, leading with example; she raised great kids. She said, "You know what I made sure of in life? That they would be good people because Allah, when he asks me about my life, is not going to ask me what university they went to, or any of that. Allah will ask me about their manners and behaviour—for them to be good human beings is what I care for."

I also think of Safaa's stories of her relationship with her grandmother, whom she described as a "powerful," "strong," and "amazing" woman. Safaa's grandmother encouraged her to continue her studies and become a medical practitioner even as she cautioned Safaa about giving so much of herself that she would become *shirko* [shared]. These familial and intergenerational stories continue to live in Safaa and reverberate in her life-making alongside others.

Rayyan, Ayesha, Zahra, Layla, and Maya also shared many stories of intergenerational and familial relationships. I think of Rayyan's stories of her father and siblings and of looking forward to visiting with extended family, especially her grandmothers. I think of Ayesha's love and continued care for her parents and siblings, and her stories of her grandmother's love and wisdom. I think of Zahra's stories of her sisters, of looking forward to her aunts' weddings and of being her grandmother's "favourite." I think of Layla's stories of growing alongside her mom and dad, sisters, brothers, aunts, uncles, grandparents, and cousins for most of her childhood and of how she continues to compose her life alongside her extended family. I think of the stories Maya shared of being in the midst of family "all the time," and her relationships with her dad, brothers, sister, Aunt Sara, and her beloved Tata (Allah yirhama). These and other stories that co-inquirers and I shared give a sense of feeling loved, supported, and sustained by intergenerational and familial relationships.

(Re)considering some of the intergenerational narrative reverberations (Young) co-inquirers and I shared, lived, and inquired into alongside each other, I think about how the stories Ayesha shared of experiencing war and displacement continue to live in her and reverberate in her relationships, life-composing, and familial curriculum-making (Huber et al., *Places*) alongside her daughters and other family members. I am reminded of Zahra listening to her mother's stories of earlier experiences in Afghanistan and Pakistan for the first time with tear-filled, wide-eyed surprise but also how months after hearing some of Ayesha's stories of conflict and displacement for the first time, Zahra said, "I was like, 'Oh my God' [at first], but I could imagine it. I could imagine myself with her." Our narrative accounts made visible that co-inquirers and I often experience(d) home as places where we learn(ed) to travel to multiple familial and intergenerational worlds (Lugones) ... and where we learn(ed) to imaginatively compose our selves and our lives *in relation* to a multiplicity of familial and intergenerational narratives.

Composing Lives *in relation* to Our Faith and Each Other ... and Imagining Possibilities

For my daughter,
I want to draw our family tree,
on the soles of your feet.
that way you will have roots
wherever you choose to go.

—Key Ballah

Reverberating across our stories of being and becoming as Muslim girls and women are resonant threads of composing our lives *in relation*—including in relation to our faith. I think of Safaa repeatedly saying "Alhamdulillah, Allah makes it easy for me" and reminding me to make duaa in the face of hardship and uncertainty; Rayyan drawing upon her faith in her resistance to arrogant perceptions and single stories; Ayesha saying, "Alhamdulillah, whatever Allah has planned, it's good;" Zahra's weekly *halaqa* (an Arabic/Islamic term for a group gathering to discuss issues related to faith) alongside other Muslim youth, and women; Layla saying she *lives* her faith unabashedly; and Maya's stories of admiring women in hijab who "[don't] care what people think." However, although co-inquirers and I are guided and sustained by our faith, our narrative accounts have shown that, for us, composing our lives with faith is not a disembodied, passive process. As our stories and Ayesha's powerful words elucidate, "Faith is good for guidance, but you still actually have to find a way to make that happen. You also need to *do* something." The stories we (re)told and (re) lived made the many ways that co-inquirers and I are sustained and guided by our faith as we actively imagine forward-looking stories (Nelson).

Co-inquirers repeatedly taught me about imaginatively composing lives *in relation* as mothers and daughters. I think of Ayesha saying that it is important to "communicate with your child as much as possible, to empathize with them—that's the hardest part sometimes—but find out what it is that they're thinking and feeling, and encourage them to grow." I think of Safaa emphasizing, "But Muna, when we plant a seed in the ground, it won't go shooting straight up. Sometimes, it wants to go over here [gesturing to the right with her hands], and we have to say, 'No, not that way' and we nudge it over, away from that area that harms them. We need to be patient and help our children to grow in the right way insha'Allah." I continue to feel resonance with Layla expressing that she wants her children "to *feel* [her] love and support. They already have enough to deal with ... they need to see their mom supporting them and telling them that they're awesome and that they can do it." I think of Rayyan, drawing upon her familial knowledge of imaginatively composing her life *in relation*, emphasizing, "You should always stand up for other people." I am still inspired by Zahra saying, "I learned that I have to stand up for myself" and by Maya asserting, "I can do anything."

As I ponder the changes to the stories co-inquirers and I live(d) *by*, *with*, and *in* over time, I think of Greene's discussion of the importance of imagination in life composition: "Of all our cognitive capacities, imagination is the one that permits us to give credence to alternative realities" (3). I think of the ways we have imaginatively composed ourselves, lives, and forward-looking stories: Safaa repeatedly expressing her desire to pursue a master's degree; Rayyan wanting to become a teacher; Ayesha planning to continue leading a support group for women; Zahra's stories of wanting to become a forensic scientist; Layla planning to travel to Lebanon with her family and continuing to face her fears and learn to swim; and Maya continuing to skate and study videos of orthodontic practices. I think of our love and support for one another— especially the profound love between mother and daughter co-inquirers—and I am reminded of Rich's words, "Before sisterhood, there was the knowledge—transitory, fragmented, perhaps, but original and crucial—of mother-and-daughterhood" (*Of Woman* 225). As co-inquirers and I imagine forward, I sense that our life-making will continue to be imaginatively composed *in relation* ... to our faith, (chosen) families, embodied knowing, and each other.

(Re)Connecting Threads

> I am constantly being encouraged to pluck out some one
> aspect of myself and present this as the meaningful whole,
> eclipsing or denying the other parts of myself.
>
> (Lorde 120)

Although the resonant threads in the preceding three chapters were identified and discussed separately, they are indelibly interconnected and interwoven with one another and other threads in the tapestry of our life-making. Co-inquirers and I are always in the process of simultaneously composing lives in the midst of arrogant perceptions, living stories of relational resistance, and imaginatively composing lives *in relation*—amid many other threads of our being and becoming. We are always in the process of facing and resisting stories of who we are and who we should be as "good (Muslim) girls and mothers" as we compose our selves and lives with embodied knowing, faith, and imagination alongside family, friends, teachers, community members, and others in the myriad worlds we travel to and inhabit.

The stories Safaa, Rayyan, Ayesha, Zahra, Layla, Maya, and I (re) told and (re)lived alongside one another in this research do not and can not tell *the* single story of who we (and other Muslim females) are and who we are always in the process of becoming. However, they do provide insights into the multiplicity of stories we live *by*, *with*, and *in* and into the ways we—and perhaps other Muslim girls, women, children, youth, and families—can be supported in our life-making. Looking forward to the next chapter, I continue to think and wonder with the stories co-inquirers and I shared and lived together as I reflect upon my growing understandings of my research puzzle ... understandings rooted in two years of narratively inquiring alongside Safaa, Rayyan, Ayesha, Zahra, Layla, and Maya.

Chapter 9

(Re)telling Our (Own) Stories

> It is impossible to talk about the single story without talking about
> power ... How they are told, who tells them, when they're told, how
> many stories are told, are really dependent on power ...
> Power is the ability not just to tell the story of another person,
> but to make it the definitive story of that person.
>
> (Adichie, "Danger")

Reflecting back to when I first imagined this study, I think of my many wonderings about the experiences of second-generation Canadian Muslim girls and their mothers during the girls' transitions into adolescence. However, reading much of the available literature from Canada and around the world about the schooling-related experiences of Muslim girls, women, children, youth, and families gave me a discomforting sense that we are often not asked to participate in framing research questions, discussions, and understandings. I was also troubled by work that seemed to dichotomize Muslim[35] and Western[36] worlds, cultures, experiences, and beliefs. This view was especially evident in literature in which second-generation

---

35 As discussed in Chapter 1, Muslim individuals and communities are often written about in monolithic ways. The vast personal, familial, national, racial, linguistic, cultural, political, and theological diversity within and across Muslim communities (Aslan; Esposito and Mogahed; Niyozov; Ramji, "Creating"; "Variable") is often ignored.

36 This is often a reductionist perception of the multiplicity of worlds, cultures, experiences, and beliefs in the West.

Muslim children and youth, as well as subsequent ones, were positioned as bridges between their familial and school worlds, whose role it is to soothe tensions that arise amid (ongoing) clashes.

As I reviewed the literature, I also gained a strong sense that discussions of/about Muslim girl/womanhood often reduced us and our experiences to the hijab—an uncomfortable and exoticizing fixation with why we do or do not don it, how we negotiate expectations related to it, and what happens when we do or do not don it. Although this focus on hijab may, at times, assist educators and Muslim women in finding and/or creating spaces of increased understanding, it is also disturbingly narrow. Deeply perturbed by these and other social narratives about Muslims—particularly single stories of Muslims (and Islam) as prone to terrorism and violence, and of Muslim women as oppressed—I wondered how my daughter Noor, close to eleven years old at the commencement of this research, has or will experience these types of stories of what it means to be a Muslim female composing a life in Canada. I wondered about how other Canadian Muslim girls and their mothers are negotiating their life-making amid larger sociopolitical narratives.

Over three years after my wonderings led to this research, Clandinin reminds me that all researchers "need to be able to answer the questions of 'So What?' and 'Who Cares?' about our studies" ("Engaging" 35). As I contemplate the wider significance of inquiring alongside other Muslim mothers and daughters for deeper understandings of our experiences, I am drawn towards the stories we shared and lived alongside one another that make visible the many ways we creatively and relationally compose(d) our lives amid a multiplicity of arrogant perceptions and single stories. I am drawn towards how, through our life-making, we challenge(d) single stories of what/who we *are* and/or *should* be as Muslim females. In the sections that follow, I discuss three ways we relationally resisted, troubled, and challenged single stories: challenging single stories of victimhood and oppression; challenging single stories of Muslims and Islam; and challenging single stories of fixed borders between familial and school worlds. Throughout this chapter, it is my intent to be in metaphoric dialogue with co-inquirers, teachers, teacher educators, writers and theorists, and other members from within and across Muslim and other communities in Canada and beyond. I do so because I want to speak *with* other (Muslim) mothers and daughters, and others from within and across Muslim and other communities, rather than *to* or *for* them.

Challenging Single Stories of Victimhood and Oppression

Do you know what it is like to represent a billion human beings every day you walk out of your house? To be looked at as a representative of an entire world religion? A world religion! Do you know what that's like? It's exhausting, and it feels so heavy. Sometimes it makes me angry, and I'm tired of it ... I am just NOT a representation.

—Sahar Ishtiaque Ullah, *The Hijabi Monologues Project*

Although Muslim girls and women are often storied as victims of oppression in mainstream Canadian media and literature (Bullock and Jaffri; Sensoy and Marshall), little is known about our diverse experiences—particularly within familial and community landscapes. The stories Safaa, Rayyan, Ayesha, Zahra, Layla, Maya, and I shared, lived, and inquired into alongside one another made visible the many ways we regularly face(d) arrogant perceptions (Lugones) and single stories (Adichie, "Danger") from within and across Muslim and other Canadian communities of who we *are* and/or *should* be. However, our stories simultaneously challenge(d) single stories of Muslim girls and women as victims. Through (re)telling and (re)living our stories, co-inquirers and I eschewed arrogant gazes and made visible the agentic and creative ways we compose our lives *in relation* (Huber).

An example of a prevalent single story of the inability of Muslim girls and women to agentically compose their lives is in the field of physical education. A basic Google Scholar search will result in multiple studies about the barriers Muslim girls face when participating in physical education classes, sports programs, and/or other extracurricular activities. However, Rayyan, Zahra, and Maya challenged this single story through their participation in a combination of the following activities: figure skating, theatre, swimming, soccer, volleyball, basketball, and art. Co-inquirers helped me to appreciate how, with awareness of different personal, familial, cultural, and faith-based/religious narratives related to dress, propriety, and/or contact with boys, they are always in the process of (re) negotiating a multiplicity of expectations, boundaries, and arrogant perceptions. Our narrative accounts highlighted how, for co-inquirers, these diverse expectations, boundaries, and arrogant perceptions are fluid, shift over time, in relation to new stories/knowing, and/or are *shifted* by co-inquirers. Alongside her mother Layla, Maya creatively shifted boundaries, expectations, and arrogant perceptions through pursuing her passion for figure skating and through slight alterations to her costumes. I am reminded of how, in the midst of feeling arrogantly perceived about not covering *enough* and/or being *too* covered, Maya wrote about Zahra Lari, a Muslim figure skater in hijab, as her (s)hero for a school assignment. While Layla's and Maya's stories of the disapproval of some female relatives make visible the arrogant perceptions and single stories they face(d) and resist(ed) alongside each other, co-inquirers were mainly supported in their participation in extracurricular activities by others within familial and school curriculum-making worlds (Huber et al., *Places*). However, reflecting upon how Muslim girls and women have sometimes been forced to choose between their hijab and the sports and activities they love,[37] I wonder about how Muslim girls and women may sometimes face multiple expectations related to 'appropriate' attire from others within and across familial, school, community, and social worlds.

I wonder about the ways these external expectations and arrogant perceptions, if imposed, can bump up against the stories *we* live by. I wonder about how these and other arrogant perceptions can shape the stories Muslim children, youth, and families live and tell within and across familial and school worlds. The stories Layla shared of not participating in overnight school camping trips as a child and youth and the stories that Ayesha and Zahra shared of Zahra's desire to attend a school dance with her friends draw attention to the need to be cautious about arrogantly determining why Muslim girls may not participate in school and community activities, dances, overnight trips, etc. Layla emphasized that the girls *and boys* in her family were not allowed to sleep outside of the house likely because her mom feared for their safety as, for her mother, it was uncommon for children to sleep anywhere other than their home. Ayesha's refusal to allow Zahra to attend a school dance stemmed from her belief that it is inappropriate

37 See: Agerholm; Bryson and Ouachtouki; CAIR "Canadian"; and Mokhtar.

for Muslim girls *and boys* to dance in a mixed-gender setting. For co-inquirers, lack of participation and/or modified participation was not indicative of unfair, gendered, and oppressive practices; rather, mother co-inquirers made visible how families worried about safeguarding their children's safety and/or honouring familial, religious, and/or cultural beliefs.

Another prevalent single story of victimhood and oppression is the notion that Muslim girls and women in hijab suffer from a lack of agency. The story Rayyan shared of being told "Don't worry, when you're eighteen you won't have to wear that [hijab] anymore" brings to mind Abo-Lughod's contention that "representations of the unfreedom of others that blame the chains of culture incite rescue missions by outsiders" (20). Abo-Lughod later asserts the following: "Veiling must not be confused with, or made to stand for, lack of agency. Not only are there many forms of covering, which themselves have different meanings in the communities where they are used, but veiling has become caught up almost everywhere now in a politics of representation—of class, of piety, and of political affiliation" (39). Although my embodied knowledge resonates with Abu-Lughod's powerful words, I would add the word "agency" to her list of the hijab's "politics of representation," since the stories co-inquirers and I (re)told and (re)lived alongside one another foregrounded our agency in choosing how we wish to express our faith—including whether or not to don the hijab. I type these words with trepidation because by focusing upon how we challenge(d) single stories of our (lack of) agency, I could be unintentionally reinforcing the reductive equation of Muslim femalehood with hijab. However, I resonate profoundly with Bullock and Jafri's assertion, "Because of this Western cultural fixation on Muslim women's dress as a symbol of oppression, Muslim women often have to focus on that aspect of their identity as well, even if they would rather talk of something else" (37). While Zahra's stories of feeling forced to wear hijab reveal that Muslim girls and women may sometimes be pressured or forced to don hijab,[38] the stories Safaa, Rayyan, Ayesha, Layla, Maya and I shared make visible that we *chose* whether or not to veil. Reflecting upon the woman's arrogant

---

38 However, Zahra later expressed her agency of how to express and live her faith in her decision to remove her hijab.

perception that Rayyan did not choose her hijab, I think about how Muslim girls and women in hijab may sometimes contend with others hijab-splaining[39] the significance and meaning of our hijabs *to us*. As discussed in Chapter 1, Muslim girls and women may choose to don hijab for reasons as diverse as we are. However, reflecting upon the stories of hijab co-inquirers and I shared and lived alongside one another and on my choice to live as a Canadian Muslim woman in hijab, I feel a profound sense of resonance with how a participant in Ahmed's study asserts that she wears hijab "for the same reason as some of my Jewish friends wear the yarmulke: as a way of openly identifying with a group that people have prejudices about and as a way of saying 'yes we're here, and we have the right to be here and to be treated equally'" (8).

However, as I reconsider the single story in mainstream media and literature of reducing Muslim girls and women to the hijab, I think about how it is ultimately a form of erasure. I think about how unfair and uncomfortable the fixation on hijab is—for Muslim girls and women who wear it and those who do not. The stories co-inquirers shared—particularly the stories Ayesha and Zahra shared of being made to feel the need to prove that they are "normal"—give a sense of how, as girls and women in hijabs, *we are hypervisible but often made to feel invisible*. For, while our hijab is an extremely visible marker of our faith, it also triggers a multiplicity of single stories about who we *are* and/or *should* be—as though the fabric covering our hair and bodies seems to also cover the eyes, ears, hearts, and minds of those who arrogantly perceive us and deny our right to full personhood. However, thinking of Zahra and Maya (and my daughter Noor), I (re)consider how unfair equating hijab with Muslim girl and womanhood is for Muslim females who choose not to wear hijab because they may be arrogantly perceived as not Muslim *enough* by others and/or held up as examples of agentic, integrated, and feminist Muslim women (Hoodfar). As I think of the interwoveness of Maya's and Zahra's faith-based beliefs and practices in their life-making, I am reminded of

---

39 In using this term, I draw inspiration from the popular culture term 'mansplaining' that is used when males "comment on or explain something to a woman in a condescending, overconfident, and often inaccurate or oversimplified manner" (dictionary.com).

Ali's contention that Muslim girls who do not wear hijab "are often no less religious or conscious of their religion" (8) than those who wear hijab. The stories co-inquirers and I lived and shared alongside each other make visible that we are infinitely more than our hijab or lack of it. They make visible the agentic and creative ways we are composing our lives ... stories that defy single stories of us as victims of oppression.

Challenging Single Stories of Muslims and Islam

> O mankind, indeed We have created you from male and female and made you peoples and tribes that you may know one another. Indeed, the most noble of you in the sight of Allah is the most righteous of you.
>
> [Qu'ran, 49:13]

Although Muslims are often discussed, critiqued, and imagined as a monolith, the stories co-inquirers and I lived and shared highlight the diversity and multiplicity of personal, cultural, familial, intergenerational, linguistic, racial, temporal, and faith-based/religious narratives we live *by*, *with*, and *in*. Barlas argued that the Qu'ran and other Islamic texts are *interpreted* texts; Muslim individuals, families, and communities interweave their embodied, experiential, and relational knowing with their interpretations of Islam.[40] However, as I think about how co-inquirers and I have struggled to comprehend the repeated devastation of terror attacks committed by those who identify as Muslim, Barlas reminds me that Islamic texts also allow for the possibility that sacred themes and principles for living with divine guidance can be *mis*interpreted. As Reza Aslan asserts in an interview:

> People don't derive their values from their religion—they bring their values to their religion. Which is why religions like Judaism, Hinduism, Christianity, [and] Islam, are experienced in such profound, wide diversity. Two individuals can look at the exact same text and come away with radically different interpretations. Those interpretations have ... everything to do with the cultural,

---

40 Perhaps I should have written *Islams* because beliefs and practices differ for the multiplicity of Muslim individuals, families, and communities.

nationalistic, ethnic, political prejudices and preconceived notions that the individual brings to the text. (qtd. in Singal)

Barlas writes, "To identify Islam inseparably with [violence and] oppression is to ignore the reality of misreadings of the sacred text" (xi). As our narrative accounts made visible, co-inquirers and I are acutely aware of single stories of Muslims as terrorists, violent, and/or suspect even as we experience(d) grief, fear, and trauma in the aftermath of continued terror attacks. I think of Maya, reacting to Layla's stories of troubling posts in their town's online comments page about Muslims being complicit in terrorism, tearfully saying, "I don't think Muslims can do that kind of stuff. They're not Muslim. But, yeah, they think we're terrorists." I think of Layla saying, "I mean, we don't know who these people are and we can't stop them, but others think we can. I wish we could, but we can't." I think of Safaa's story of her daughter Sadia confronting her high school social studies teacher following his remarks about Islam and terrorism: "She confronted that teacher, and she was upset. She told him, 'That hurts me; you can't say that.'" I think of Rayyan and her sister Marwa sharing the story of their eldest sister (who wears hijab) being told "Go back to your country! You don't belong here!" by a belligerent man on a bus and of Rayyan saying, "Not every Muslim is like what you see in the news." I think of how, after repeated terror attacks in late 2015, Ayesha expressed, "I am so tired of this. With Paris and now this, it is too much! I try not to think about it, but it is hard." Her words reminded me of how Zahra said, "What happened in Paris made me so upset and scared. I still think about it. I'm traumatized by it."

However, although we regularly contended with grief, trauma, and fear in the wake of terror attacks, vitriol, and rhetoric, we actively and passionately resisted single stories of Muslims. I am reminded of Zahra saying, "We can't be afraid. We need to be honest and keep speaking up." I think of Ayesha saying, "I can't defend any of those things. It's not my responsibility to defend it, and I can't. I just don't understand why people do such bad things. But we can't live in fear." I remember how Safaa, in the wake of her eldest daughter being verbally attacked on a bus, cautioned against single-storying others, "But we cannot say all society acts like that." I think of how Rayyan asserted, "Even if you're not Muslim, you should always stand up for people," and of Maya tearfully saying, "Just because one person does it [engage in

STORIES WE LIVE AND GROW BY

terrorist acts], doesn't mean everyone will." I once again wonder about when/how/if to discuss single stories of Muslims with children and youth as I think about how, after noticing Maya's tears, Layla questioned, "*Yimkin flitna bi'l hakee shway* [an Arabic phrase for "Maybe we let our conversation get out of hand"]." But she then powerfully asserted, "But they have to know about it too. I always tell them don't ever be ashamed of who you are."

I experienced great tension in writing this section because I am fearful of centring yet another discussion of Muslims and Islam around terrorism. I am fearful that I will invite arrogant gazes and construct-ions in ways similar to (mis)representations of Muslims and Islam in mainstream media and literature. However, while the stories we lived and shared alongside one another give a sense of our strength in relationally resisting and challenging single stories of Muslims and Islam, *they also make visible that we are always living in relation to these pervasive constructions.* I wonder about the short- and long-term reverberations in our life-making and in the life-making of other Muslim children, youth, families, and communities, as we experience ongoing trauma—of continued terror attacks, of being made to feel linked to terrorism/violence, and of possible retaliatory attacks against us. Although our narrative accounts revealed that single stories of Islam and Muslims were only some of the single stories co-inquirers and I live in relation to, they also made visible our embodied knowing of potential danger—particularly those who are visibly or identifiably Muslim or who *look* like they may be Muslim[41]—in the aftermath of large-scale terror attacks. Co-inquirers and I regularly spoke of fear and unease as we learned of the stories of Canadian Muslims—many of whom were women in hijab—being threatened or attacked in the wake of several terror attacks in the last few years.[42] We were collectively shocked and terrified as we learned of the horrific murder on 30 January 2017 of six Muslim men in in a Quebec City mosque by an extremist with Islamophobic views (McKenna and Montpetit). However, while these stories remind us of the need to be aware of potential danger, they cannot be represented as *the* single story of our experiences as Canadian Muslims. The stories co-inquirers and I lived

41 See Basu; Abhasakun.
42 See: CBC News, "Suspect"; Chin; Da Silva; Pelletier.

and shared—and the stories of Canadians of all backgrounds standing alongside their Muslim family, friends, and neighbours in the wake of hate crimes and terror attacks committed by perpetrators of all backgrounds—call attention to how we, alongside multitudes, are standing up and speaking out to condemn discrimination and other forms of hatred and violence.

Challenging Single Stories of Fixed Borders between Familial and School Worlds

> We see the necessity of honouring two worlds of
> curriculum making, the familial and
> the school worlds and the importance of
> dialogue between the worlds.
>
> (Huber et al., *Places* 149)

While many studies in the literature about Muslim children, youth, and families in relation to schools and schooling give a sense of fixed borders between school and familial worlds fraught with tension-filled attempts at border-crossing, our narrative accounts showed that—although we at times experienced moments of tension—co-inquirers and I did not experience our travels across familial and school curriculum-making worlds (Huber et al., *Places*) in this way.[43] Our stories made visible the multiple ways that our familial and school curriculum-making worlds met and overlapped.

In their research alongside children, youth, families, and teachers, Huber et al. discuss learning "how easily arrogant perception can cause children, families, and teachers to overwrite one world of curriculum making." They further state:

> We see the dangers of making it impossible for children and families to compose forward-looking stories when school curriculum making becomes too dominant and assumes a kind of arrogant perception of familial curriculum making. We also

43 It is not my intention to deny that others may feel this way. Rather, it is my intention to make visible that the stories *co-inquirers and I* shared do not give a sense of fixed borders.

recognize the dangers of arrogant perception when familial curriculum making may overwrite school curriculum making. (*Places* 149)

Although co-inquirers and I shared many stories drawing attention to the importance school curriculum-making has been in our life-making, our stories foregrounded the centrality of our familial relationships and knowing to our stories of being and becoming. This should not be perceived as suggestive of the need to only prioritize familial curriculum-making in the lives of Muslim girls (and boys), women (and men), and families. In foregrounding our familial curriculum-making experiences, I purposely attempted to illuminate a world of curriculum-making that is often not seen or recognized (Huber et al., *Places*)—particularly for (female) Muslim children, youth, and families.

I am drawn to how for Safaa familial curriculum-making is a relational, reciprocal, creatively co-composed process alongside her husband, children, extended (and chosen) family, friends, teachers, and community members. Alongside living a familial curriculum of the right and responsibility to advocate for themselves and others in the face of racial, religious, cultural, social, and gendered arrogant perceptions and single stories, Safaa also teaches her children the importance of reconnecting with family as often as possible in her repeated efforts to travel to America to visit with extended family. Having grown up in the midst of a very large extended family, familial relationships are important to Safaa because of mutual love and care and because they are imbued with educative spaces: "That's how I grew up, nobody ever told me, 'Do this, and do that.' It was through lived examples; that's how we learn. It's through living." Reflecting upon her parenting practices alongside her husband in their relatively smaller family unit in Canada, Safaa drew upon her experiences growing up in Somalia and Kenya:

There, we say it takes a community to raise a child; so there was minimal interaction between the parents and the child because the child belongs to *all* the community, whereby here you have long interactions, one-on-one interactions. We grew up in a *rich* community whereby we learned from everybody, but for [our kids] it's just you, and how much teaching can you give them by yourself to grow as you grew?

However, Safaa later expressed appreciation for how values like honesty and politeness within "Canadian culture" have shaped her children's knowledge and their familial curriculum-making practices. Safaa's stories made visible that, while her children are learning and growing in different ways and places than she did, she has "*made* a family" in Canada, which includes members of her children's Islamic school community—one of the places they call home.

Whether within public or Islamic school environments, mothers and daughters shared many stories of the ways school curriculum-making practices shape(d) their familial curriculum-making. However, I am drawn to their stories of the ways their personal and familial knowledge and practices have (re)shaped school curriculum-making worlds. I think of how guided by their belief in the Two R's of rights and responsibilities, Safaa and Rayyan shared familial curriculum resources within school curriculum-making worlds in their stories of resisting bullying, discrimination, and racism. I think of how Layla and Safaa drew upon their knowledge of familial languages to teach within school curriculum-making worlds. I think of Safaa's stories of encouraging her children to advocate for prayer spaces in schools and of her work as a multicultural consultant alongside many children, youth, families, and school educators. I think of Ayesha teaching Rayyan "how to win [teachers'] trust" and of Ayesha volunteering in her daughters' school library. I think of how Maya, drawing upon her embodied knowledge, confidently spoke up in defence of others who had been unfairly judged and/or bullied. Co-inquirers and I made visible the ways that familial and intergenerational knowing live in us ... and how, while our lives are profoundly shaped by the worlds (Lugones) we inhabit, we also (re)shape myriad worlds in our ongoing and creative life-making.

Returning to reflect upon how co-inquirers and I face(d) and challenge(d) a multiplicity of single stories and arrogant perceptions, I think about how family, friends, teachers, and other community members help(ed) support us in our resistance to these stories. For Ayesha, resisting single stories and arrogant perceptions includes co-composing a curriculum of choice(s) alongside her daughters. Ayesha purposefully create(s/d) spaces for choices through listening to her daughters in their nightly routine of bedtime talks. This resonates in how Ayesha repeatedly spoke of appreciating the ways that Zahra's grade seven social studies teacher discussed single stories of Muslims with Zahra and her classmates: "Her teacher makes people aware about the things that happen and talks about how we should react, which is so good, right?" I am reminded of Layla receiving a gift of flowers with an encouraging note from an anonymous friend/community member after the Paris attacks in November 2015. I think about how Zahra described being troubled in class by a candidate for the federal Progressive Conservative Party discussing his views that women in niqab should not be allowed to take the ceremonial oath of Canadian citizenship if they do not remove their niqab, and how she felt more at ease when another candidate responded, "We don't ask you to take your turban off, shame on you!" I think of how Maya said she does not experience discrimination as a Muslim in school because "in school we talk about that, like my teacher is against people doing and saying mean things to other people because of things like culture." However, I also think of the story Safaa shared of how she and her daughter Sadia confronted Sadia's grade ten social studies teacher for his hurtful rhetoric about Muslims as perpetrators of terror attacks: "I believe it's not only her who feels like that, you have more [students] than her who are of the Muslim faith, and they don't feel good about what you're saying." Although our narrative accounts made visible that we draw upon our embodied knowledge to resist single stories and arrogant perceptions, they also made visible that this profoundly hard and necessary work often requires allies.[44] They made visible how allies can help co-compose conversational spaces (Clandinin at al., "Reverberations") where we can speak *with* each other and listen *to* each other—spaces imbued with possibilities for world-travel with loving perception ... and possibilities for (re)shaping our world(s).

As the stories Safaa shared of her experiences confronting teachers alongside her daughters made visible, co-inquirers and I sometimes experienced tensionality in our movement between familial and school curriculum-making worlds. We shared many stories of bullying, racism, and discrimination *from other girls and youth*—many of whom were Muslim—within school worlds. However, the stories we shared made visible the many ways we draw upon personal, familial, and

44 I resonate with MuslimGirl.com founder Amani Al-Khatahtbeh's conception of how to be an ally against Islamophobia (Kahn).

relational knowledge in our resistance to bullying, racism, discrimination, single stories, and arrogant perceptions from within and across the multiplicity of worlds we travel to and inhabit. I think about how we found and/or created borderland spaces (Anzaldúa) of liminality and possibility within, between, and across curriculum-making worlds—spaces that are continually shifting and shifted through our living. As Gloria Anzaldúa elucidates, "Borders are set up to define the places that are safe and unsafe, to distinguish us from them. A border is a dividing line, a narrow strip along a steep edge. A borderland is a vague and undetermined place created by the emotional residue of an unnatural boundary. It is in a constant state of transition" (3). Ruminating on fluid boundaries permeated with borderland spaces between our familial and school curriculum-making worlds (Menon and Saleh), I wonder at how constructions in the literature, and sometimes in practice, of fixed borders between familial and school worlds suggest a lack of agency for familial and school learners/ educators to (re)shape the curriculum-making worlds we inhabit—a suggestion that co-inquirers and I challenged alongside multiple friends, educators, and community members.

However, Safaa's stories of her work as a multicultural consultant remind me that co-inquirers and I are all fluent in the English language and have been blessed with many different kinds of familial, community, material, and school supports in our life-making. Discussing her work as a multicultural consultant with the Canadian Somali community, Safaa ruminated on her work alongside families and teachers to co-compose (borderland) spaces of increased understanding:

> I go to some schools and teachers will tell me that they haven't seen a parent the whole year, but maybe they have reasons. Like this mom is a single working mom. She is still learning English. The father died back home. She's raising four kids, and one of them [is] now diagnosed with schizophrenia. She has so many other things to think about ... Also, in [our] culture, the mother will tell her child, "Oh you did this today? I'm going to tell your teacher," and the teacher will discipline the child. That's the power that schools had ... so that's where these women are coming from. They don't even get involved with the children's school.

Safaa's words call attention to the need for continual dialogue between learners/educators[45] from within and across familial and school curriculum-making worlds. Her words call attention to the need for learners/educators within both curriculum-making worlds to travel with loving perception within and across a multiplicity of worlds.

Reflecting Back … and Imagining Forward

> The encounter with persons, one by one,
> rather than categories and generalizations,
> is still the best way
> to cross the lines of strangeness.
>
> (Bateson, *Full* 81)

By engaging in this inquiry alongside co-inquirers, I attempted to foreground additional dimensions to the literature and to wider narratives and discourses that are too often *about* Muslim girls and women, yet do not acknowledge us as integral to framing and shaping discourses in relational, experiential, and profoundly complex and interconnected ways. Through our narrative inquiries, Safaa, Rayyan, Ayesha, Zahra, Layla, Maya, and I made visible many of the stories we live *by*, *with*, and *in* as Canadian Muslim girls, youth and women in the midst of ongoing life transitions. The stories we (re)told and (re)lived alongside each other made visible the many ways co-inquirers and I are creatively composing our lives *in relation* to a multiplicity of people, places, and stories. They made visible the personal, familial, intergenerational, faith-based/religious, and relational knowing we draw upon in relationally resisting arrogant perceptions and single stories. They made visible the many ways that we are agentically and relationally (re)shaping our familial and school curriculum-making worlds, the multiplicity of our selves, and the stories we live *by*, *with*, and *in*. They made visible that we are always in the process of composing forward-looking stories alongside one another, family, friends, school and community members, and others. The stories we (re)told and (re) lived alongside one another call attention to the need to be cautious

---

45 I purposely do not separate learners from educators here, for as Huber et al. ("Places") notes, these labels are fluid and shift depending upon the context.

about single-storying us and our experiences ... and the need for educators, researchers, and community members from within and across Muslim and other Canadian communities to listen to, foreground, and amplify *our* voices rather than presuming to speak *to*, *about*, and/or *for* us.

As I reflect upon our narrative inquiries alongside one another I think of how blessed I have been to inquire alongside Safaa, Rayyan, Ayesha, Zahra, Layla, and Maya during this time of multiple life transitions. I think of all that I have learned and the many understandings and wonderings that continue to live and grow in me as I ruminate about the many changes to our selves and the stories we lived *by*, *with*, and *in* for over two years. As co-inquirers and I continue to imagine forward, I wonder about the changes future seasons will bring ... and those *we* will bring into being.

Works Cited

Abhasakun, T. "When You "Look Muslim": Middle Eastern Minorities Also Targets of Anti-Muslim Bigotry." *Conatus News*, 1 April 2017, www.conatusnews.com/when-you-look-muslim-middle-eastern-minorities-too-are-targets-of-anti-muslim-bigotry/. Accessed 13 Sept.2018.

Abo-Lughod, L. *Do Muslim Women Need Saving?* Harvard University Press, 2013.

Adichie, C. N. "The Danger of a Single Story." *ted.com*, July 2009, www.ted.com/talks/chimamanda_adichie_the_danger_of_a_single_story.html. Accessed 13 Sept. 2018.

Adichie, C. N. *Dear Ijeawele, or a Feminist Manifesto in Fifteen Suggestions.* Alfred A. Knopf Canada, 2017.

Agerholm, H. "Burkini Ban: French Police Continue to Target Women in Islamic Clothing Despite Court Ruling." *The Independent*, 28 August 2016, www.independent.co.uk/news/world/europe/burkini-ban-france-french-police-muslim-women-hijab-burka-latest-news-court-ruling-a7213856.html. Accessed 13 Sept. 2018.

Ahmed, L. *A Quiet Revolution: The Veil's Resurgence from the Middle East to America.* Yale University Press, 2011.

Ali, S. *The Experiences of Arab Muslim Girls with Curriculum/Schooling in Public Secondary Schools in Ontario, Canada.* University of Toronto Press, 2012.

Anzaldúa, G. E. *Borderlands/La Frontera: The New Mestiza.* Aunt Lute Books, 1999.

Asad, M. "The Message of the Quran: Translated and Explained by Muhammad Asad." *usc.edu*, 1980, http://www.muhammad-asad.com/Message-of-Quran.pdf. Accessed 13 Sept. 2018.

Aslan, R. *No God but God: The Origins and Evolution of Islam.* Delacorte Press, 2011.

Austin, H., and L. Carpenter. "Troubled, Troublesome, Troubling Mothers: The Dilemma of Difference in Women's Personal Motherhood Narratives." Narrative Inquiry, vol. 18, no. 2, 2008, pp. 378-392, doi:10.1075/ni.18.1.10aus.

Ballah, K. *Preparing my Daughter for Rain*. Key Ballah, 2014.

Barlas, A. *"Believing Women" in Islam: Unreading Patriarchal Interpretations of the Qu'ran*. University of Texas Press, 2002.

Basso, K. H. *Wisdom Sits in Places: Landscape and Language Among the Western Apache*. University of New Mexico Press, 1996.

Basu, M. "15 Years after 9/11, Sikhs Still Victims of Anti-Muslim Hate Crimes." *CNN*, 15 Sept. 2016, www.cnn.com/2016/09/15/us/sikh-hate-crime-victims/. Accessed 13 Sept. 2018.

Bateson, M. C. *Composing a Life*. A Plume Book, 1989.

Bateson, M. C. *Peripheral Visions: Learning Along the Way*. Harper Collins, 1994.

Bateson, M. C. *Full Circles, Overlapping Lives*. Ballantine Books, 2000.

Belenky, M. F., et al. *Women's Ways of Knowing: The Development of Self, Voice, and Mind*. BasicBooks, 1997.

Brown, B. *Daring Greatly: How the Courage to be Vulnerable Transforms the Way We Live, Love, Parent, and Lead*. Penguin Books, 2012.

Brown, L. M., and C. Gilligan. *Meeting at the Crossroads: Women's Psychology and Girls' Development*. Harvard University Press, 1992.

Bruner, J. "Life as Narrative." *Social Research*, vol. 71, no. 3, 2004, 691-710, www.jstor.org/stable/40971721?origin=JSTOR-pdf. Accessed 13 Sept. 2018.

Bullock, K. H., and G. J. Jafri. "Media (Mis)representations: Muslim Women in the Canadian Nation." *Canadian Woman Studies*, vol. 20, no. 2, 35–40, 2000, www.pi.library.yorku.ca/ojs/index.php/cws/article/view/7607/6738. Accessed 13 Sept. 2018.

Bush, Laura. "The Weekly Address Delivered by the First Lady." *The American Presidency Project*, 17 Nov. 2011, www.presidency.ucsb.edu/ws/?pid=24992. Accessed 13 Sept. 2018.

Bryson, J. S., and S. Ouachtouki. "The Hijab Hurdle in Sports." *Contending Modernities*, 2011, www.contendingmodernities.nd.edu/gender-state-society/the-hijab-hurdle-in-sports/. Accessed 13 Sept. 2018.

Caine, V. "Narrative Beginnings: Traveling to and Within Unfamiliar Landscapes." *Qualitative Health Research*, vol. 20, no. 9, 2010, 1304–1311, doi: 10.1177/1049732310367500.

"Canadian Muslim Girls Banned from Karate Tournament Over Hijab." *Cair*, 15 April 2007, www.cair.com/canadian_muslim_girls_banned_from_karate_tournament_over_hijab. Accessed 13 Sept. 2018.

Carr, D. *Time, Narrative and History*. Indiana University Press, 1986.

CBC News. "Wildfire Forces Evacuation of Fort McMurray: Residents Seek Shelter after Evacuation of the Oilsands City." *CBC News*, 8 May 2016, www.cbc.ca/news/canada/photos/wildfire-forces-evacuation-of-fort-mcmurray-1.3562195. Accessed 13 Sept.2018.

CBC News. "Suspect in Custody after Women Wearing Hijabs Threatened with Noose at LRT Transit Station." *CBC News*, 6 Dec. 2016, www.cbc.ca/news/canada/edmonton/edmonton-hijab-noose-threat-1.3884501. Accessed 13 Sept. 2018.

Clandinin, D. J. *Engaging in Narrative Inquiry*. Left Coast Leaf Press, 2013.

Clandinin, D. J., and F. M. Connelly. *Narrative Inquiry: Experience and Story in Qualitative Research*. Jossey-Bass Publishers, 2000.

Clandinin, D. J., and F. M. Connelly. "Teacher as Curriculum Maker." *Handbook of Research on Curriculum*, edited by P. W. Jackson, Macmillan, 1992, pp. 363-401.

Clandinin, D. J., and F. M. Connelly. "Teachers' Professional Knowledge Landscapes: Teacher Stories, Stories of Teachers, School Stories, Stories of Schools." *Educational Researcher*, vol. 25, no. 3, 1996, 24-30, www.jstor.org/stable/1176665. Accessed 13 Sept. 2018.

Clandinin, D. J., et al. *Relational Ethics of Narrative Inquiry*. Taylor and Francis Ltd, 2017.

Clandinin, D. J., et al. *Composing Diverse Identities: Narrative Inquiries into the Interwoven Lives of Children and Teachers*. Routledge, 2006.

Clandinin, D. J., et al. "Reverberations of Narrative Inquiry: How Resonant Echoes of an Inquiry with Early School Leavers Shaped Further Inquiries."*Educacao, Sociedade and Culturas*, vol. 36, 2012, pp. 7-24, www.fpce.up.pt/ciie/revistaesc/ESC36/ESC36_D.Jean_SeanandVera.pdf. Accessed 13 Sept. 2018.

Clandinin, D. J., and S. Murphy. "Relational Ontological Commitments in Narrative Research." *Educational Researcher* vol. 38, no. 8, 2009, pp. 598-602, doi: 10.3102/0013189X09353940

Coles, R. *The Call of Stories: Teaching and the Moral Imagination*. Houghton Mifflin, 1989.

Connelly, F. M., and D. J. Clandinin. *Teachers as Curriculum Planners: Narratives of Experience.* Teachers College Press, 1988.

Connelly, F. M., and D. J. Clandinin. *Shaping a Professional Identity: Stories of Educational Practice.* Teachers College Press, 1999.

Connelly, F. M., and D. J. Clandinin. "Narrative Inquiry." *Handbook of Complementary Methods in Education Research*, edited by J. Green, et al, 3rd ed., Lawrence Erlbaum, 2006, pp. 375-385.

Crites, S. "The Narrative Quality of Experience." *Journal of the American Academy of Religion,* vol. 39, no. 3, 1971, pp. 291-311, www.jstor.org/stable/1461066. Accessed 13 Sept. 2018.

Da Silva, M. "Tolerant Toronto? Think Again. Attacks on Muslim Women on the Rise." *Now Toronto*, 28 June 2016, www.nowtoronto.com/news/tolerant-toronto-think-again-attacks-on-muslim-women-on-the-rise/. Accessed 13 Sept. 2018.

Dearden, L. "Israel-Gaza Conflict: 50-Day War by Numbers." *Independent*, 27 Aug. 2014, www.independent.co.uk/news/world/middle-east/israelgaza-conflict-50day-war-by-numbers-9693310.html. Accessed 13 September 2018.

Dewey, J. *Experience and Education.* The Macmillan Co, 1938.

Dostoevsky, F. *The Brothers Karamazov.* Woodsworth Editions Ltd, 2007.

Downey, C. A., and D. J. Clandinin. "Narrative Inquiry as Reflective Practice: Tensions and Possibilities." *Handbook of Reflection and Reflective Inquiry: Mapping a Way of Knowing for Professional Reflective Practice*, edited by N. Lyons, Springer, 2010, pp. 285-397.

Eid, M., and K. Karim. "Ten Years After 9/11—What Have We Learned?" *Global Media Journal: Canadian Edition*, vol. 4 no. 2, 2011, pp. 1-12.

Eliot, G. *"Middlemarch: A Study of Provincial Life."* Chicago and New York: Belford, Clark and Co., 1885, www.books.google.vu/books?id=GmlhAQAACAAJ. Accessed 13 Sept. 2018.

Elliot, A. "Family Members of Chapel Hill Shooting Victims Continue Push for Hate Crime Charge." *Time Warner Cable News*, 22 Dec. 2015, www.twcnews.com/nc/triangle-sandhills/news/2015/12/16/family-members-of-chapel-hill-shooting-victims-continue-push-for-hate-crime-charge.html. Accessed 13 Sept. 2018.

Ely, M. "In-forming Re-presentations." *Handbook of Narrative Inquiry: Mapping a Methodology*, edited by D. J. Clandinin, Sage Publications, 2007, pp. 567-598.

Esposito, J. L., and D. Mogahed. *Who Speaks for Islam?: What a Billion Muslims Really Think*. Gallup Press, 2007.

Gibran, K. *The Prophet*. 1923. Random House, 2006.

Gilligan, C. et al. *Making Connections: The Relational Worlds of Adolescent Girls at Emma Willard School*. Harvard University Press, 1990.

Goodwin, S., and K. Huppatz. *The Good Mother*. Sydney University Press, 2010, pp. 1-24.

Gonzales, M. "The Alchemy of Storytelling." *YouTube*, 2013, www.youtube.com/watch?v=l7S7Xk639nQ. Accessed 13 September 2018.

Gore, A. "High Risk: Who a Mother Should Be." *Maternal Theory: Essential Readings*, edited by A. O'Reilly, Demeter Press, 2007, pp. 756-760.

Greene, M. *Releasing the Imagination: Essays on Education, the Arts, and Social Change*. Jossey Bass, 1995.

Heilbrun, C. *Women's Lives: The View from the Threshold*. University of Toronto Press, 1999.

Hoodfar, H. "The Veil in Their Minds and on Our Heads: The Persistence of Colonial Images of Muslim Women." *Resources for Feminist Research*, vol. 22, no. 3/4, pp. 5-18, 1993, doi:10.1007/978-1-137-04830-1_22.

Huber, J. "Stories Within and Between Selves—Identities in Relation on the Professional Knowledge Landscape." *Collections Canada*, 2000, www.collectionscanada.gc.ca/obj/s4/f2/dsk1/tape3/PQDD_0014/NQ59973.pdf. Accessed 13 Sept. 2018.

Huber, J., et al. *Places of Curriculum Making: Narrative Inquiries into Children's Lives in Motion*. Emerald, 2011.

Johnson, M. "Embodied Knowledge." *Curriculum Inquiry*, vol. 19, no. 4, 1986, pp. 361-377. doi:10.2307/1179358.

Kahn, M. "Not Sure How to Fight Islamophobia? MuslimGirl Founder Amani Al-Khatahtbeh Has Some Suggestions." 25 Jan. 2017, *Elle*. www.elle.com/culture/career-politics/news/a42435/how-to-be-muslim-ally-muslim-girl-video/. Accessed 13 Sept. 2018.

Keddie, A. "Identity Politics, Justice and the Schooling of Muslim Girls: Navigating the Tensions Between Multiculturalism, Group Rights and Feminism." *British Journal of Sociology of Education*, vol. 35, no. 3, pp. 353-370, 2014, doi:10.1080/01425692.2013.776930.

Khan, F. *"Can I Not Wear My Hijab in Peace?": Understanding Young Muslim Girls' Reasons for and Experiences of Wearing the Hijab*. Master's

Thesis. Ryerson University, 2009.

Kubota, H., et al. "A Narrative Conception of Professional Development as a Nested Community." *LEARNing Landscapes*, vol. 9, 2015, pp. 161-176, www.learninglandscapes.ca/index.php/learnland/article/view/751/751. Accessed 13 Sept. 2018.

Lev-Wiesel, R. "Intergenerational Transmission of Trauma Across Three Generations: A Preliminary Study." *Qualitative Social Work*, vol. 6, no. 1, 2007, pp. 75-94, doi:10.1177/1473325007074167.

Lopez, B. *Crow and Weasel*. North Point Press, 1990.

Lorde, A. *Sister Outsider: Essays and Speeches by Audre Lorde*. 1984. Crossing Press, 2007.

Lugones, M. "Playfulness, 'World'-Travelling, and Loving Perception." *Hypatia*, vol. 2, no. 2, 1987, pp. 3-19, doi:10.1111/ j.1527-2001.1987.tb01062.x.

Macdonald, N. "The Barbaric Cultural Practice of Election Pronouncements: A Steady Throb of Anti-Muslim Sentiment Appears to Be Running Through the Current Campaign." *CBC News*, 6 Oct. 2015, www.cbc.ca/news/politics/canada-election-2015-neil-macdonald-muslims-1.3257892. Accessed 13 Sept. 2018.

MacLachlan, P. *What You Know First*. HarperCollins, 1995.

Mattson, I. "Of Fences and Neighbours: An Islamic Perspective on Interfaith Engagement for Peace." *ingridmattson.com*, Oct. 2013, www.ingridmattson.org/article/of-fences-and-neighbors/. Accessed 13 Sept. 2018.

Mattson, I. "Rooting a Canadian Muslim Identity." *ingridmattson.com*, Mar. 2014, www.ingridmattson.org/video/ingrid-mattson-rooting-a-canadian-muslim-identity/. Accessed 13 Sept. 2018.

McKenna, K., and J. Montpetit. "Suspect in Mosque Shooting a Moderate Conservative Turned Extremist, Say Friends, Classmates." *CBC News*, 31 Jan. 2017, www.cbc.ca/news/canada/montreal/quebec-city-mosque-alexandre-bissonnette-profile-1.3959581. Accessed 13 Sept. 2018.

Menon, J., et al. "Embracing Lived Multiplicities as Beginning Narrative Inquirers." *Creative Approaches to Research*, vol. 8, no. 3, 2015, pp. 80-101, http://creativeapproachestoresearch.net/wp-content/uploads/CAR8_3_fullissue.pdf. Accessed 13 Sept. 2018.

Menon, J., and M. Saleh. "Borders." *Keywords in the Social Studies: Concepts and Conversations*, edited by D. G. Krutka, et al., Peter Lang Publishing, 2018, pp. 53-64.

Mickelson, J. R. *Our Sons are Labeled Behaviour Disordered: Here Are the Stories of Our Lives.* Dissertation, University of Alberta, 1995.

Mokhtar, H. "Banned from Basketball: Why the NCAA's First Veiled Muslim Woman Can't Play Pro." *muslimgirl.com*, 22 Aug. 2016, www.muslimgirl.com/28879/banned-basketball-ncaas-first-veiled-muslim-woman-cant-play-pro/. Accessed 13 Sept. 2018.

Nagra, B. "'Our Faith Was Also Hijacked by Those People': Reclaiming Muslim Identity in Canada in a Post-9/11 Era." *Journal of Ethnic and Migration Studies*, vol. 37, no. 3, 2011, pp. 425-441, doi:10.10 80/1369183X.2011.526781

Nelson, Hilde L. "Resistance and Insubordination." *Hypatia*, vol. 10, no. 2, 1995, pp. 23-40.

Niyozov, S. "Teachers and Teaching Islam and Muslims in Pluralistic Societies: Claims, Misunderstandings, and Responses." *Journal of International Migration and Integration,* vol. 11, no. 1, 2010, pp. 23-40, doi: 10.1007/s12134-009-0123-y.

Okri, B. *A Way of Being Free.* Phoenix House, 1997.

O'Reilly, A., ed. *Maternal Theory: Essential Readings.* Demeter Press, 2007.

Pelletier, J. "Montreal Man Charged with Inciting Hatred After Anti-Muslim Video Emerges." *CBC News*, 18 Nov. 2015, www.cbc.ca/news/canada/montreal/montreal-police-arrest-man-mask-joker-muslims-1.3324089. Accessed 13 Sept. 2018.

"The Changing Global Religious Landscape: Muslims." *Pew Forum*, 2017, www.pewforum.org/2017/04/05/the-changing-global-religious-landscape/. Accessed 13 Sept. 2018.

Ramji, R. "Creating a Genuine Islam: Second Generation Muslims Growing Up in Canada." *Canadian Diversity*, vol. 6, no. 2, 2009, pp. 104-109, www.connection.ebscohost.com/c/articles/34736977/creating-genuine-islam. Accessed 13 Sept. 2018.

Ramji, R. "A Variable but Convergent Islam: Muslim Women." *Growing up Canadian: Muslims, Hindus, Buddhists*, edited by P. Beyer, and R. Ramji, McGill-Queen's University Press, 2013, pp. 112-144.

Rath, T., and D. O. Clifton. *How Full Is Your Bucket?: Positive Strategies for Work and Life.* Gallup Press, 2004.

Rich, A. *On Lies, Secrets, and Silence.* W. W. Norton and Company, 1979.

Rich, A. *Of Woman Born.* W. W. Norton and Company, 1976.

Sa'di, A. H., and L. Abu-Lughod, editors. *Nakba: Palestine, 1948, and the Claims of Memory.* Columbia University Press, 2007.

Said, E. *Orientalism.* Random House, 1978.

Saleh, M., et al. "Stories to (Re)Name By: Relationally living (and Inquiring) within the Multilayered Midst." *LEARNing Landscapes,* vol. 11, no. 2, 2018, pp. 331-344, https://www.learninglandscapes.ca/index.php/learnland/article/view/966/963. Accessed 13 Sept. 2018.

Saleh, M., et al. "Autobiographical Narrative Inquiry: Tellings and Retellings." *LEARNing Landscapes,* vol.7, no. 2, 2014, pp. 271-282, , www.learninglandscapes.ca/. Accessed 13 September 2018.

Sarbin, T. R. "The Role of Imagination in Narrative Construction." *Narrative Aanalysis: Studying the Development of Individuals in Society,* edited by C. Daiute, and C. Lightfoot, Sage, 2004.

Sarris, G. *Keeping Slug Woman Alive: A Holistic Approach to American Indian Texts.* University of California Press, 1993.

Schwab, J. "The Practical 3: Translation into Curriculum." *The School Review,* vol 81, no. 4, 1973, pp. 501-522, www.jstor.org/stable/1084423. Accessed 13 Sept. 2018.

Sensoy, O., and E. Marshall. "Save the Muslim Girl!" *Rethinking Schools Online,* vol. 24, no. 2, 2009, www.rethinkingschools.org/archive/24_02/24_02_muslim.shtml. Accessed 13 Sept. 2018.

Shweder R. A., et al. "The Cultural Psychology of Development: One Mind, Many Mentalities." *Handbook of Child Development,* edited by W. Damon, 2006, pp. 716-792, doi:10.1002/9780470147658.chpsy0113.

Silko, L. M. *Yellow Woman and a Beauty of the Spirit.* Simon and Schuster, 1996.

Singal, J. "Q & A: Reza Aslan on What the New Atheists Get Wrong About Islam." *New York Magazine,* 14 Oct. 2014, www.nymag.com/scienceofus/2014/10/reza-aslan-on-what-the-new-atheists-get-wrong.html. Accessed 13 Sept. 2018.

Smith, D. "Curriculum and Teaching Face Globalization." *International Handbook of Curriculum Research,* edited by W. Pinar, Lawrence Erlbaum, 2003, pp. 35-51.

Talbot, M. "The Story of a Hate Crime: What Led to the Murder of Three Muslim Students in Chapel Hill?" *The New Yorker,* 22 June 2015, www.newyorker.com/magazine/2015/06/22/the-story-of-a-hate-crime. Accessed 13 Sept. 2018.

Taylor, J. L. "Treaty Research Report—Treaty Six (1876)." *Treaties and Historical Research Centre, Indian and Northern Affairs Canada,* 1986, www.aadnc-aandc.gc.ca/eng/1100100028706/1100100028708. Accessed 13 September 2018.

"What Is Islamophobia?" *The Bridge Initiative,* www.bridge. georgetown.edu/about/. Accessed 13 Sept. 2018.

Thurer, S. L. "The Myths of Motherhood." *Maternal Theory: Essential Readings,* edited by A. O'Reilly, Demeter Press, 2007, pp. 331-344.

Waheed, N. *Salt.* Createspace, 2013.

Waheed, N. *Nejma.* Createspace, 2014.

Watters, H. "C-51, Controversial Anti-Terrorism Bill, Is Now Law. So, What Changes?" *CBC News,* 18 June 2015, www.cbc.ca/news/politics/c-51-controversial-anti-terrorism-bill-is-now-law-so-what-changes-1.3108608. Accessed 13 Sept. 2018.

Young, M. *Pimatisiwin: Walking in a Good Way—A Narrative Inquiry into Language as Identity.* Pemmican Publications, 2005.

Yuhas, A., and M. Sidahmed. "Is this a Muslim Ban? Trump's Executive Order Explained." *The Guardian,* 31 Jan. 2017, www. theguardian.com/us-news/2017/jan/28/trump-immigration-ban-syria-muslims-reaction-lawsuits. Accessed 13 Sept. 2018.

Glossary of Arabic and/or Islamic Terms

A3mo: Colloquial way of saying "uncle" in Arabic.

A3mto: Colloquial way of saying "auntie" in Arabic.

Alhmadulillah: A word that is said in instances of gratitude. It means "All praise is for Allah (SWT)."

Allah (SWT): Allah is the Arabic word for God. For Muslims around the world, the acronym SWT usually accompanies the verbal or written mention of Allah (SWT). It stands for *Subhanahu Wa Ta'la*, meaning "Glory be to Allah (SWT), the Exalted."

Allah yirhama: May God have mercy on her.

Allah yirhamu: May God have mercy on him.

Amanah: An *Amanah* is the Arabic word for 'a trust.' In Islam, the concept of an *Amanah* signifies a faith-based, moral obligation to uphold and carry out a sacred obligation.

Baligh: Ali describes this as "a term used in Islam to refer to one's coming of age, signified by reaching puberty" (8).

Bism'Allah: This is a shortened version of "Bism'Allah Al-Rahman Al-Raheem," which means, "In the name of God, The Most Gracious, The Dispenser of Grace" (as translated by Muhammad Asad). This invocation is used by Muslims throughout the world before praying, eating, writing, reading, and myriad other activities, including embarking upon a challenging task.

Burqa: A long garment covering a woman's body, except for her eyes.

Duaa: This is a word that signifies supplication or a prayer to Allah (SWT). Duaa is viewed as an integral form of worship in Islam.

Eid: The two Muslim festivals are celebrated to commemorate important events in the Islamic lunar calendar. Eid Al-Fitr is celebrated after the completion of the holy month of Ramadan and a few months later, Eid Al-Adha is celebrated after the completion of the annual Hajj pilgrimage, during the holy month of Dhul Hijjah.

Eid Mubarak: This is a common Islamic saying during one of the two Eid celebrations. It means, "May you have a blessed Eid."

Haram: Forbidden.

Habibty: My beloved.

Hijab: Although many scholars are careful to differentiate between the terms headscarf/veil and hijab—arguing that the concept of hijab is infinitely broader than a piece of fabric meant to cover a woman's hair, I use the terms headscarf/veil and hijab interchangeably. I do this purposely because this is the term many veiled Muslim women use to refer to their headscarf/veil. However, the concept of hijab includes a requirement for men and women to observe modesty in demeanour and dress. The headscarf/veil is considered a form of hijab, and Islamic scholars from diverse Muslim communities differ in their opinions as to whether the headscarf is required to fulfill hijab for women.

Hijabi: This is a colloquial term for women who wear hijab that Muslim women often use with one another. It is considered derogatory by some Muslim women, but as a Muslim woman in a hijab, I use it with co-inquirers and friends in a loving and playful manner.

Inna li'Allah wa Inna Ilayhi Raj'oon: This is an Arabic and Islamic saying that is commonly used upon news of death: "We belong to Allah and to Him we are destined to return."

Insha'Allah: God willing.

Insha'Allah khair: May this be good/bring blessings, God willing.

Jazakum Allahu Khairan: An Islamic saying that translates to "May Allah reward you with all that is good."

Jiddee/Jiddo: A colloquial way of saying Grandfather.

Jihad: This means to struggle, or strive in the way of the Creator, including the struggle against turning away from the Creator and striving against oppression and injustice (Aslan, 2011).

Ka3k: For my family, *ka3k* are a hybrid between a cookie and cake.

Khalee: Maternal uncle.

Khalto: A colloquial way of saying maternal aunt. I was also taught to refer to elder female family friends as *Khalto* as a sign of respect.

Masjid: This usually refers to a mosque, a congregational place of worship for many Muslims.

Mash'Allah: This is an Arabic phrase used to express appreciation for Allah's (SWT) blessings and/or creation.

Nakba: An Arabic word used to refer to the "Catastrophe" of the Palestinian experience following the 1948 War.

Nikah: Islamic word for marriage.

Sabr: The concept of *sabr* in Islam is one of patience, perseverance, and acceptance of Allah's (SWT) Will. Praying for *sabr* in the face of hardship is a common Muslim invocation.

Sittee/Sitto: A colloquial way of saying grandmother.

Subhan Allah: This is an Arabic phrase that means "Glory be to God." This phrase is used to connote wonder and amazement.

SWT: For Muslims around the world, the abbreviation SWT usually accompanies the verbal or written mention of Allah (SWT). It stands for *Subhanahu Wa Ta'la*, meaning Glory be to Allah (SWT), the Exalted.

Ummah: An Islamic concept of Muslims being intricately connected to each other as one body, one community.

Wajib: Duty/responsibility.

Wallah: A way of expressing truthfulness and/or sincerely, wallah means, "I swear by God."

Qur'an: Muslims consider the Qur'an to be the holiest, foundational Islamic text.

About the Author

Dr. Muna Saleh is an Assistant Professor in the Faculty of Education at Concordia University of Edmonton. Drawing upon her experiences as a Canadian Muslim woman, mother, educator, and researcher, Muna's doctoral research was a Killam Trusts-funded narrative inquiry into the experiences of Canadian Muslim girls and their mothers. Prior to engaging in graduate studies, she was an elementary and secondary school teacher and leader. Her research interests include multiperspectival narrative inquiry, mothering and motherhood, conceptions of curriculum, familial curriculum-making, and research alongside children and youth with exceptionalities and their families.